On the Formal Way to Chinese Languages

On the Formal Way to Chinese Languages

edited by
Sze-Wing Tang
Chen-Sheng Luther Liu

CSLI
PUBLICATIONS
Center for the Study of
Language and Information
Stanford, California

Center for the Study of Language and Information
Leland Stanford Junior University
Printed in the United States
06 05 04 03 02 1 2 3 4 5

Library of Congress Cataloging-in-Publication Data

On the formal way to Chinese languages /
edited by Sze-Wing Tang, Chen-Sheng Luther Liu.
p. cm.
Includes bibliographical references and index.

ISBN 1-57586-370-7 (paper : alk. paper)
ISBN 1-57586-369-3 (alk. paper)

1. Chinese language–Grammar.
I. Tang, Sze-Wing. II. Liu, Chen-Sheng Luther, 1964–
PL1231.5 .O5 2002
495.1′5–dc21 2002074142
CIP

∞ The acid-free paper used in this book meets the minimum requirements of the American National Standard for Information Sciences—Permanence of Paper for Printed Library Materials, ANSI Z39.48-1984.

CSLI was founded early in 1983 by researchers from Stanford University, SRI International, and Xerox PARC to further research and development of integrated theories of language, information, and computation. CSLI headquarters and CSLI Publications are located on the campus of Stanford University.

CSLI Publications reports new developments in the study of language, information, and computation. In addition to lecture notes, our publications include monographs, working papers, revised dissertations, and conference proceedings. Our aim is to make new results, ideas, and approaches available as quickly as possible. Please visit our web site at
http://cslipublications.stanford.edu/
for comments on this and other titles, as well as for changes and corrections by the author and publisher.

Contents

Preface

The papers in this book arose from 'On the Formal Way to Chinese Languages' held at the University of California, Irvine, December 12-14, 1997, which was organized by Irvine Linguistics Students Association (ILSA). 21 papers were presented at the conference; 11 of those are in this book. The original motivation of the conference was to provide a forum for discussion on Chinese linguistics in theoretical approaches. Participants were from the Canada, Germany, Hong Kong, Taiwan, United Kingdom, and the United States. This book represents an attempt to present readers with the main thrust of research on Chinese languages from the perspective of formal linguistics.

We would like to thank the many people who helped to make the conference a success. First, our deeply gratitude goes to Jim Huang and Moira Yip for offering advice and assistance. Funding for the conference was provided by a grant from the School of Social Sciences of the University of California, Irvine, which we gratefully acknowledge. We thank the very patient anonymous reviewers who had to read a good number of abstracts in a short time. Thanks also go to the volunteers in Irvine who helped with registration, food, and all other important details, particularly to Jonah Lin who originally suggested the title of the conference.

Each paper submitted to this book was reviewed at least by two reviewers anonymously. The anonymous reviewers of this book were invited from the United States, Hong Kong, Taiwan, and Japan, all of whom we are thankful to. This book has been a very long time in the making. Due to so many unexpected difficulties and problems, the editorial work was behind our schedule. Thanks most of all to the authors herein for their time and effort in submitting these papers and patient cooperation. Finally, we would like to thank CSLI for assistance in preparing the manuscripts and for helping to harvest the book.

Sze-Wing Tang and Chen-Sheng Luther Liu

Part I

Syntax and Semantics

Tense as a Grammatical Category in Chinese*

MIAO-LING HSIEH
National Taiwan Normal University

0. Introduction

Recent studies of Chinese syntax such as Y.-H. Li (1990) and B. Chiu (1993) claim that Chinese sentences bear tense. Y.-H. Li distinguishes finite from non-finite (i.e. infinitives) clauses. Following C. L. Tsang (1981), she takes the two modals hui 'will' and yao 'want, surely' to be future tense markers, and claims that they cannot occur in infinitives because infinitives do not have tense. On the other hand, B. Chiu (1993) claims that the verbal suffix -le is a past tense marker, which heads a TP (Tense Projection).

In contrast, Cheng & Tang (1996) (C & T) argue against the above views, and claim there is no syntactic projection of Tense. The three arguments that they provide are as follows. First, not all verbs can occur with hui, yao and -le. For example,

*The author is grateful for the audience at the "On the Formal Way to Chinese Languages' held at University of California, Irvine (December, 1997). Special thanks go to B. Comrie, C.-T. James Huang, Y.-H. Audrey Li, Binfu Lu, and an anonymous reviewer who provided useful suggestions.

On the Formal Way to Chinese Languages.
Sze-Wing Tang and Chen-Sheng Luther Liu (eds.).

(1) a. *Ta mingtian hui/yao neng lai.
he tomorrow will/surely can come
'He will can come tomorrow.'
b. *Ta qunian zai-le Meiguo.
he last:year be:located-ASP America[1]
'He was in America last year.'

Sentence (1a) contains the modal neng 'can,' which can occur with neither hui nor yao. This is not surprising because the English counterpart is also ungrammatical. Modals do not seem to be able to be marked with future tense. Sentence (1b) shows that the verbal suffix -le is not compatible with a stative verb such as zai 'be located.' This is also expected because not all of the stative predicates can occur with the verbal -le as discussed in the literature (Smith 1991, among others).

Another argument is based on the contrast between (2) and (3):

(2) a. He was at home yesterday/*right now/*tomorrow.
b. John would/should/might/must/can go to school *yesterday/now/tomorrow.

(3) a. Ta zuotian/xianzai/mingtian zai jia.
he yesterday/now/tomorrow be:located home
'He were/is/will be home yesterday/now/tomorrow.'
b. Ta zuotian/xianzai/mingtian keyi/yinggai/keneng/
he yesterday/now/tomorrow can/should/may/need/can
bixu/neng lai.[2]
need/can come
'He can/should/may/need/can come yesterday/now/tomorrow.'

According to C & T, if Chinese does have overt tense markers, the difference between Chinese and English cannot be accounted for in a principled way. We will discuss the contrast between (2a) and (3a) in

---

[1] The abbreviations used in this paper are as follows:
ASP: aspectual marker, CL: classifier, DE: structural particle de, PART: sentence-final particle.

[2] One difference between the modals in Chinese and those in English is that some modals in Chinese can precede hui 'will,' while this is not possible in English:

(i) Ta mingtian keneng/yinggai hui lai.
he tomorrow may/should will come
'It may/should be the case that he will come tomorrow.'

(ii) *He may/should will come tomorrow.

Section 3, where we discuss the tense interpretations of sentences that do not have any aspect or tense marker. The contrast between (2b) and (3b) is potentially problematic for the claim that Chinese has tense. However, if modals are treated as verbs as in Lin & Tang (1991), then they are not predicted to behave like modals in English.

Finally, C & T claim that 'the fact that epistemic modals themselves carry the meaning of future possibility does not mean that they should be analyzed as tense morphemes.' In the first section of this paper, we will show that hui, but not yao, should be analyzed as a tense morpheme, marking (relative) future tense. This will be followed by the discussion of the manner in which time adverbs interact with hui in Section 2. Section 3 discusses the tense interpretations of sentences that are not marked by hui. Finally, Section 4 concludes the paper.

1. (Relative) Future Tense

There are two modals in Chinese, hui 'will' and yao 'surely,' which have future time reference:

(4) Nar hui hen leng.
There will very cold.
'It will be cold there.'

(5) a. Huoche kuai yao lai le.
train soon surely come ASP
'The train will soon be coming.'

b. Kan yangzi mingtian yao xia yu.
see appearance tomorrow surely fall rain
'Looks like it will rain tomorrow.'

As we mentioned above, C. L. Tsang (1981) claims that both hui and yao should be considered relative future tense markers. In this section, we will argue that only the former can be considered a (relative) future tense marker.

Like Chinese, the so-called future tense in English is indicated by modals, i.e. 'will' and 'shall.' It is a controversial issue in the literature on English whether these expressions of future time reference are in fact distinct tense forms or merely forms with more general meanings subsuming future time reference. While some agree that English has a future tense, this view is rejected either explicitly or implicitly by others.[3] This issue is discussed in Comrie (1985, pp. 47-48; 1989), in which it is suggested that English has a separate grammatical category of future time reference, i.e. future tense. Comrie (1985) points out that the so-called future tense is

---

[3] For a review of early literature on this subject, please see Wekker (1976).

clearly distinct from the modal use because the former makes a clear prediction about some future state of affairs, while the latter only makes reference to alternative worlds. Compare (6a) with (6b).

(6) a. It will rain tomorrow.
b. It may rain tomorrow.

Sentences (6a) and (6b) are distinct because the former is 'a very definite statement about a state of affairs to hold at a certain time subsequent to the present moment,' and the latter is 'simply a claim about a possible world in which there is rain tomorrow.' (p.44) The two are different in the way their truth conditions are evaluated. According to Comrie, the truth conditions of the former can be tested at that future time by seeing whether it does in fact rain or not, yet those of the latter cannot be evaluated in the same manner. Thus future tense is distinct from the modal use.

In addition, Comrie gives two pieces of evidence suggesting that English marks future tense. The first piece of evidence has to do with the distinction between scheduling and future time reference. In English, a matrix clause which bears future time reference does not have to be marked by the auxiliary 'will' if it refers to a situation that is scheduled to happen. Thus, (7a) is acceptable because departing can be scheduled, while (7b) is not since raining cannot be scheduled.

(7) a. The train departs at five o'clock tomorrow morning.
b. It will rain/*rains tomorrow.

The ungrammatical example in (7b) would be acceptable if, according to Comrie, one imagines a context in which rain is scheduled, e.g., if God is talking, or advances in meteorology make it possible for human beings to schedule rain. Crucially, the contrast between (7a) and (7b) cannot be explained if one does not make explicit separate references to scheduling and future time reference.

The second piece of evidence comes from the use of the auxiliary 'will' in temporal and conditional clauses. In general, the auxiliary 'will' with future time reference is normally excluded from these contexts even when scheduling is not possible. Consider the examples in (8).

(8) a. If it *will rain/rains tomorrow, we will get wet.
b. If he will go swimming in dangerous waters, he will drown.

As shown in (8a), the auxiliary 'will' cannot occur in a conditional clause. Sentence (8b) is possible only with the modal meaning of 'will.' Thus, the uses of 'will' with future time reference are GRAMMATICALLY distinct from the modal uses of 'will' in these subordinate clauses. This again suggests that the grammar must refer to future time reference independent of the modal meaning.

Now let us consider Chinese data. There are cases where neither hui nor yao is required for the indication of future time reference:

(9) Wo qu.
I go
'I go/want to go/I will go.'

(10) a. Huoche wu dian kai.
train five o'clock leave
'The train departs at five o'clock.'

b. Wo zai jia.
I be:located home
'I am at home.'

One might want to argue that Chinese, like many European languages, simply does not distinguish present and future. In those languages, the so-called present tense, the normal verb form, can be used to indicate future time reference, despite the fact that these languages do also have specific constructions with exclusively future reference (Comrie 1985). For example, in German both (11a) and (11b) are acceptable:

(11) a. Ich gehe morgen.
I go tomorrow
'I will go [literally: I go] tomorrow.'

b. Ich werde gehen.
I will go
'I will go.'

Sentence (11b) is normally only used where there would otherwise be danger of misunderstanding in the direction of present time reference. In these languages, then, it is reasonable that the only tenses distinguished grammatically are past and non-past.

However, Chinese is different from these European languages because there are clear cases in which a future tense marker is required:

(12) a. Mingtian *(hui) xia yu.[4]
tomorrow will fall rain
'It will rain tomorrow.'

---

[4] The sentence without hui might be acceptable if it were uttered by a weatherman.

b. Ta mingtian *(hui) zhidao na-jian shi.
he tomorrow will know that-CL matter
'He will know that matter tomorrow.'

Note that in the above cases the presence of the time adverb mingtian 'tomorrow' is insufficient to indicate future time reference.

Now the question is why in the earlier examples neither hui nor yao is needed for indicating future time reference. In (9), it is reasonable to believe that the future time reference derives from the volitional interpretation (M.-L. Hsieh 2001). Now consider the contrast between the sentences in (10) and those in (12). The former but not the latter can be scheduled. Thus, the former do not need an auxiliary, while the latter are ungrammatical without the presence of hui 'will.'

In what follows we will provide evidence to show that hui, but not yao, is a relative future tense marker.

1.1 Hui

Hui 'will,' just like 'will' in English, is excluded in conditional clauses:

(13) a. *(Yaoshi) mingtian hui xia yu dehua, women jiu hui
if tomorrow will fall rain that:case we then will
linshi. [5]
get:wet
'If it rains tomorrow, we will get wet.'

b. *(Yaoshi) ta mingtian hui zhidao na-jian shi dehua, ta hui
if he tomorrow will know that-CL matter that:case
hen shengqi.
very angry
'If he knows that matter tomorrow, he will be very angry.'

The fact that hui is not allowed in these contexts strongly suggests that in Chinese, just as in English, future time reference must be referred to independently of the modal meaning.

---

[5] A reviewer has pointed out that sentence in (i) is good in contrast to the sentence discussed in the text.

(i) Yaoshi mingtian hui xia yu dehua, wo jiu gei ni yiqian kuai qian.
if tomorrow will fall rain if I then give you one:thousand money
'If it is possible to rain tomorrow, I will give you one thousand dollars.'

However, unlike the sentence in the text, example (i) refers to a highly hypothetical situation. While the former is neutral about whether it will rain tomorrow, (i) strongly implies it is not possible for it to rain tomorrow. Thus, the use of hui in (i) should be considered a modal one.

On the other hand, there is evidence suggesting that the future tense in Chinese is relative. We follow Comrie (1985) in defining tense as the grammaticalization of location in time and in distinguishing two subtypes: absolute and relative tense. The former locates the situation in question at, before, or after the present moment, while the latter locates it at, before, or after a point of reference given by the context. The examples in (14) show that hui can locate the situation after a point of reference in the past. Given this possibility, hui should be considered a relative future tense marker rather than an absolute one.

(14) a. Zhangsan qiantian hen danxin
Zhangsan the:day:before:yesterday very worried
zuotian Lisi hui zhidao na-ge mimi.
yesterday Lisi will know that-CL secret
'Zhangsan was worried the day before yesterday that Lisi would know about that secret yesterday.'

b. Wo qiantian zai dianshi li kandao zuotian
I the:day:before:yesterday in TV inside see yesterday
taifeng hui lai de baodao.
typhoon will come DE report
'I saw on TV the day before yesterday the report that the typhoon would come yesterday.'

In summary, if 'will' and 'shall' in English can be considered future tense markers, hui in Chinese is qualified to be a relative future tense marker. Now the question is why hui has the absolute tense reading in matrix clauses such as (12). We will return to this in Section 2.

1.2 Yao

It is commonly held that yao 'surely' in Chinese also indicates future tense. Yao, however, behaves differently from hui 'will' in several ways. First, yao, but not hui, can occur with the sentence-final particle le indicating imminent future as shown in the examples below:

(15) a. Huoche kuai yao lai le.
train soon surely come ASP
'The train is coming soon.'

b. *Huoche hui lai le.
train will come ASP
'The train is coming.'

However, as shown in (16), yao in this pattern is not obligatory as long as there are adverbs such kuai 'soon' or jiu 'immediately':

(16) a. Huoche kuai lai le.
train soon come ASP
'The train is coming soon.'
b. Huoche jiu lai le.
train immediately come ASP
'The train is coming in no time.'

In the cases where the sentence-final particle le does not occur, the use of yao indicating future time reference is highly restricted. Yao must occur in contexts in which there is some indication in the present that the future event in question will happen, a constraint that hui is not subject to. Consider the contrast between hui and yao in (17), and that between (17) and (18).

(17) a. Mingtian hui/*yao xia yu.
tomorrow will/surely fall rain
'It will rain tomorrow.'
b. Ta mingtian hui/*yao danxin.
he tomorrow will/surely worried
'He will be worried tomorrow.'
c. Ta mingtian hui/*yao shengbing.
he tomorrow will/surely sick
'He will get sick tomorrow.'
(18) a. Kan yangzi mingtian yao xia yu.
see appearance tomorrow surely fall rain
'Looks like it will rain tomorrow.'
b. Ta mingtian you yao danxin.
he tomorrow again surely worried
'He will be worried again tomorrow.'
c. Ta mingtian kending yao shengbing.
he tomorrow definitely surely sick
'He will definitely be sick tomorrow.'

The fact that yao co-occurs with expressions such as kan yangzi, you, and kending in (17) suggests that a felicitous occurrence of yao may require some present indication of the future event. This difference between yao and hui is very similar to the difference between 'will' and 'be going to' in English as exemplified in (19): sentence (19a) is oriented toward the future, while (19b) focuses on the preparatory state which leads to a future state.

(19) a. It'll rain this afternoon.
b. It's going to rain this afternoon.

Comparing the difference between the two sentences, Wekker (1976, p. 124) observes that while (19a) sounds odd as it stands, (19b) sounds perfectly normal. He points out when (19a) is used, there would normally be at least some implication of an association with something else in the context of the situation. For this reason, (19a) is felicitous if it is followed by a discourse fragment such as 'so don't go out without a good raincoat.' In contrast, (19b) does not have this same implication. Its implication, according to Wekker, is that some present situation indicates the future event in question will occur. Present indications are 'facts and circumstances existing at the present moment, from which the speaker infers a future happening, or on which he bases his prediction.' Wekker points out that this is the reason why (19b) tends to be preceded by the following sentences: 'Look at those clouds,' or 'I can see the black clouds gathering.' In other words, (19a) is a simple prediction, and its orientation is toward the future, whereas (19b) refers to the preparatory state that characteristically precedes the event described by the predication of the sentence.

The difference between yao and hui is further demonstrated by the contrast in (20).

(20) a. Zhangsan qinyan kanjian huoche you yao kai.
Zhangsan with:own:eye see train again surely leave
'Zhangsan with his own eyes saw the train about to depart again.'

b. *Zhangsan qinyan kanjian huoche hui kai.
Zhangsan with:own:eye see train will leave
'Zhangsan with his own eyes saw the train will leave.'

While (20a) is perfectly grammatical with the interpretation involving direct perception, sentence (20b) is ungrammatical. Sentence (20a) shows again that yao does not mark a future event. If yao denoted future tense, Zhangsan would not be able to see anything. In contrast, sentence (20a) is possible because the preparations leading to a future situation could be seen.

Thus far, we have pointed out several differences between hui and yao. These differences do not necessarily disqualify the latter from being a tense marker. However, there is indeed evidence suggesting that only the former, but not the latter, should be treated as a future tense marker. First, yao can occur in conditional clauses as shown in (21).

(21) a. Mingtian yao xia yu dehua, women jiu hui linshi
tomorrow surely fall rain that:case we then will get:wet
'If it rains tomorrow, we will get wet.'

b. Ta mingtian yao zhidao na-jian shi dehua,
he tomorrow surely know that-CL matter that:case
ta hui hen shengqi.
he will very angry
'If he knows that matter tomorrow, he will be very angry.'

This contrasts with hui in (13), repeated here.

(22) a. *(Yaoshi) mingtian hui xia yu dehua, women jiu hui linshi.
if tomorrow will fall rain that:case we then will get:wet
'If it rains tomorrow, we will get wet.'

b. *(Yaoshi) ta mingtian hui zhidao na-jian shi dehua, ta hui
if he tomorrow will know that-CL matter that:case
hen shengqi.
very angry

'If he knows that matter tomorrow, he will be very angry.'

Thus, unlike hui, the future time reference uses of yao do not seem to be distinct from its modal uses.

Further evidence that suggests yao should not be treated as a tense marker comes from negation and question formation. First, when yao is negated by bu 'not' as shown in (23), it does not have the future reference reading. Instead, it only has the imperative reading:

(23) a. Danyuan mingtian bu-yao xia yu.
hopefully tomorrow don't fall rain
'I hope it will not rain tomorrow.'
*'It will not rain tomorrow.'

b. Ni jinnian dongtian bu-yao shengbing.
you this:year winter don't get:sick
'Don't get sick this winter.'
*'You will not get sick this winter.'

Moreover, yao cannot form A-not-A questions directly:

(24) a. *Mingtian yao-bu-yao xia yu?
tomorrow surely-not-surely fall rain
'Will it rain tomorrow?'

b. *Ta jinnian dongtian yao-bu-yao sheng bing?
he this:year winter surely-not-surely grow sickness
'Will he be sick this winter?'

An A-not-A question with yao can only be formed using the copula shi 'be':

(25) a. Mingtian shi-bu-shi yao xia yu?
tomorrow be-not-be surely fall rain
'Will it rain tomorrow?'
b. Huoche shi-bu-shi yao kai le?
train be-not-be surely leave ASP
'Is the train going to leave?'

In contrast, hui can be negated directly, and it can be used to form an A-not-A question:

(26) a. Mingtian bu hui xia yu.
he tomorrow not will fall rain
'It will not rain tomorrow.'
b. Ta mingtian hui bu hui zhidao na-jian shi?
he tomorrow will not will know that-CL matter
'Will he know about that matter tomorrow?'

The above evidence suggests yao is not a future tense marker. If it were, there would be no reason why it could not be negated, or form an A-not-A question directly. These facts can be explained, however, if it is analyzed as a modal, since modals tend to act differently from verbs with respect to negation and question formation. To compare, let us consider the modal dei 'must.' As shown in (27), dei cannot be negated by bu, or form an A-not-A question directly.

(27) a. Wo (*bu) dei qu.
I not must go
'I must go.'
b. *Ni dei-bu-dei qu?
you must not must go
'Must you go?'

Finally, consider the two sentences taken from S. Lü (1991) in (28). They show that when hui and yao are present in a sentence, the former precedes the latter.

(28) a. Kan yangzi hui yao xia yu.
see appearance will surely fall rain
'It looks like it will rain.'

b. Bu guan shiji yiwei man gan hui yao shibai de.
not care reality obstinate hard do will surely fail DE
'You will fail if you disregard reality and persist obstinately.'

This fact cannot be accounted for if both hui and yao mark future tense. If hui marks relative future tense as we have argued above, yao cannot be a relative tense marker.

In summary, the above study suggests that yao should not be treated as a future tense marker, in contrast to C. L. Tsang's (1981) position in which both hui and yao are considered relative future tense markers.

2. Tense Interpretations and Time Adverbs

In this section, we consider the manners in which time adverbs interact with hui. If our claim that hui marks (relative) future tense is correct, the time adverb should be able to denote a point of reference in time, and hui should be able to locate the situation before this point of reference denoted by the time adverb (cf. Comrie 1985, p. 64). However, as shown in the example below, hui cannot locate the situation relative to the reference point denoted by a time adverb in the same clause.

(29) a. Ta mingtian hui zhidao na-jian shi.
he tomorrow will know that-CL matter
'He will know about that matter tomorrow.'

b. Ta zuotian benlai hui you weixian.
he yesterday originally will have danger
'Originally he was in danger yesterday.'

The time adverb mingtian 'tomorrow' in (29a) cannot be taken to be a point of reference in time, and thus the situation referred to cannot be located after the reference point denoted by the time adverb. Similarly, the relative future reading in (29b) is also missing. The only reading that is possible is the epistemic possibility reading. The results are the same when the time adverb is detached from the rest of the clause.

(30) a. Mingtian ta hui zhidao na-jian shi.
tomorrow he will know that-CL matter
'He will know about that matter tomorrow.'

b. Zuotian ta hui you weixian.
yesterday he will have danger
'It is possible that he was in danger yesterday.'

A possible analysis explaining why relative tense makers do not take time adverbs in the same clause as their reference point is that there is a general tendency in language for the present moment to be taken as the reference point.[6] This accounts for the fact that in the following hui behaves like an absolute tense marker.

(31) Ta hui zhidao na-jian shi.
he will know that-CL matter
'He will know about that matter.'

In embedded clauses, as in the sentences in (14), repeated here, the tense of the closest verb is taken as a point of reference:

(32) a. Zhangsan qiantian hen danxin
Zhangsan the:day:before:yesterday very worried
zuotian Lisi hui zhidao na-ge mimi.
yesterday Lisi will know that-CL secret
'Zhangsan was worried the day before yesterday that Lisi would know about that secret yesterday.'

b. Wo qiantian zai dianshi li kandao zuotian
I the:day:before:yesterday in TV inside see yesterday
taifeng hui lai de baodao.
typhoon will come DE report
'I saw on TV the day before yesterday the report that the typhoon would come yesterday.'

In summary, hui is a relative tense marker. When it occurs in an embedded sentence, the tense of the closest verb serves as the reference time. But when it is not embedded, the reference time is the time of utterance.

3. Aspect and Tense Interpretations

In the case of sentences in which there are no tense markers, it is conceivable that time reference is determined by several distinctions, including time adverbs, verbal aspect (stative vs. eventive), grammatical aspect (progressive vs. perfective), mood, and clause type (finite clause vs. infinitive). Take Japanese as an example. Japanese has a basic past/non-past distinction because it lacks any verb form that specifically refers to future time. According to Comrie (1989), in the absence of other contextual

---

[6] This suggestion is due to B. Comrie.

indicators, the most likely interpretation of sentences with non-past tense is determined mainly by grammatical aspect and verbal aspect. Thus the sentence with the progressive form in (33a) below will usually be assigned present time reference and thus means '(he) is going.' On the other hand, (33b) can either have a habitual interpretation, or it can be assigned future time reference and mean '(he) will go.' This future time reference is assigned because it is not possible for a complete act of going to take place entirely in the present.

(33) a. it-te i-ru
go-progressive-nonpast
'(he) is going'
b. ik-u
go-nonpast
'(he) will go'

Stative sentences with no overt adverbial can have both possible time references, as in the following sentence:

(34) Taroo-ga koko-ni i-masu. (Ogihara 1996)
Taro-NOM here-at be-PRES (progressive)
'Taro is here now' or 'Taro will be here.'

Note that sentence (34) is considered by Ogihara (1996) to be genuinely ambiguous. This is because it cannot be used to assert that John is here at some non-past time. In other words, the speaker must decide whether a claim is being made about the current time or about some future time.

We have argued above that hui is a (relative) future tense marker in Chinese. In the case that hui does not appear (nor other modals), then a sentence must have either past time reference or present time reference. In the following, we will discuss the manner in which aspect and situation type determine the tense interpretations of a sentence in Chinese.

3.1 Sentences with Perfective Markers

As shown in (35), sentences with the perfective marker -le or -guo denote past:

(35) a. Ta kan-le san-ben shu.
he read-ASP three-CL book
'He read three books.'
b. Ta qu-guo Beijing.
he go-ASP Beijing
'He has been to Beijing.'

This is expected because both -le and -guo are perfective, and it is not possible for a complete event to take place entirely in the present.

When a resultant state is involved, the most natural interpretation of a sentence with -le is present time reference, though past time reference is still an available interpretation.

(36) a. Nar gua-le yi-zhang hua.
there hang-ASP one-CL painting
'Here is/was a painting hanging on the wall.'
b. Nar ting-man-le che.
there park-full-ASP car
'That place is/was full of cars.'

Contrasting with (35a), the sentences in (36) refer to the resultant state of a relevant action. The present time reference interpretation, in addition to the past time reference interpretation, is available because the resultant state may still be ongoing at the time of utterance.

English uses different tenses for similar situations. For example, seeing a broken window lying on the floor, (37a) can be used if it is the resultant state that is focused. On the other hand, if it is the event that is focused, (37b) is more appropriate. One difference between the two sentences lies in tense. The former sentence is in present tense because the resultant state is ongoing. The second sentence, however, is in past tense because for the sentence to be felicitous the event must have taken place.

(37) a. The window is broken.
b. The window was broken by John.

3.2 Sentences with Imperfective Markers

The most natural tense interpretation for sentences with the imperfective marker zai or -zhe is the present tense. However, these sentences can also have past time reference:

(38) a. Ta zai renzhen de kan shu.
he ASP diligent DE read book
'He is/was studying diligently.'
b. Na-kuai heiban shang xie-zhe zi.
that-CL blackboard top write-ASP word
'There are/were a lot of words written on the blackboard.'

That imperfectives can have present time reference is expected because they do not have the same restriction as perfectives. Thus imperfective sentences can have either present or past time reference.

3.3 Sentences with no Overt Aspectual Markers

In Chinese, some of the sentences that are not overtly aspectually marked are stative sentences, including habituals and generics. Generic sentences are considered to be true at all times, and thus the issue of tense does not arise. Habitual sentences, on the other hand, can be interpreted as either in the past or in the present, just like other stative sentences:

(39) a. Ta tiantian kai che.
he everyday drive car
'He drove/drives everyday.'
b. Na-ben shu hen gui.
that-CL book very expensive
'That book is/was expensive.'

Thus it is not surprising that there is a contrast between (2a) and (3a), repeated here, as pointed out by Cheng & Tang (1996).

(40) a. He was at home yesterday/*right now/*tomorrow.
b. Ta zuotian/xianzai/mingtian zai jia.
he yesterday/now/tomorrow be:located home
'He were/is/will be home yesterday/now/tomorrow.'

As for non-stative types of sentences, there are two subtypes that do not bear aspectual markers. In one subtype the presence of perfective markers is prohibited or marginal. In the other subtype perfective markers and imperfective markers are optional. As an example of the first subtype, consider (41).

(41) a. Wo tingshuo(*-le) ta zou le.
I hear-ASP he leave ASP
'I heard that he left.'
b. Ta hen limao de ba ta jieshao(?-le) gei women.
he very polite DE BA he introduce-ASP to us
'He introduced him to us very politely.'

There are several reasons that (41a) should be considered to bear past time reference. First, it is unlikely that the sentence in (41a) is something that will be scheduled. Second, it is unlikely that (41a) refers to a habitual situation because there are no adverbs such as changchang 'often.' Finally, the imperfective reading is also unlikely. Given these, past time reference is the only possibility remaining. Similarly, the matrix verb in (41b) can only bear past time reference.

For the second subtype, consider the examples in (42). The examples in (42) show that aspectual markers can be optional.

(42) a. Ni mai (-le) shenme shu?[7]
he buy-ASP what book
'What book did you buy?'
b. Ni nar (zai) xia(-zhe) yu ma?
you place in fall-ASP rain PART
"Is it raining at the place where you are?'
c. Ni shou shang na(-zhe) shenme?
you hand top take-ASP what
'What are you holding in your hand?'

The first sentence in (42a) can be used when the speaker presupposes that the hearer has bought book(s), and when the speaker wants to know what book(s) the hearer bought. Sentence (42b) can be used felicitously when the speaker is interested in knowing the current weather condition in the hearer's location. The former sentence is perfective, whereas the latter sentence is imperfective. Thus the former bears past time reference, and the most natural interpretation for the imperfective sentence is the present time reference. Finally, (42c) can be used when the speaker presupposes that the hearer is holding something and thus the sentence bears present time reference.

4. Conclusions

Our study supports the claim that Chinese has tense. However, contrast to the studies done by C. L. Tsang (1981) and Y.-H. Li (1990), we claim that hui 'will', but not yao 'surely,' marks (relative) future tense. The tense interpretations of sentences that are not marked by hui are also discussed.

References

Cheng, Lisa L.-S., and C.-C. Jane Tang. 1996. On the Syntactic Projection of Tense in Mandarin Chinese. Paper presented at The Eighth North American Conference on Chinese Linguistics, University of Illinois, Urbana-Champaign.

---

[7] Without -le, this sentence can refer to a future situation since the volitional interpretation is available.

Chiu, Bonnie H.-C. 1993. *The Inflectional Structure of Mandarin Chinese.* Ph.D. Dissertation, University of California at Los Angeles.

Comrie, Bernard. 1985. *Tense.* Cambridge: Cambridge University Press.

Comrie, Bernard. 1989. On Identifying Future Tenses. *Tempus-Aspekt-Modus: Die Lexikalischen und Grammatischen Formen in den Germanischen Sprachen.* Herausgegeben von Werner Abraham und Theo Janssen. Tübingen: Max Niemeyer Verlag.

Hsieh, M.-L. 2001. Form and Meaning: Negation and Question in Chinese. Doctoral Dissertation, University of Southern California.

Li, Y.-H. Audrey. 1990. *Order and Constituency in Mandarin Chinese.* Dordrecht/Boston/London: Kluwer.

Lin, J.-W., and C.-C. J. Tang. 1991. Modals in Chinese. Paper presented at The Third North American Conference on Chinese Linguistics, Cornell University.

Lü, Shuxiang. 1991. *Xiandai Hanyu Babai Ci.* Hong Kong: Shangwu Yinshuguan.

Ogihara, Toshiyuki. 1996. *Tense, Attitudes, and Scope.* Dordrecht: Kluwer.

Smith, Carlota. 1991. *The Parameter of Aspect.* Dordrecht: Kluwer.

Tsang, Chui Lim. 1981. *A Semantic Study of Modal Auxiliary Verbs in Chinese.* Doctoral Dissertation, Stanford University.

Wekker H. Chr. 1976. *The Expression of Future Time in Contemporary British English: An Investigation into the Syntax and Semantics of Five Verbal Constructions Expressing Futurity.* Amsterdam, New York and Oxford: North-Holland Publishing Company.

Distributivity and Reflexivity

C.-T. JAMES HUANG
Harvard University

In this paper I consider some peculiar properties of reflexive sentences in Mandarin, indicating that the bare reflexive *ziji* exceptionally induces distributivity on a plural antecedent—in both local binding and long-distance binding.* Despite the appeal of a uniform explanation for the distributivity effects, it will be argued that the distributivity of a local plural binder should be derived from a different source than the distributivity of a long-distance antecedent. This is in line with a non-uniform approach which treats the locally bound *ziji* as an instance of a syntactic anaphor, and the long-distance *ziji* as a logophor. The correctness of our account of distributivity then lends further support to the non-uniform approach.

*The ideas pursued in this paper were first presented at two NSF sponsored workshops that took place during the 1997 Linguistic Institute at Cornell University: the Workshop on Long-Distance Reflexives and the Workshop on Parameters in Semantic Theory. An earlier version of the paper was presented at a colloquium at National Tsing Hua University. For their support and/or very useful comments I am indebted to Yue-chin Chang, Gennaro Chierchia, Peter Cole, Francesca Del Gobbo, Audrey Li, Yafei Li, Jonah Lin, Jowang Lin, Luther Liu, Kuang Mei, Sze-Wing Tang, Dylan Tsai, Matthew Whelpton, and Di Wu. This research has been supported, in part, by NSF Grant #SBR-9729519 and by a fellowship from the Center for Advanced Study in the Behavioral Sciences (1997-1998).

On the Formal Way to Chinese Languages.
Sze-Wing Tang and Chen-Sheng Luther Liu (eds.).

1. Two Distributivity Puzzles

1.1 Plurals and Distributivity

It is generally agreed that English plural noun phrases admit of both a collective and a distributive reading, as illustrated in (1):

(1) a. They bought a car.
  b. John and Bill read two books.

According to (1a) they may have bought a car together, or they may have each bought a car; and in (1b) John and Bill may have read a total of two books (the collective reading), or they may have each read two, for a total of four, books (the distributive reading).

In Chinese, however, plural NPs generally do not exhibit the distributive reading without a special marker for distributivity. Thus, the Chinese counterparts of (1) are unambiguous, admitting of only a collective reading each:

(2) a. Tamen mai-le yi-liang che.
  They buy-PERF one-CL car
  'They bought a car.' (Collective reading only.)

  b. Zhangsan he Lisi kan-le liang-ben shu.
  Zhangsan and Lisi read-PERF two-CL book
  'Zhangsan and Lisi read two books.'
  (Collective reading only.)

A distributive reading requires the presence of *dou* 'all' or *ge* 'each'.[1]

---

[1] Both *dou* 'all' and *ge* 'each' have the force of universal quantification and of distributivity. The English glosses for these words do not capture their differences adequately. One way to talk about the differences between *dou* and *ge* is that whereas the former is a 'mass' distributor, the latter is a 'count' distributor (or, in the words of Lin (1998), that *ge* distributes over extensional classes while *dou* operates on intensional expressions). In terms of the 'relational' theory of distributivity developed in Choe (1987), *ge* 'each' requires a c-commanding plural term representing the 'sorting key' and an indefinite quantity expression in its c-domain representing the 'distributive share'. In (i) the sorting key is *tamen* 'they' and the distributive share is '3 books'. For *ge*, the sorting key must be a plural term and the distributive share an indefinite one. Both must be count NPs:

(i) tamen ge mai-le san-ben shu.
  They each buy-PERF three-CL book
  'They each bought three books.'

(3) a. Tamen dou/ge mai-le yi-liang che.
They all/each buy-PERF one-CL car
'They all/each bought a car.'
(Distributive reading only.)

b. Zhangsan he Lisi dou/ge kan-le liang-ben shu.
Zhangsan and Lisi all/each read-PERF two-CL book
'Zhangsan and Lisi both/each read two books.'
(Distributive reading only.)

(ii) *tamen ge mai-le shu.
they each buy-PERF book
For: 'They each bought books.'

(iii) *tamen ge mai-le na-ben shu.
they each buy-PERF that-CL book
For: 'They each bought that book.'

(iv) *ta zheng ben shu ge kan le.
he whole volume book each read PERF
For: 'He read the entire book.'

(v) *ta shui ge he le.
he water each drink PERF
For: 'He drank all the water.'

The occurrence of *dou* is much freer. All of (i-iv) are well-formed if *ge* is replaced by *dou*:

(vi) tamen dou mai-le san-ben shu.
they all buy-PERF three-CL book
'They all bought three books.'

(vii) tamen dou mai-le shu.
they all buy-PERF book
'They all bought books.'

(viii) tamen dou mai-le na-ben shu.
they all buy-PERF that-CL book
'They all bought that book.'

(ix) ta zheng ben shu dou kan le.
he whole volume book all read PERF
'He read the entire book.'

(x) ta shui dou he le.
he water all drink PERF
'He drank all the water.'

While *ge* distributes over atomic entities each of which corresponds to a count noun, *dou* is able to distribute over molecules that make up sub-lattices of singular atoms, plurals, or masses. In (vii)-(viii) the distributive share is provided by indefinite slices of the kind 'books' or copies (tokens) of the singular object 'that book'. In (ix) and (x), *dou* distributes over sub-lattices of NP denotations as its sorting key and (possibly) sub-events (or properties) as its distributive share. For discussion of the properties of *ge*, see T.-H. Lin (1998). For the semantics of *dou*, see S. Huang (1996), Li (1997), J. Lin (1998) and references cited there.

This is clearly a systematic contrast of considerable comparative significance, and is the subject of investigation for J. Lin (1996, 1998), S. Huang (1996) and X. Li (1997). Li highlights the Chinese-English contrast by comparing an English sentence of the sort studied in Heim, Lasnik and May (1991, HLM) with its Chinese counterpart. HLM observed that 5 different readings may be obtained from the English sentence (4), depending on whether the matrix subject or the embedded subject, or both, are interpreted collectively or distributively.

(4) John and Mary argue that they will win $100.
  a. [John and Mary]1 argue that they1 will win $100.
  b. [John and Mary]1 argue that [they1 D2] will win $100.
  c. [[John and Mary]1 D2] argue that they1 will win $100.
  d. [[John and Mary]1 D2] argue that [they1 D3] will win $100.
  e. [[John and Mary]1 D2] argue that they2 will win $100.

According to (4a), John and Mary together claim that they, together, will win $100.[2] According to (4b), they claim "We will each win $100." In (4c-e), John and Mary both make the following claims, respectively: "We (together) will win $100," "We will each win $100," and "I will win $100."

In sharp contrast, the Chinese sentence in (5) has only one reading, that corresponding to (4a).

(5) Lao Zhang he Lao Li shuo tamen hui zhong yibai yuan.
Lao Zhang and Lao Li say they will hit 100 dollar
Lao Zhang and Lao Li argued that they would win $100.

The distributive readings indicated in (4b-e) are obtained only if *dou* (or *ge*) is inserted in the position corresponding to D in (4):

(6) Lao Zhang he Lao Li shuo tamen dou hui zhong yibai yuan.
Lao Zhang and Lao Li say they all will hit 100 dollar

---

[2] Here *together* means 'regarded collectively', not 'occurring at the same time or at the same place'. A collective reading may be true of many scenarios, not limited to those where participants are involved 'together' in any spatial or temporal sense. For example, the collective reading of (2b) may be true of the scenario where one of the readers read one whole book and half of another, and the other reader finished the other half of the second book. Similarly, the collective reading represented in (4a) (and the Chinese sentence (5) below) is true not only of the scenario where John and Bill make the joint statement, "We will win $100," but also true where John says, "I will win $80" and Bill says, on a different occasion, "I will win $20." The semantics of plurals and group readings is a complex subject which goes beyond the scope of this note.

Lao Zhang and Lao Li argued that both of them would win $100.

(7) Lao Zhang he Lao Li dou shuo tamen hui zhong yibai yuan.
Lao Zhang and Lao Li all say they will hit 100 dollar
Both Lao Zhang and Lao Li argued that they would win $100.

(8) Lao Zhang he Lao Li dou shuo tamen dou hui zhong yibai yuan.
Lao Zhang and Lao Li all say they all will hit 100 dollar
Both Lao Zhang and Lao Li argued they would both win $100.

(9) Lao Zhang he Lao Li dou shuo ziji hui zhong yibai yuan.[3]
Lao Zhang and Lao Li all say self will hit 100 dollar
Both Lao Zhang and Lao Li argued, "I will win $100."

This behavior of Chinese plurals seems to hold quite generally, except where the predicates inherently resist a collective reading. For example, to cry or have swollen eyes is an event that can only happen to singular individuals. The ability or tendency to cry is not a property of a group. So if it is true that a group of people are crying or have swollen eyes, then it is also that each of them is crying or has swollen eyes. In the following sentences, the distributive reading is available even though *dou* is not present:

(10) Tamen ku-de yanjing zhong-le qilai.
they cry-DE eye swell-PERF up
'They cried so much that their eyes got swollen.'

The addition of *dou* following the plural in (10) adds no content to the sentence with respect to its distributivity; it simply adds the force of universal quantification, emphasizing that the event occurred without exception to all members of the group that the subject denotes. In other

---

[3] (9) and (4e) represent the bound reading of the embedded subject. Under this reading the embedded subject must be rendered by a reflexive. Although for many speakers the singular pronoun *ta* may be used as a bound variable with a singular antecedent like 'everybody', with a plural antecedent neither a singular nor a plural pronoun is acceptable:

(i) mei-ge ren$_i$ dou shuo ta$_i$ meiyou kong.
Every-CL person all say s/he not-have leisure
'Everybody says that s/he has no time.'

(ii) *[Zhangsan gen Lisi]$_i$ dou shuo ta$_i$/tamen$_i$ meiyou kong.
Zhangsan and Lisi all say he/they not-have leisure
'Both Zhangsan and Lisi say that he/they have no time.'

words, a sentence may be inherently distributive, and as such the distributivity need not be signaled by *dou*.

1.2 Puzzle One: Local Reflexive

Now, let's consider reflexive sentences with plural subject antecedents:

(11) a. They praised themselves.

b. John and Mary criticized themselves.

Like (1) and (4) above, both English sentences in (11) may be said to be ambiguous between a distributive and a collective reading, although the nature of distributivity is somewhat different between these and the earlier examples. In the earlier examples, an indefinite expression denoting the 'distributive share' (*a car*, *one hundred dollars*, etc., see note 1) appears in the predicate, so that a distributive reading on a plural subject would entail a multiplied quantity of the distributive share (a total of 2 cars bought, 4 books read, etc.). We can easily distinguish between the collective and distributive readings by pointing to the multiplication, or lack thereof, of the distributive share. In (11), however, the plural subject is not related to an indefinite expression in the predicate, but to an anaphor coindexed with it. Under no circumstances will these sentences convey the meaning that the denotation of the plural subjects engaged in the praising or criticism of a multiple of themselves. However, a significant distinction can still be made between the distributive and collective readings, as follows.

One specific scenario which makes the sentences in (11) true is when each member of the set {they} or of {John, Mary} was engaged in an action of self-praise or self-criticism (e.g., each of them says, "I am great" or both John and Mary say, "I am wrong."). This is the distributive reading. The 'sorting key' (see note 1) is the plural subject in each case, and the distributive share may be said to be one "self," even though the object is actually expressed by a plural term, *themselves*. In this way we could say that the distributive reading does involve a multiple of selves.[4] Note that under the distributive reading, each atomic event involving a singular member of the plural subject is an event of self-praise or self-criticism.

The sentences in (11) can have the collective reading and be true under many other scenarios. For (11a), it may be that each member of the group {they} praises the entire group (including himself or herself). Or it may be

[4] In other words, the plural *themselves* is an example of what is known as the 'dependent plural' in the literature. See Roberts (1987) for a review.

that each member praises *at least* one member of his/her own group *and* is also praised by at least one member of the group.[5] (In the former situation each might say, "We are marvelous," and in the latter each might say "She is great" or "You are great", etc.) Or it may be any scenarios intermediate between these two extremes. Note that for the collective reading, each atomic event (if we are to look into smaller sub-events of each scenario) need not be an event of self-praise or self-criticism. In fact, the collective reading may be true of a scenario where members of a group actually praise or criticize *each other* (hence, the group reading includes the reciprocal reading). Such an event of mutual praise or criticism by a group's members, when viewed externally, is an event of self-praise or self-criticism by the group as a whole.

Let's turn now to Chinese reflexive sentences with *ziji*. Given the contrasts with English we saw, we expect that they should only admit of the collective reading. The fact, however, is just the opposite. The following sentences only have a distributive reading:

(12) a. Zhangsan he Lisi zai piping ziji.
Zhangsan and Lisi at criticize self
'Zhangsan and Lisi are criticizing themselves.'

b. Tamen you zai kuajiang ziji le.
They again at praise self ASP
'They are praising themselves again.'

According to (12a), both Zhangsan and Lisi are engaged in some act of self-criticism, and according to (12b), each of *tamen* 'them' is praising himself/herself. The sentences would not be appropriate for scenarios where members of a group are each praising or criticizing the whole group or each other. The following contrast between English and Chinese illustrates the same point. Although pragmatic considerations strongly favor a collective reading (as in the English example (13a)), (13b) is understood in distributive sense:

(13) a. John and Bill lifted a piano.

[5] These represent the "strong symmetric" and "weak symmetric" versions of the collective reading in Gil's (1982) terminology.

b. Zhangsan he Lisi tai-qi-le ziji-de gangqin.
Zhangsan and Lisi lift-up-PERF self's piano
'Zhangsan and Lisi [respectively] lifted their pianos.'

The point can also be seen by comparing (12) with (14), where instead of the bare reflexive *ziji* we have the compound form *pronoun + ziji*.

(14) a. Zhangsan he Lisi zai piping tamen-ziji.
Zhangsan and Lisi at criticize themselves
'Zhangsan and Lisi are criticizing themselves.'

b. Tamen you zai kuajiang tamen-ziji le.
They again at praise themselves ASP
'They are again praising themselves again.'

These sentences are more on a par with their English counterparts in (11) in readily allowing a group reading. To obtain a clear distributive reading, *dou* can be added:

(15) a. Zhangsan he Lisi dou zai piping tamen-ziji.
Zhangsan and Lisi all at criticize themselves
'Both Zhangsan and Lisi are criticizing themselves.'

b. Tamen you dou zai kuajiang tamen-ziji le.
They again all at praise themselves ASP
'All of them are praising themselves again.'

However, even in (15) the distributive reading should still be distinguished from that observed with (12). In (15) only the plural subjects are interpreted distributively, but not the objects. So these sentences can still be true where each individual denoted by the subject criticizes or praises the entire group (e.g., saying "We are wrong," etc.). In (12), however, distributivity extends to both the subject and the reflexive object, so that only a one-one relationship of self-praise or self-criticism is intended in each case. These sentences in (12) are strongly distributive, in that both the 'sorting key' and the 'distributive share' are singularized.

We have thus observed a peculiar property of the bare reflexive *ziji*, which raises the following question: What is it about the bare reflexive *ziji* that makes a sentence (strongly) distributive?

1.3 Puzzle Two: Long-Distance Reflexive

Now let us turn to sentences in which the bare reflexive is long-distance bound. It has been well known that the bare *ziji* can have an antecedent outside of its governing category:

(16) Zhangsan$_i$ shuo Lisi$_j$ piping-le ziji$_{i/j}$
Zhangsan say Lisi criticize-PERF self
Zhangsan said that Lisi criticized him/himself.

Y.-H. Huang (1984) made an early observation that long-distance binding is not free, but subject to blocking under certain circumstances. For example, a local first- or second-person NP prevents a remote third-person NP from being a long-distance antecedent, so in contrast to (16), neither (17) nor (18) permits long-distance binding:

(17) Zhangsan$_i$ shuo wo$_j$ piping-le ziji$_{*i/j}$
Zhangsan say you criticize-PERF self
Zhangsan said that I criticized *him/myself.

(18) Zhangsan$_i$ shuo ni$_j$ piping-le ziji$_{*i/j}$
Zhangsan say you criticize-PERF self
Zhangsan said that I criticized *him/myself.

Tang (1989) noted that although a plural local subject does not block a singular remote antecedent:

(19) Zhangsan$_i$ shuo tamen$_j$ piping-le ziji$_{i/j}$.
Zhangsan say they criticize-PERF self
Zhangsan said that they criticized him/themselves.

a singular local subject does seem to block a plural remote antecedent:

(20) Tamen$_i$ shuo Zhangsan$_j$ piping-le ziji$_{*i/j}$
They say Zhangsan criticize-PERF self
They said that Zhangsan criticized *them/himself.

If the plural remote antecedent is followed by *dou* 'all' and hence interpreted distributively (and singularly), long-distance binding again becomes possible.

(21) Tamen$_i$ dou shuo Zhangsan$_j$ piping-le ziji$_{i/j}$
They all say Zhangsan criticize-PERF self
'Every one of them said that Zhangsan criticized him/himself.

It turns out, however, that (19)-(21) do not represent the whole picture. Rather than a generalization about blocking, the real generalization seems to be that a plural NP simply cannot serve as the long-distance antecedent of *ziji*, unless it is overtly marked to be distributive.[6] Thus, consider (22), where the embedded and matrix subjects are both third-person plural. Although no blocking effects are expected, *ziji* still cannot be bound by the higher *tamen* 'they':

(22) Tamen$_i$ shuo tamen$_j$ chang piping ziji$_{*i/j}$. (i ≠ j)
they say they often criticize self
'They$_i$ said that they$_j$ often criticize self$_{*i/j}$.'

But if the matrix subject is marked for distributivity by *dou*, then long-distance binding becomes possible again:

(23) Tamen$_i$ dou shuo tamen$_j$ chang piping ziji$_{i/j}$. (i ≠ j)
they all say they often criticize self
'Each of them$_i$ said that they$_j$ often criticize him$_i$/themselves$_j$.'

The real generalization is similar to the one we arrived at in the preceding sub-section. Like locally bound *ziji*, long-distance *ziji* allows a plural remote antecedent, but requires such an antecedent to be interpreted distributively. The important difference is that, unlike the local plural binder, distributivity for the long-distance binder must be marked by an overt distributor like *dou*, and this difference constitutes a second puzzle. In this respect the long-distance plural NP is not exceptional; it is normally interpreted collectively unless explicitly marked for distributivity. The puzzle is why a reflexive *ziji* induces distributivity on its local and remote antecedents in such different ways.

2. *Ziji* is Singular?

Why does the bare reflexive *ziji* induce distributivity? One suggestion that quickly comes to mind is the hypothesis that the bare reflexive *ziji*, which

[6] See also Xu (1993) for a similar point.

lacks any overt specification of its phi-features, is inherently (lexically) specified as [-plural]. Under this hypothesis, distributivity is forced upon the Chinese sentences in (12) because a singular anaphor cannot take a plural antecedent.

While I think the idea that *ziji* has to do with atomicity is on the right track, the simple hypothesis that it is lexically singular will not work to explain the puzzles. This hypothesis basically amounts to saying that *ziji* is covertly equivalent with the Chinese counterparts of *himself, herself, myself,* or *yourself,* but not to *themselves, ourselves,* or *yourselves*. The obligatoriness of the distributive reading in (12a) is then likened to the ungrammaticality of **They criticized himself.* The problem here is that (12a) is itself fully grammatical, but becomes fully ungrammatical once the bare reflexive is replaced with an overt singular *taziji*:

(24) *Zhangsan he Lisi zai piping taziji.
Zhangsan and Lisi at criticize himself
'*Zhangsan and Lisi are criticizing himself.'

This is the case even if distributivity is explicitly signaled by the presence of *dou* 'all':

(25) *Zhangsan he Lisi dou zai piping taziji.
Zhangsan and Lisi all at criticize himself
'*Zhangsan and Lisi are both criticizing himself.'

In fact, even under the distributive reading, a compound reflexive taking a plural antecedent must take the plural form *tamen-ziji* 'themselves':

(26) Zhangsan he Lisi (dou) zai piping tamen-ziji.
Zhangsan and Lisi (all) at criticize themselves
'Zhangsan and Lisi are (both) criticizing themselves'

In other words, the fact remains that (12a) is grammatical but has only a distributive reading. The distributive reading cannot be reduced to the supposed singularity of the bare reflexive. In fact, given the facts in (24)-(26), the grammaticality of (12a) suggests that if the bare reflexive were to be assigned number features, it must be possible for it to have the [+plural] feature, regardless of whether the antecedent is to be interpreted collectively or distributively. The same point can be made with (compound) reflexives or bound variable pronouns with plural antecedents interpreted distributively:

(27) They each criticized themselves.

(28) The contestants each think that they are the best.

Here *themselves* and *they* are examples of what have been known as 'dependent plurals' in the literature, on a par with the following (see, e.g., Roberts 1987 and references cited).

(29) a. They have bleeding noses.

b. *They have a bleeding nose.

All of these sentences on their distributive reading would involve objects that are semantically singular, even though the objects themselves are expressed in the plural form.

Thus, although the singularity/plurality of an argument may affect the singularity/plurality of another (especially if they are coindexed), it does not seem to affect the distributivity of the latter. Given that a bare reflexive can occur with a plural subject grammatically, it must be possible to assign the feature [+plural] to *ziji* in such environments. The question then remains why, unlike the compound reflexives and other plural bound pronouns, the bare reflexive requires a distributive reading of its plural subject.

3. *ziji* and LF-Raising

Although the singularity/plurality of an object does not affect the distributivity of its subject, the singularity of a *predicate* may entail the distributivity of its subject. If a predicate denotes an atomic event or property, which by its nature can only be attributed to one individual at a time, then any plural subject occurring with such a predicate will necessarily be distributive. This is true of cases like (10) above. Below are a few more examples:

(30) a. John and Bill coughed.

b. They are shaving themselves.

c. They have bloody noses.

These sentences must have a distributive reading, since the property of coughing, shaving oneself or having a bloody nose is the property of a single human being, and this is the case even if John and Bill synchronize their action and cough, shave, or have bloody noses exactly at the same time in the same place. In this connection, note that a lexical reflexive predicate has exactly this property of denoting an atomic event or property, forcing distributivity on a plural subject. This is true of both English and Chinese *self*-prefixed predicates:[7]

(31) a. By self-inflicting these wounds, they tried to win our sympathy.

b. Their self-appraisals were rather self-serving.

c. They are overly self-criticizing.

(32) a. Zhangsan he Lisi zai ziwo-piping.
Zhangsan and Lisi at self-criticize
'Zhangsan and Lisi are engaged in self-criticism.'

b. Tamen zi-sha le.
They self-kill ASP
'They committed suicide.'

These sentences contrast with those in which a compound reflexive, like *themselves* or *tamen-ziji*, occurs as a separate co-argument (see (11) and (15)). Thus according to (31a) each of them must have inflicted wounds upon himself/herself, whereas a sentence like *They inflicted wounds upon themselves* may be true of a scenario where members of a group actually inflicted wounds on each other. Similarly, (32a) is true only of a scenario where both Zhangsan and Lisi are engaged in an act of self-criticism, but not where they criticize each other.[8]

Recall that our first puzzle is that the bare *ziji*, but not the compound *tamen-ziji*, induces distributivity.

(12a) Zhangsan he Lisi zai piping ziji.
Zhangsan and Lisi at criticize self
'Zhangsan and Lisi are criticizing themselves.'

---

[7] In English, *self*-prefixed predicates are usually adjectival or nominal, but rarely verbal (as in (31c), due to Matthew Whelpton, personal communication). In Chinese, *zi-* and *ziwo-* can easily occur as verbal prefixes.

[8] Remember that there is also the "group-as-individual" reading for both (32a) and sentences like (11) and (15). In this case, the plural subject is treated as a singular entity, and the issue of distributivity does not arise.

(14a) Zhangsan he Lisi zai piping tamen-ziji.
Zhangsan and Lisi at criticize themselves
'Zhangsan and Lisi are criticizing themselves.'

In this respect, the bare *ziji* behaves like a lexical reflexive predicate, in contrast to the compound reflexive.

Why should a predicate containing a *bare* reflexive argument behave like a lexical reflexive predicate? I suggest that this is because such a predicate is indeed a lexical reflexive predicate at the level of LF, much as first proposed by Lebeaux (1983) and Chomsky (1986). In particular, at LF, the bare reflexive *ziji*, but not the compound *taziji* or *tamen-ziji*, raises and left-adjoins to the governing or immediately c-commanding verb, so that at the level of LF, (12a) has the representation in (33):

(33) Zhangsan he Lisi zai $ziji_i$-piping t_i.
Zhangsan and Lisi at self-criticize
'Zhangsan and Lisi are engaged in self-criticism.'

In other words, the bare reflexive which appears as a postverbal argument in overt syntax, is in fact an LF-prefix, just like the prefix *ziwo* in (32a), as part of a lexical reflexive predicate. Given that a reflexive predicate denotes an atomic event attributable only to singular but not plural individuals, we may say that the bare reflexive, by forming a reflexive predicate in LF, "singularizes" a predicate, forcing it to denote atomic events.

The LF raising analysis thus provides the following answer to the first puzzle. Plural subjects in Chinese are normally interpreted collectively, except when they take predicates that are inherently distributive, such as those exemplified in (30)-(32), including but not limited to lexical reflexive predicates. Bare reflexives form lexical reflexive predicates in LF, so they force a distributive interpretation on their plural subjects as well. In other words, in the case of locally bound bare reflexives, distributivity of the subject is derivative of singularity of the predicate.

The LF raising analysis originates, of course, with Lebeaux (1983) and Chomsky (1986), and has been extended by Pica (1987), Battistella (1987) and Cole et al.(1990) and others in accounts of long-distance anaphora. However, our account must differ from these previous proposals in two crucial respects.

First, unlike Lebeaux and Chomsky, but in line with Pica, Battistella, and Cole et al, I assume that only the *bare* reflexive, but not the compound reflexive, undergoes LF head-movement to V. This must be the case, for our present purposes, because only the bare reflexive, but not the compound reflexive, induces distributivity. This is also supported by general considerations of movement theory. Since the movement is an instance of head-movement, it involves only the bare reflexive, an X^0 element, but not the compound reflexive, an XP.

Second, unlike Pica, Battistella and Cole et al, I assume that the bare reflexive only moves locally, to an immediately c-commanding verb, but does not move further beyond to a higher domain. This must be the case, for our present purposes, given the fact we saw above that a long-distance plural antecedent of the bare reflexive must be marked for distributivity by an appropriate element like *dou*. Some relevant examples are repeated below (cf. (20) and (21)):

(34) *Tamen$_i$ shuo Zhangsan piping-le ziji$_i$.
They say Zhangsan criticize-PERF self
They said that Zhangsan criticized them.

(35) Tamen$_i$ dou shuo Zhangsan piping-le ziji$_i$.
They all say Zhangsan criticize-PERF self
'Everyone of them said that Zhangsan criticized him/her.

If *ziji* were to move (successive cyclically) to the higher verb in (34), the following LF representation would result:

(36) Tamen$_i$ ziji$_i$-shuo Zhangsan piping-le t$_i$.
They self-say Zhangsan criticize-PERF

Since the matrix verb is now a lexical reflexive predicate, we expect it to force a distributive reading on the subject without the aid of *dou*, but as indicated by the contrast between (34) and (36), this expectation is not fulfilled.

The assumption that *ziji* only raises to the local verb is also justified on general considerations as well. It is well known that head-movement is generally bounded within the domain of a finite clause, and obeys strict minimality and island conditions (more than XP-movement does). It is therefore desirable to limit the head-movement of *ziji* to the local clause.[9]

---

[9] As is required by some appropriate minimality conditions, e.g., the Head-Movement Constraint of Travis (1984). Sze-Wing Tang (personal communication) observes an interesting contrast between bare noun phrases and numeral classifier phrases with respect to the interpretation of *ziji*.

To summarize, we have seen that the problems posed in Section 1 receive an explanation under the assumption that the bare reflexive raises to a local c-commanding verb in LF. It forms an LF reflexive predicate with the local verb, thus deriving distributivity of a local plural subject unmarked by *dou*. Because head-movement is clause-bounded, *ziji* does not form a reflexive predicate with a higher verb, and therefore it does not remove the need of *dou* to mark the distributivity of the remote plural antecedent. This, then, leaves the question still unanswered as to why a plural long-distance antecedent of *ziji* must have distributive interpretation. Let us turn to this question now.

4. Long-Distance *ziji*, Variable Binding and Attitudes

I claim that the answer to this question comes from the semantics of logophoricity and the assumption that the long-distance *ziji* is a logophor. More specifically, a logophoric *ziji* has the status of an A-bar variable at LF and semantic representation, bound by an operator that ranges over individuals capable of '*de se* beliefs' in the sense of Lewis (1979). To

---

(i) Tamen yanzou-le ziji de gequ.
they play-PERF self DE song
'They played their songs.'

(ii) Tamen yanzou-le yi-shou guanyu ziji mingyun de gequ.
They play-PERF one-CL about self destiny DE song
They played a song about their destiny.

In particular, while the salient reading of (i) is that they played different songs (the distributive reading), it is possible to get a group reading in (ii), according to which they played the song which is about the destiny of *tamen* 'they' as a group. An acceptability contrast obtains when a collective predicate is used:

(iii) ??Tamen he-xie-le ziji de shu.
they join-write-PERF self DE book
'They wrote a book about themselves in collaboration.'

(iv) Tamen he-xie-le yiben youguan ziji de shu.
they join-write-PERF one-CL about self DE book
'They wrote a book about themselves in collaboration.'

The ill-formedness of (iii) suggests that distributivity is being unnaturally forced upon a collective (plural) predicate. The acceptability of (iv) shows that the collective reading is allowed, according to which the book they collaborated on was one about themselves.

Why should a collective reading be allowed when *ziji* is embedded within a numeral classifier phrase? Tang suggests that this is due to minimality and the possibility that a numeral or classifier may head a functional projection of its own. Given this possible structure, the functional categories (Num and Cl) within the nominal phrases in (ii) and (iv) will block the LF movement of *ziji*. No reflexive predicate is formed in this case, and the subject is not required to be distributive.

make this point clear, I must briefly describe the theory of long-distance *ziji* assumed here.

Despite various previous attempts at providing a uniform syntactic or pragmatic account of the bare reflexive *ziji*, many scholars have now converged on the viewpoint that local and long-distance reflexives deserve different treatments. In particular, it is believed that many instances of long-distance binding should not be brought under the standard theory of anaphor binding (cf. Chomsky's Binding Condition A), but should be treated as instances of logophoric binding. The core cases of logophoricity are those where the antecedent of a (long-distance) reflexive refers to an individual who has first-hand knowledge of particular events being described and is disposed to describe such events using the first-person pronoun. Huang et al. (1984), following Kuno (1972), made an early attempt to characterize the long-distance *ziji* as originating from the pronoun *wo* 'I/me' in a direct-discourse underlying representation. Thus, (37) has the representation (38):

(37) Zhangsan shuo Lisi chang piping ziji.
'Zhangsan said that Lisi often criticized self.'

(38) Zhangsan shuo, "Lisi chang piping wo."
Zhangsan said, "Lisi often criticized me."

Chierchia (1989), drawing on Lewis (1979), developed a formal account of interpretive semantics that treats the intended reading of (37) as representing a *de se* belief of Zhangsan.[10] Central to Chierchia's proposal is that under this sort of reading the complement clause has the structure of secondary predication and operator binding. Following this approach, Huang and Liu

[10] Lewis' *de re* vs. *de se* distinction may be illustrated with a sentence like (i), where *his* and *Pavarotti* are coindexed:

(i) Pavarotti$_i$ said that his$_i$ pants were on fire.

The *de re* reading simply describes the speaker's knowledge of the co-reference relation, but makes no claim as to whether Pavarotti himself was aware of this co-reference relation, i.e., that it was his own pants that were on fire. The *de se* reading, on the other hand, refers to the specific scenario where Pavarotti was actually aware of his own pants being on fire. Under the *de re* scenario, Pavarotti might have said, "His pants are on fire," and under the *de se* scenario, he would be disposed to say, "My pants are on fire!". Chierchia argues that these two readings should be semantically represented as in (ii)-(iii):

(ii) λx (said (x, x's pants were on fire)) (P) (*de re*)

(iii) said (P, λx (x's pants were on fire)) (*de se*)

(1999) propose that (37) has the following structure at LF, with *ziji* IP-adjoined to the complement clause, binding its trace as a bound variable.[11]

(39) Zhangsan shuo [ziji$_i$ [Lisi chang piping t$_i$]].
Zhangsan say self Lisi often criticize

The operator *ziji* corresponds to a lambda operator in semantic representation:

(40) Zhangsan shuo (λ_x (Lisi chang piping x))

(41) said (Z, λ_x (often-criticize (L, x)))

These are structures of secondary predication subject to what Chomsky (1986) called 'strong binding', by which the operator is coindexed with the subject *Zhangsan* and has its *range* determined by it.

Returning now to the question of plural antecedents for the long-distance *ziji*, as illustrated in (42), recall that the problem is that the plural antecedent must be understood in the distributive sense and be overtly marked by *dou*.

(42) Tamen$_i$ dou shuo Zhangsan piping-le ziji$_i$
They all say Zhangsan criticize-PERF self
'Everyone of them said that Zhangsan criticized him/himself.

Under the intended reading, (42) has the LF structure (43):

(43) Tamen$_i$ dou shuo [ziji$_i$ [Zhangsan piping-le t$_i$]]
They all say self Zhangsan criticize-PERF
'Everyone of them said that Zhangsan criticized him/her.'

The '*de se* operator' (as we shall call the IP-adjoined *ziji*) is subject to strong binding by the plural subject in order to obtain its range. What we need to do is ensure that this operator ranges over individual members of 'they', but not over groups. It seems that this can be stipulated as a matter

[11] For more details see Huang and Liu (1999) and the references cited. I shall only present a minimum part of the relevant analysis here. Note that the IP-adjunction of *ziji* is a case of XP-movement. The bare reflexive is an N^0 under NP. Hence *ziji* may be head-moved as an N^0 or it may be IP-adjoined as XP.

of definition since, normally, only individuals but not groups are capable of having inner feelings like *de se* beliefs:[12]

(44) A *de se* operator ranges over individuals, not over groups.

Strictly speaking, an individual with *de se* attitudes is one who thinks, "I am such and such," but not one who thinks, "We are such and such," or one of a group who think of each other as being such and such. Recall that a group reading would include scenarios where members have certain beliefs about each other, but such beliefs fall outside of the definition of *de se* beliefs. In other words, a true *de se* belief entails the interpretation of the long-distance (logophoric) *ziji* as a variable strongly bound by an antecedent that is (semantically) singular.[13] To qualify as such a binder, the plural subject in (43) must be distributed. Note that the matrix verb is not reflexivized and does not obligatorily denote atomic events. And since Chinese plurals do not distribute without an overt marker, the obligatory occurrence of *dou* is explained.

That the *de se* requirement on a long-distance *ziji* drastically reduces the range of possible interpretations of a sentence can also be appreciated by looking at the earlier example (4) again:

(4) John and Mary argue that they will win $100.
   a. [John and Mary]1 argue that they1 will win $100.
   b. [John and Mary]1 argue that [they1 D2] will win $100.
   c. [[John and Mary]1 D2] argue that they1 will win $100.
   d. [[John and Mary]1 D2] argue that [they1 D3] will win $100.
   e. [[John and Mary]1 D2] argue that they2 will win $100.

Recall that (4a-e) represent the following 5 readings for (4): (4a) represents the group reading for both the matrix and the embedded subject, while (4d)

---

[12] One might suggest that there is no need for (44), and that the distributivity of the long-distance antecedent of *ziji* simply follows from *ziji* being a bound variable. This alternative suggestion is not sufficient to ensure our desired result, though, because the semantic atomicity of a variable depends on what its operator ranges over. An operator may range over groups, and so a variable need not always denote a singular atom.

[13] What about the group-as-individual reading, including cases where a group of people constitute an organization or institution? While such cases do qualify for the requirement of being a "singular individual", the collective body made up of the members is not itself a natural holder of *de se* beliefs, since groups by themselves cannot believe. A group can have a certain mental attitude by virtue of everyone of its members having that mental attitude. But in that situation we can say that the *de se* reading comes from each member having a *de se* belief, not the group by itself.

represents the distributive reading for both subjects. In (4b), the matrix subject is collective and the embedded subject distributive, while in (4c) this situation is reversed. Finally, in (4e) the matrix subject is distributed and the embedded subject is a variable bound by the distributed matrix subject. Recall also that these 5 readings are rendered in the following distinct forms, respectively:

(5) Lao Zhang he Lao Li shuo tamen hui zhong yibai yuan.
Lao Zhang and Lao Li say they will hit 100 dollar
Lao Zhang and Lao Li argued that they would win $100.

(6) Lao Zhang he Lao Li shuo tamen dou hui zhong yibai yuan.
Lao Zhang and Lao Li say they all will hit 100 dollar
Lao Zhang and Lao Li argued that both of them would win $100.

(7) Lao Zhang he Lao Li dou shuo tamen hui zhong yibai yuan.
Lao Zhang and Lao Li all say they will hit 100 dollar
Both Lao Zhang and Lao Li argued that they would win $100.

(8) Lao Zhang he Lao Li dou shuo tamen dou hui zhong yibai yuan.
Lao Zhang and Lao Li all say they all will hit 100 dollar
Both Lao Zhang and Lao Li argued they would both win $100.

(9) Lao Zhang he Lao Li dou shuo ziji hui zhong yibai yuan.
Lao Zhang and Lao Li all say self will hit 100 dollar
Both Lao Zhang and Lao Li argued, "I will win $100."

What is particularly significant at this point is that, of all these sentences, only (9) permits (in fact requires) the use of *ziji* as its embedded subject. All of (5)-(8) require the plural pronoun *tamen* 'they' as their embedded subjects. In particular, (5) becomes ill-formed when *tamen* 'they' is replaced by *ziji,* which cannot take a plural, undistributed antecedent.

(5') ??Lao Zhang he Lao Li shuo ziji hui zhong yibai yuan.
Lao Zhang and Lao Li say self will hit 100 dollar

The ungrammaticality is even more severe when *ziji*, as a variable ranging over singular individuals, is itself forced to be distributed by *dou* (but cannot be), as in (6') and (8'):

(6') *Lao Zhang he Lao Li shuoziji dou hui zhong yibai yuan.
Lao Zhang and Lao Li say self all will hit 100 dollar

(8') *Lao Zhang he Lao Li dou shuo ziji dou hui zhong yibai yuan.
Lao Zhang and Lao Li all say self all will hit 100 dollar

And in (7), if the embedded subject is replaced by *ziji*, so the result will be indistinguishable from (9) in form, the interpretation is also necessarily identical to (9):

(7') Lao Zhang he Lao Li dou shuo ziji hui zhong yibai yuan. (= 9)
Lao Zhang and Lao Li all say self will hit 100 dollar
Both Lao Zhang and Lao Li argued, "I will win $100."

That is, (7') cannot preserve the meaning of (7), with *ziji* interpreted collectively. (7') cannot be true of the scenario where both Zhang and Li said "We will win $100.").

The ungrammaticality of all of (5')-(8') follows if we say that the long-distance *ziji* is a variable bound by a '*de se* operator' ranging over singular individuals only, but not over groups.

If this general idea of an operator that ranges over singular individuals is on the right track, we expect that logophors in other languages may exhibit similar strict distributivity effects as well. This expectation is fulfilled by the Italian possessive logophor *proprio*.[14] Thus (45) has only the strict distributive reading:

(45) Pavarotti e Domingo hanno detto che i propri pantaloni sono in fiamme.
'Pavarotti and Domingo have said that self's pants are on fire.'

That is, the sentence only means that both Pavarotti and Domingo said, "My pants are on fire." The sentence does not have the meaning according to which Pavarotti and Domingo said, either separately or as a group, "Our pants are on fire." Another example showing the same point:

(46) Francesca e Maria hanno detto che i propri articoli sono pronti.
Francesca and Maria have said that self's articles are ready.

Again, only the strict distributive reading is available: both Francesca and Maria said, *Il mio articolo e'pronto* 'My article is ready' or *I miei articoli sono pronti* 'My articles are ready'. That these sentences have only the

---

[14] Data from Francesca Del Gobbo (personal communication).

distributive reading can again be reduced to the fact that *de se* beliefs hold of singular individuals, not of groups.[15]

5. Conclusion

In this paper, we observed that the bare reflexive *ziji* exceptionally induces distributivity on a plural subject antecedent, but in a way that distinguishes local and long-distance binding of the reflexive. It was shown that these exceptional properties follow from a grammar that treats local *ziji* as a case of syntactic anaphora and long-distance *ziji* as an instance of logophoricity. The local reflexive undergoes head-movement and forms a lexical reflexive predicate in LF. The reflexive predicate denotes atomic events and its subject, if plural, is interpreted distributively. The long-distance reflexive undergoes IP adjunction as an LF operator ranging over individual holders of *de se* beliefs, again forcing a distributive reading on a remote plural antecedent. The LF adjunction process does not, however, reflexivize or otherwise singularize the matrix predicate. Nothing in the predicate therefore automatically forces a distributive reading on any plural argument. To qualify as the antecedent of the *de se ziji*, a plural NP must rely on an overt marker like *dou*.

Our account of the two distributivity puzzles relies crucially on a distinction we make of the local and the long-distance reflexive: the former a syntactic anaphor which reflexivizes a local predicate and the latter a logophor representing *de se* attitudes of its antecedent. Needless to say, to the extent that this account of distributivity is correct, it lends important further support to the non-unitary approach to local and long-distance reflexives as developed, for example, in Huang and Liu (1999).

References

Battistella, Edwin. 1987. Chinese Reflexivization: A Movement to Infl Approach. *Linguistics* 27, 987-1012.

---

[15] Unlike Chinese plurals, Italian plural NPs do in general allow for both collective and distributive readings. This is why (45)-(46) can have the distributive reading without being marked by *sia* 'both'. The strict distributive reading is of course available with *sia* as well:

(i) Sia Pavarotti che Domingo hanno detto che i propri pantaloni sono in fiamme.
'Both Pavarotti and Domingo have said that self's pants are on fire.'

(ii) Sia Francesca che Wu Di hanno detto che i propri articoli sono pronti.
'Both Francesca and Wu Di said that self's articles are ready.'

Chierchia, Gennaro. 1989. Anaphora and Attitudes *de se*, in R. Bartsch, J. van Benthem and P. van Emde Boas, eds., *Semantics and Contextual Expression*, Foris Publications, Dordrecht, pp. 1031.

Choe, Jae-Woong. 1987. *Anti-Quantifiers and a Theory of Distributivity*. Ph.D. dissertation, University of Massachusetts, Amherst.

Chomsky, Noam. 1981. *Lectures on Government and Binding*. Foris Publications.

Chomsky, Noam. 1986. *Knowledge of Language: Its Nature, Origin, and Use*. Praeger, New York.

Cole, Peter, Gabriella Hermon, and Li-May Sung. 1990. Principles and Parameters of Long-Distance Reflexives. *Linguistic Inquiry* 21, 1-22.

Cole, Peter and Li-May Sung. 1994. Head Movement and Long-Distance Reflexives. *Linguistic Inquiry* 25, 355-406.

Gil, David. 1982. Quantifier Scope, Linguistic Variation, and Natural Language Semantics. *Linguistic and Philosophy* 5, 421-472.

Heim, Irene, Howard Lasnik and Robert May. 1991. Reciprocity and Plurality. *Linguistic Inquiry* 22, 63-102.

Huang, C.-T. James, Yun-Hua Huang, Te-Hsiang Teng, and Robyne Tiedeman. 1984. Reflexives in Chinese and the Teaching of Chinese. *Proceedings of the First World Conference on Chinese Language*, pp. 205-215.

Huang, C.-T. James, and Luther C.-S. Liu. 1999. Logophoricity, Attitudes and *ziji* at the Interface, to appear in Peter Cole, et al. eds., *Long-Distance Reflexives*, Syntax and Semantics Vol. 33, Academic Press, New York.

Huang, C.-T. James and C.-C. Jane Tang. 1991. The Local Nature of the Long-Distance Reflexives in Chinese, in J. Koster and E. Reuland, eds., *Long-Distance Anaphora*, 263-282. Cambridge University Press. Also in *Proceedings of NELS 19* (1989).

Huang, Shizhe. 1996. *Quantification and Predication in Mandarin Chinese: A Case Study of* Dou. Ph.D. dissertation, University of Pennsylvania.

Huang, Yun-Hua. 1984. Reflexives in Chinese. *Studies in English Literature and Linguistics* 10.

Kuno, Susumu. 1972. Pronominalization, Reflexivization, and Direct Discourse. *Linguistic Inquiry* 3, 161-195.

Kuno, Susumu. 1987. *Functional Syntax*. University of Chicago Press, Chicago, Illinois.

Lebeaux, David. 1983. A Distributional Difference between Reciprocals and Reflexives. *Linguistic Inquiry* 14, 723-730.

Lewis, David. 1979. Attitudes *de dicto* and *de se*. *The Philosophical Review* 88, 513-543.

Li, Xiaoguang. 1997. *Deriving Distributivity in Chinese*. Ph.D. dissertation, University of California, Irvine.

Lin, Jowang. 1996. *Polarity Licensing and Wh-Phrase Quantification in Chinese*. Ph.D. dissertation, University of Massachusetts, Amherst.

Lin, Jowang. 1998. Distributivity in Chinese and Its Implications. *Natural Language Semantics* 6, 201-243.

Lin, Tzong-Hong. 1998. On *Ge* and Other Related Problems, in Liejiong Xu, ed., *The Referential Properties of Chinese Noun Phrase*, Collection des Cahiers de Linguistique, Asie Oriental 2, Reg. Recettes Cahiers de Linguistique, Paris.

Pica, Pierre. 1987. On the Nature of the Reflexivization Cycle, in *Proceedings of NELS* 17, 483-499.

Roberts, Craige. 1987. *Modal Subordination, Anaphora, and Distributivity*. Ph.D. dissertation, University of Massachusetts, Amherst.

Tang, C.-C. Jane. 1989. Chinese Reflexives. *Natural Language and Linguistic Theory* 7, 93-121.

Travis, Lisa. 1984. *Parameters and Effects of Word Order Variation*. Ph.D. dissertation, MIT, Cambridge, Massachusetts.

Xu, Liejiong. 1993. The Long-Distance Binding of *ziji*. *Journal of Chinese Linguistics* 21, 123-141.

Word Order, Structure, and Relativization*

YEN-HUI AUDREY LI
University of Southern California

1. Introduction

Nominal systems appear to have significant differences cross-linguistically. Take English and Chinese nominal expressions for instance[1]. Prominent differences between them include the fact that nouns in English generally do not occur in the "bare" form but those in Chinese can.[2] Moreover, a bare noun in Chinese can be interpreted as definite, indefinite or generic; these different interpretations of an English nominal phrase rely on the occurrence of the definite article *the*, indefinite article *a* or some other determiners. Take a definite expression for instance. Chinese is sufficient with a bare noun [N], such as *shu* 'book'; whereas English requires the definite article [*the* N] *the book(s)* or its equivalent.[3] A very interesting question that arises from such a difference concerns the structure of nominal phrases in these languages. An article/determiner in English, for instance, plays a key role in the structural representation: a nominal phrase is represented as a Determiner Phrase (DP), headed by a Determiner (D) (see Abney 1987, for instance). The definite article *the* can be in the D

*Many thanks to Tom Ernst, Jim Huang, Yafei Li , Bingfu Lu, Sze-Wing Tang, Zoe Wu and Patricia Schenider-Zioga for their help with this work.
[1] Chinese in this work refers to Mandarin Chinese.
[2] Mass nouns in English can occur in the bare form.
[3] Demonstratives, possessives etc. also make a nominal phrase definite, which we disregard here.

On the Formal Way to Chinese Languages.
Sze-Wing Tang and Chen-Sheng Luther Liu (eds.).

position (see Longobardi 1994, Chierchia 1998, among others). In other words, *the book* can have the structure in (1), headed by *the*:[4]

```
(1)            DP
               /\
              D  NP
             /     \
          the      book
```

What, then, is the structure of a definite expression such as *shu* in Chinese? Is it like (1) with a null D head (where N might move to)? Or, does it have a simpler structure, such as (2)?

```
(2)            NP
               |
              shu
```

The answers are anchored in important theoretical and empirical issues. Theoretically, if *shu* is interpreted in the same way as *the book*, should they have the same structure? Both positive and negative answers to this question have been explored. On the one hand, it is assumed that syntax-semantics mapping is a one-to-one relation. Mapping rules remain constant cross-linguistically. An N is always a property-denoting expression (predicate-type) and a D is always an individual-denoting expression (argument-type). A bare noun in an argument position in languages like Chinese, therefore, needs to be projected as a DP, not simply an N(P) (see Li 1998, 1999a, b). The structure in (2), for instance, should be further projected as a DP when the definite nominal *shu* is in an argument position. On the other hand, it is possible to assume that a one-to-one syntax-semantics mapping relation need not exist. Type-shifting can take place in some languages (see Chierchia 1998). A bare noun interpreted as definite in an argument position, for instance, has undergone type-shifting and taken on the role of an argument, rather than a predicate. Because type-shifting has taken place, (2) can be a representation for a definite nominal expression in an argument position. Theoretically, then, the choice between (1) and (2) relies on whether a one-to-one syntax-semantics mapping relation is to be retained or whether type-shifting is an option in such cases.

[4] In this work, we do not concern ourselves with the functional projections between D and N; see Carstens (1991), Ritter (1991, 1995), Valois (1991), for instance, for discussions on some of such projections. See Tang (1990), Li (1998, 1999a,b), Cheng and Sybesma (1999) among others for the functional projections within nominal phrases in Chinese.

The empirical question is even more interesting. Is there empirical evidence helping us to determine if a DP structure is projected in languages like Chinese? Does the availability of a DP projection, in addition to an NP, more adequately capture empirical generalizations than an analysis that does without a DP projection? Li (1998, 1999a, b) argues for a positive answer, based on the facts concerning word order and constituent structures within nominal expressions, the distribution of nominal phrases within a sentence, and the distribution of the collective/plural marker *–men* in Mandarin Chinese. Indeed, many interesting facts are derived by the presence of D and an N-to-D raising process. On the other hand, Fukui and Takano (2000), based on a theory of universal phrase structure proposed by Takano (1996) and Fukui and Takano (1998) and a prohibition against right-adjunction structures (Kayne 1994), argue that the linear ordering between a relative clause and the head it modifies (the relative head) in different types of languages can be derived from a contrast in nominal structures. They argue that there are Japanese type and English type languages. In the English type, a DP is projected and a process of N-to-D raising must take place. Such a raising process places a relative clause, which is base-generated as left-adjunction to the head N, after this N.[5] In contrast, the type of languages like Japanese, which uses bare nouns as definite, indefinite and generic expressions, does not have a D projection. Because of the lack of a D projection, an N-to-D raising process cannot take place. A relative clause therefore maintains to be left-adjoined to the head N and, accordingly, surfaces on the left of this N. Such a parametric difference between these two types of languages, according to Fukui and Takano, is not only manifested in the contrast in ordering between a relative clause and its head but also reflected in how relative clauses are formed and licensed in these two different types of languages.

Fukui and Takano's analysis of English and Japanese relative structures appears to provide strong empirical support for the absence of a DP projection and N-to-D raising in languages like Japanese. It also poses interesting challenges to Li's claim that Chinese does project a DP and that N-to-D movement does take place in this language. After all, Chinese and Japanese have identical word order with respect to a relative clause and the head it modifies, both being head-final. Chinese relativization also seems to have similar properties as Japanese relativization, in addition to the fact that both languages allow a bare noun in an argument position. Chinese appears

[5] Kayne (1994) further developed the promotion analysis by Schachter (1973) and Vergnaud (1974) and proposed that English relativization is a promotion process which raises the relativized nominal to the Spec of a relative CP. The relative CP is a complement of D [$_{DP}$ D CP]. In such a structure, the head modified by the relative clause is not the syntactic head of the structure. We do not concern ourselves with the English structure in this paper. For simplicity, we continue using the term "head" to refer to the noun (phrase) modified by a relative clause.

to belong to the Japanese type of languages, rather than the English type, at least with respect to the ordering of a relative clause and its head and the form/interpretation of bare nouns. This raises the question of whether Chinese, indeed, projects a DP and allows an N-to-D raising process, as Li has claimed.

In this work, I will show that the various empirical generalizations claimed to be derivable from the parametric differences in nominal structures between Japanese and English types of languages discussed in Fukui and Takano do not hold true in Chinese relativization structures. The correlation between N-to-D raising and the ordering between a relative clause and its head cannot be upheld considering the Chinese data. Consequently, there is no evidence against the existence of a DP projection and N-to-D raising in Chinese. Further evidence will be provided to support the existence of a DP projection based on the interpretation of relative clauses.

2. Word order and the structure of relative clauses

A major claim of Fukui and Takano's (2000) work is that the ordering between a relative clause and the head modified by the relative clause is due to the absence or presence of D and the subsequent movement of N to D when D is present. Adopting Kayne's proposal that only left-adjunction is allowed in the grammar, Fukui and Takano claim that a relative clause is always left-adjoined to the head: [CP N].[6] A Japanese relative construction, illustrated in (3), has the structure in (4) after the relative clause is left-adjoined to the head.

(3) John-ga kinoo mita syasin
John-Nom yesterday saw picture
'the/a picture that John saw yesterday'

(4)
```
      N1
     /\
   CP  N1=syasin
```

Because a Japanese nominal phrase does not contain a D projection or other functional categories according to Fukui and Takano, (4) will not merge

[6] Fukui and Takano (2000) label the relative clause CP and the head, N. Left adjunction of the relative clause to the head, thus, is [$_{NP}$ CP N]. Such an account does not distinguish complementation structures from adjunction structures: a complement XP is also a sister of N and has the same structure [$_{NP}$ XP N]. See the next note concerning the structure containing an head and a complement of head.

further and it is the full representation for the relative construction illustrated in (3). A slight modification of (4) has been made by Fukui and Takano: the relative clause should be an IP (TP), not a CP, a claim to which we will return shortly.

In contrast, an English nominal phrase must project a D. A phrase marker like (4) must further merge with a D in order to generate a well-formed nominal structure in English. After D is merged with the phrase markers, N-to-D raising must take place in order for the N to check the features in D. An English relative construction as illustrated in (5), therefore, has the structure in (6).

(5) a picture which John saw yesterday.[7]

(6)

```
        DP
        / \
      a   D'
           /\
  picture  D'
             /\
            N  D
           /\
         CP  N=t_picture
         /\
  which ...
```

The following generalization thus emerges according to Fukui and Takano's analysis: the word order [relative clause + relative head] indicates that N-to-D raising has not applied and the reverse order [relative head + relative clause] indicates that N-to-D raising has applied. The former is illustrated by Japanese and the latter by English.

Fukui and Takano note further that there is a cluster of differences between English type and Japanese type languages which can "fall out in a simple and elegant fashion, based solely on the single parametric difference between the languages: English exhibits N-to-D raising, while Japanese does not (simply because the latter language lacks the category D)." (Fukui and Takano 2000, 219)..[8] The differences discussed are briefly described in

[7] Fukui and Takano (1998, 2000) assume with Takano (1996) that a complement is generated to the left of a head.

[8] Fukui and Takano's proposal requires N-to-D movement to apply in all cases in English. This contrasts with, for instance, the analysis of Chierchia (1998) or Longobardi (1994) which does not raise N to D when an article occurs (at least overtly). In these analyses, an article occupies

the following subsections.

2.1. Relative pronoun

According to Fukui and Takano, the absence of a relative pronoun (as in Japanese), or its possible presence (such as *which* in (5)) can be derived from the structural contrast between (6) and (4). Assuming that a relative pronoun must be bound by a relative head, they claim that a relative pronoun in a structure like (6) in English is legitimate because in this structure, the relative head (the raised N) c-commands the relative pronoun *which*. The relative pronoun *which* is, therefore, properly bound and thus, English allows a relative pronoun in a relative clause. In contrast, because N_1 has two segments in (4), the relative head does not c-command CP, if the definition of c-command in May (1985), Chomsky (1986), and Kayne (1994) is adopted, which incorporates the notion of segments and exclusion.[9] If the relative head does not c-command the relative clause CP, it cannot c-command a relative pronoun in the CP. In order for (4) to be well-formed, the relative clause cannot contain a relative pronoun; otherwise, such a relative pronoun would not be c-commanded and properly bound by the relative head. Consequently, Japanese does not and cannot have a relative pronoun in its relative construction. The contrast between the structures in (6) and (4) captures the contrast between the existence of a relative pronoun in English and the lack of one in Japanese.

2.2. Operator movement

The lack of a relative pronoun, according to Fukui and Takano, indicates that a Japanese relative clause is not "operator-oriented." It is not licensed as a modifier of the relative head through the mediation of a relative pronoun functioning as an operator creating an open position within the relative clause. Instead, it is licensed by an "aboutness" relation between the relative clause and the relative head. They claim that such an aboutness condition is not peculiar to the licensing of the Japanese relative clause. It can also be seen in the licensing of certain topic constructions in Japanese and English:

the D position and N stays in the N position, N being a property-denoting, predicate type of expressions. Fukui and Takano place the definite article *the* in a position higher than the Spec of D position which hosts the raised N, N-to-D raising being a substitution process.

[9] The definition adopted in Fukui and Takano is this:

(i) X c-commands Y iff X excludes Y and every element that dominates X dominates Y.

(ii) X excludes Y iff no segment of X dominates Y.

The two-segmented category [N_1, N_1] is the relative Head. The Head does not exclude CP. The upper N_1, a segment of [N_1, N_1], dominates the CP.

(7) sakana-wa tai-ga ii
fish-Top red-snapper-Nom good
'As for fish, a red-snapper is the best.'

(8) As for sports, I like baseball best.

Attributing the insight to Kuno (1973) and Murasugi (1991), Fukui and Takano argue that such an aboutness condition licenses relative clauses in Japanese. Thus, in the following example, the relative clause can be interpreted as being about a picture.

(9) John-ga kinoo mita syasin
John-Nom yesterday saw picture
'the/a picture John saw yesterday'

Being in an aboutness relation with the relative head, the relative clause is properly licensed.

Furthermore, because there is no operator movement in Japanese relativization and an aboutness condition is sufficient to license a relative clause, it follows that gapless relative clauses are possible in this language, such as (10), and relativization is not subject to island conditions as demonstrated in (11), where the relativized nominal has originated from within a complex NP.

(10) [syuusyoku-ga taihen na] buturigaku
employment-Nom difficult is physics
'physics (that) finding a job is difficult'

(11) [pro kiteiru yoohuku-ga yogoreteiru] sinsi
is.wearing suit-Nom is.dirty gentleman
'the/a gentleman who the suit that (he) is wearing is dirty'

2.3. Relative complementizer

Another contrast following from the proposed structural and movement differences is that a relative clause in Japanese, unlike an English one, has a TP structure, rather than a CP structure. Japanese relative clauses do not need a CP: because of the lack of N-to-D raising, Japanese relative clauses must not be operator-oriented. The fact that an operator is not needed makes the Spec of CP unnecessary. Following Diesing's (1990) suggestion that a functional category is present in a structure only when it is necessary, Fukui and Takano claim that a CP is not necessary in a Japanese relative clause and thus is not projected. The lack of a CP projection means the lack of a C to host a complementizer. This captures the fact that Japanese does not have the counterpart of the complementizer *that* in the English relative clause *a picture* ***that*** *John saw yesterday.*[10] A relative clause, accordingly, is not a CP in Japanese. It is an IP/TP (Murasugi 1991).

2.4. Internally Headed Relative Clause

Finally, Fukui and Takano note that only languages of the Japanese type allow Internally Headed Relative Clauses (IHRC). Following Cole's (1987) proposal that an IHRC has a head that is a null pronominal co-referential with the internal head, they note that if the English structure (6) were to instantiate an IHRC, it would violate Binding Principle C because the head *pro* would be co-indexed with, and c-command the internal head. In contrast, a pro in the relative head position does not c-command the internal head in (4), the proposed structure for Japanese. Consequently, only Japanese allows an IHRC.

Briefly summarizing Fukui and Takano's claims, the contrast between the English structure (6) and the Japanese structure (4), as manifested in the different ordering between a relative clause and a relative head, derives the different properties of English and Japanese relative clauses with respect to the availability of a relative pronoun, operator movement, a complementizer and an internally headed relative clause. The lack of operator movement is related to the availability of an aboutness condition licensing a relative clause, which does not obey island conditions. The lack of operator movement and the availability of licensing by an aboutness condition also make a gapless relative clause possible.

Though not discussed in Fukui and Takano, a number of other Japanese linguists have also made the observation that Japanese relative clauses do not involve operator movement. Saito (1985), for instance, shows that the lack of operator movement is manifested in the absence of long-distance relativization of reason/manner adjuncts. Such relativization is clause-bound (Murasugi 2000):

[10] Their argument is not easy to follow here. Even though an operator in the Spec of a CP is not needed, it does not mean that the head is not needed and therefore it does not mean that a CP projection is not needed. Consider the English example (i):

(i) That he is here is important.

In this sentence, there is no requirement of the presence of an operator in Spec of CP. Nonetheless, the complementizer *that* must be present. The fact that a Spec of CP is not needed does not mean that the head C is also not needed.

(12) a. [[Mary-ga e_i kaetta] riyuu$_i$]
Mary-Nom left reason
'the reason$_i$ Mary left e_i'

b. *[[Mary-ga [John-ga e_i kaetta to] omotteiru] riyuu$_i$]
Mary-Nom John-Nom left C think reason
'the reason$_i$ Mary thinks [that John left e_i]'

c. [[Mary-ga e_i mondai-o toita] hoohoo$_i$]
Mary-Nom problem-Acc solved method
'the method$_i$ Mary solved the problem e_i'

d. *[[Mary-ga [John-ga e_i mondai-o toita to] omotteiru] hoohoo$_i$]
Mary-Nom John-Nom problem-Acc solved C think method
'the method$_i$ Mary thinks [that John solved the problem e_i]'

Murasugi (1991) argues that the relativization of manner/reason adjuncts is not true relativization. According to her, a true relative clause contains a gap; the expressions in (12) do not contain a gap. The acceptable expressions in (12a, c) are just like other gapless cases:

(13) [[sakana-ga yakeru] nioi]
fish-Nom burn smell
'the smell that a fish burns (the smell of fish-burning)'

The interpretation of (12a), for instance, parallels the English (14). Such examples are derived by base-generation.

(14) the reason for John's leaving

The unacceptable examples in (12b,d) cannot be base-generated with a pro in place of the adjunct gap 'e' in the embedded clause, because a pro appears only in argument positions. Indeed, a stronger claim has been made: Japanese relative clauses simply are not derived by any type of movement. The following example from Hoji (1985, discussed in Murasugi 2000) shows the lack of reconstruction in cases involving an anaphor:

(15) *[$_{NP}$ [John$_i$-ga e_J taipu-sita] [zibun$_i$-no ronbun]$_J$]
John-Nom typed self-Gen paper
'self$_i$'s paper that John$_i$ typed'

These observations support the claim that Japanese relative clauses are not derived by movement of any kind and do not contain an operator.

When relevant Chinese facts are considered, however, the correlated properties just mentioned do not fall out as predicted. Word order facts would suggest that Chinese should be like Japanese. On the other hand, most of the other related properties suggest Chinese to be more like English. The mixture of the clustering of properties raises doubt on the correctness of the typological claims we have just seen.

3. Correlated properties?

A first look at Chinese relative constructions may suggest that they are just like their Japanese counterparts. Like Japanese that only allows a relative clause to precede the relative head, Chinese also requires a relative clause to precede the relative head. In other words, according to the proposal discussed in the previous sections, Chinese should belong to the Japanese type of languages and have the structure in (6). If Chinese has the structure in (6), should we, then, expect Chinese relative clauses to have the properties in 2.1.-2.4? Unfortunately, closer examination of the facts concerning Chinese relative constructions suggests that the correlated properties observed in Japanese relative constructions are not true with their counterparts in Chinese.

3.1. Relativization processes

Before demonstrating how the properties in 2.1-2.4 are absent in Chinese relative clauses, we begin with the discussion on how relative clauses are formed in Chinese.

3.1.1. Movement

There is evidence that relativization in Chinese can be derived from movement of the relative head directly (see Schachter 1973, Vergnaud, 1974, Kayne 1994). For instance, part of an idiomatic expression can become a relative head:

(16) a. [[ta kai t_i de] dao_i] dou hen chenggong
he open De knife all very successful
'All the operations he performed were successful.'
(kai-dao 'open knife=operate')

b. [[ta chi t_i de] cu_i] bi bieren duo.
he eat De vinegar compare others more
'He is more jealous than the others.'
(chi-cu 'eat vinegar= be jealous')

c. [[ta you t_i de] mo_i] meiren ting-de-dong.
he hu- De –mor nobody listen-able-understand
'Nobody can understand his humor.'
(you-mo, transliteration of *humor*)

Long distance movement is possible and the movement is sensitive to island conditions:

(17) a. [[ta renwei [wo yinggai kai t_i] de] dao_i] dou hen nan.
he think I should open De knife all very difficult
'The operations that he thinks I should perform are all difficult.'

a'. *[[ta kai e] hen zhongyao de] dao] ---subject island
he open very important De knife
'the operation that it is important that he performs.'

b. [[ta renwei [wo keyi chi t_i] de] cu_i] hai bu zhi zhexie.
he think I can eat De vinegar still not only these
'The vinegar that he thinks I can eat is even more than this (=He thinks I can be even more jealous).'

b'. *[[ruguo ta chi t_i, wo hui hen shengqi de] cu_i] ---adjunct island
if he eat I will very angry De vinegar

c. [[ta renwei [wo keyi you t_i] de] mo_i] you henduo.
he think I can hu- De -mor have much
'The -mor he thinks I can hu- is a lot (=The humor he thinks I can make is a lot).'

c'. *[[[[t_j you t_i de] ren_j] zai zher de] mo_i] ---complex NP island
hu- De man at here De -mor

The possibility of a relative head being part of an idiomatic expression in the relative clause suggests that the relative head has been raised from the relative clause. This derivation is not the only possible option, however. In the following instances, the relative head cannot be moved directly from inside the relative clause because the relative head is nominal and the corresponding expression in the relative clause is a PP:

(18) a. ta xiu che de **na-ge fangfa**.
he fix car De that-Cl method
'the way (how) he fixed the car'

a'. ta **yong na-ge fangfa** xiu che.
he use that-Cl method fix car
'He fixed the car at that place.'

b. ta xiu che de **na-ge liyou**.
he fix car De that-Cl reason
'the reason why he fixed the car'

b'. ta **yinwei na-ge liyou** xiu che.
he because that-Cl reason fix car
'He fixed the car because of that reason.'

Ning (1993) argues that a Chinese relative clause can be derived by a null operator movement that is equivalent to *wh*-movement in the formation of English relative constructions. Evidence for an operator movement comes from the fact that Chinese relative clauses are acceptable only when they correspond to English relative clauses that can have a single-word relative pronoun (without an accompanying preposition, such as *with which*). For instance, the acceptable Chinese relative clauses in (20) must correspond to English relative clauses like (19) which contain a relative pronoun.

(19) a. the man **who** came here
b. the work **which** he did
c. the place **where** he went
d. the time **when** he left
e. the way that (**how**) he fixed the car[11]
f. the reason **why** he left

[11] Ning (1993, 53) notes that *the way how* is only acceptable in some dialects.

(20) a. lai zher de ren
come here De man
'the man who came here'

b. ta zuo de gongzuo
he do De work
'the work which he did'

c. ta qu de difang
he go De place
'the place where he went'

d. ta likai de shijian
he leave De time
'the time when he left'

e. ta xiu che de fangfa
he fix car De way
'the way that (how) he fixed the car'

f. ta likai de yuanyin
he leave De reason
'the reason why he left'

On the other hand, Chinese does not have a counterpart of such English relative clauses as those in (21) where the relative pronoun must occur with a preposition:

(21) a. the girl with whom she danced
b. the dog behind which he walked
c. the pliers with which he fixed the car

(22) a. *[ta tiaowu de] guniang[12]
he danced De girl

[12] Certain expressions similar to those in (22) are acceptable, such as (i):

(i) [ta tiaowu de] duixiang
he dance De partner
'partner for his dancing'

Such expressions are not true relative clauses. They are more like the equivalents of [$_{NP}$ NP PP] in English, as discussed in more details later in this section. Similarly, (22c) can be acceptable because of the same reason. If it is changed to a form not analyzable as the equivalent of [$_{NP}$ NP PP] in English, such as (ii), all speakers consulted by us find it unacceptable:

b. *[ta zou de] gou
he walked De dog

c. *[ta xiu che de] qianzi
he fix car De pliers

Ning argues that the relativization in (22a-c) is not acceptable when the corresponding English sentences in (21a-c) cannot just make use of a single-word *wh*-operator and a preposition needs to occur with the *wh*-operator. Ning concludes that relativization in Chinese must involve movement of a null operator which is equivalent to a *wh*-operator in English. (21a-c) require one more element than a *wh*-operator; they therefore do not have acceptable counterparts in Chinese.

Further evidence for the existence of movement comes from the locality conditions that such structures are sensitive to. The sentences in (23) show that long distance movement is possible.

(23) a. zhe jiu shi [[wo tingshuo [ta yao qu baifang t_i] de] ren_i].
this exactly is I hear he want go visit De person
'This is the person who I heard he was going to visit'

b. zhe jiu shi [[women juede [ta yinggai qu t_i nianshu] de] $difang_i$]
this exactly is we feel he should go study De place
'This is the place where we feel he should go study'

c. zhe jiu shi [[ta renwei [nimen t_i yinggai likai] de] $yuanyin_i$]
this exactly is he think you should leave De reason
'This is the reason why he thinks you should leave'

The following sentences show the relevance of island conditions.

(24) a. *zhe jiu shi [[[ni xihuan [t_i pengyou] de] ren_i]
this exactly is you like friend De person
'This is the person who you like (his) friend.'

b. *zhe jiu shi [[[[ta xihuan [t_i nian guo shu] de] ren] de] $difang_i$]
this exactly is he like read Asp book De person De place
'This is the place where he likes the person that has studied

(ii) *zhe jiu shi [[wo kandao [ta xiu che]] de [qianzi]]
this exactly is I see he fix car De pliers
'These are the pliers that I saw him fix cars.'

(there)'

c. *zhe jiu shi [[[ruguo ta t_i shengqi] ni hui bu gaoxing] de]
this exactly is if he angry you will not happy De
yuanyin$_i$]
reason
'This is the reason(x) that you will not be happy if he gets angry (because of) x'

(24a) is a violation of the left branch condition, (24b), the complex NP constraint and (24c), the adjunct island constraint.

Even though there are sentences which may suggest relativization does not obey island conditions, such as (25), apparent violations always involve an island in a subject position (or a topic position, see Gasde and Paul 1998).

(25) [[[t_i chuan de] yifu] hen piaoling de] nage ren$_i$
wear De clothes very pretty De that-Cl person
'the person$_i$ that the clothes that (she$_i$) is wearing are pretty.'

When the island occurs in an object position, the effect of island conditions reappears:

(26) *[wo xihuan [[t_i chuan de] yifu] de] nage ren$_i$
I like wear De clothes De that-Cl person
'the person$_i$ that I like the clothes that (she$_i$) is wearing'

Certainly, we do not want to claim that island conditions are relevant in some cases but not in some others. The acceptability of (25) should be due to some other derivation than movement. Indeed, this is what Huang (1982) argues for. He claims that Chinese allows an empty *pro*, which is subject to an identification condition: a *pro* must be identified by the most local c-commanding antecedent. In (25), the most local c-commanding antecedent is the relative head.[13] In (26), the most local c-commanding antecedent is the subject of the relative clause. A *pro,* thus, is properly identified in (25) but not so in (26). The contrast between (25) and (26) argues for the relevance of island conditions when movement applies and the existence of a properly-bound *pro* when movement does not apply.

[13] An interesting problem that needs to be raised but will not be further pursued in this work is the failure of the head to c-command the relative clause according to the definition of c-command incorporating the notion of exclusion and segments, see note (9).

Note that for all those unacceptable sentences ruled out by island conditions or by the identification requirement on a *pro,* an overt pronoun in place of the empty category makes these sentences acceptable.[14]

(27) a. zhe jiu shi [[[ni xihuan [ta_i pengyou] de] ren_i]
this exactly is you like he friend De person
'This is the person who you like his friend.'

b. zhe jiu shi [[[ta xihuan [zai nar_i nian guo shu] de] ren de] $difang_i$]
this exactly is he like at there read Asp book De person De place
'This is the place where he likes the person that studies (there).'

c. [wo xihuan [[ta_i chuan de] yifu]] de] nage ren_i
I like she wear De clothes De that-Cl person
'the $person_i$ that I like the clothes that she_i is wearing.'

There is still another possibility to derive relative clauses --- those without a gap or a resumptive pronoun in the relative clause, the so-called gapless relative clauses. This is illustrated by the following examples:[15]

(28) a. zhe jiu shi [[ta kao-shi de] jieguo]
this exactly is he take-exam De result
'The is the result of his exam-taking.'

b. zhe jiu shi [[ta chang-ge de] shengyin]
this exactly is he sing-song De voice
'This is his singing voice (the voice with which he sings).'

[14] Note that, even though there are no pronouns corresponding *zenme/ruhe* 'how' for *fangfa* 'way, method', *yangzi* 'manner' and *weishenme* 'why' for *yuanyin/liyou* 'reason', it is possible to use the relevant *wh*-words as "resumptive" expressions (see Li 2001 for an account of such the distribution and constraints of such "resumptive" *wh*):

(i) ta **ruhe/zenme**$_i$ xiu che de $fangfa_i$, meiren zhidao.
he how fix car De method nobody know
'Nobody knows the way (how) he fixed the car.'

(ii) ta **weishenme**$_i$ bu lai de $yuanyin_i$, meiren zhidao.
he why not come De reason nobody know
'Nobody knows why he fixed the car.'

[15] The discussion here is based on an on-going joint work by James Huang, Yafei Li and Audrey Li.

c. zhe jiu shi [[ta zuo-e de] houguo]
this exactly is he do-evil De consequence
'This is the consequence of his evil-doings.'

d. zhe jiu shi [[ta sha zhe-ge xiaohai de] jiama]
this exactly is he kill this-Cl child De price
'This is the price for him killing the child.'

In such instances, the relative head cannot be related to any position within the relative clause. Instead, it is related to the entire relative clause. Interestingly, such relative clauses are much more limited. The head noun must be related to the entire relative clause, rather than an embedded clause inside the relative. Therefore, (29a) is not acceptable because the voice is unable to be related to the embedded clause within the relative clause. Neither is (29b) is acceptable because the consequence is unable to be related to the embedded clause.

(29) a.*zhe jiu shi [[wo xihuan [ta chang-ge] de] shengyin]
this exactly is I like he sing-song De voice
'This is the voice of my liking him singing (with).'

b. *zhe jiu shi [[wo tingshuo [ta zuo-e] de] houguo]
this exactly is I hear-say he do-evil De consequence
'This is the consequence of my hearing him do evil.'

This type of "relative clause" in fact may not be the typical relative clause that we are familiar with. To be more concrete, we note that this pattern, rather than being a counterpart of the English [Head + Relative clause], is more like a head noun with a PP in English, such as [*the price* [*for him killing the boy*]], [*the sound* [*of his singing*]], [*the consequence* [*of his evil doing*]] etc.[16] Just like the English cases where the entire PP bears a direct relation with the head noun, the head noun in (28)-(29) must also be related to the entire "relative clause," not just a subpart of it (such as an embedded clause, as in (29)). It is a direct modification relation. It is not mediated through the coindexation of the relative head and an operator in the relative clause. (29a-b) can be contrasted with (30a-b), which also

[16] It is not surprising that the Chinese counterpart of English [NP [P XP]] is [XP *de* NP]. The prepositions in question are generally quite empty: *the sound of his singing, the result of his evil doing* etc. Chinese rarely uses such empty prepositions within nominal expressions (except for *dui* that occurs with some complements, see Fu 1994). Chinese always has modifiers to the left of N and English to the right of N. *De* appears after a modifier within a Chinese nominal expression. The question, of course, is whether the prenominal modifier is a tensed clause or a gerundive expression. The distinction is not easily made in Chinese. See Fu (1994) for relevant discussions.

contain complex clauses but are acceptable. They are acceptable because the voice is related to my imagination (my imagining him singing with the voice, not necessarily the real voice with which he sings) and the consequence is related to my liking him to do evil:

(30) a. zhe jiu shi [[wo xiangxiang ta chang-ge de] shengyin]
this exactly is I imagine he sing-song De voice
'This is the voice of my imagining him singing (with).'

b. zhe jiu shi [[wo xihuan ta zuo-e de] houguo]
this exactly is I hear-say he do-evil De consequence
'This is the consequence of my liking him to do evil.'

The precise nature of such expressions put aside, it is clear that the type of "relative" clauses in (28) is quite different from the type of relative clauses in (16) or (20).

In brief, relative clauses in Chinese are derived in different ways. It can be derived by moving an NP directly to the head position, as in the cases of (16) containing idioms (the promotion analysis proposed by Vergnaud 1974 and Kayne 1994 for English relative clauses). It can be derived by a process similar to *wh*-operator movement in English, as in (20) (the operator movement analysis proposed by Chomsky 1977 for English relative constructions).[17] These movement structures allow long distance dependency relations and are sensitive to island conditions. There are also structures that seem to be generated by a "pseudo" relativization process, as in (28), which is more like the counterpart of the English $[_{NP}$ N $[_{PP}$ Prep XP]], where the entire PP, not just a sub-constituent of it, modifies the head noun.[18]

If the type of structures in (28) is more like an XP directly modifying a nominal head corresponding to the English structure $[_{NP}$ N $[_{PP}$ P XP]]

[17] See Li (2001) for the application of two different strategies to derive relative constructions in Chinese.

[18] Murasugi (1991) notes the locality condition on "gapless" relative clauses in Japanese. She and some other Japanese linguists take such relative clauses as the basic construction and try to derive all other relative clauses by resorting to the same mechanism of non-movement and aboutness licensing. In contrast, we claim that the so-called gapless relative clauses are different from other relative clauses and should be analyzed separately. Moreover, it is worth pointing out that the so-called gapless relative clauses should be distinguished into two categories: one being a direct XP modifier as shown in the text and the other with a part-whole relation between the head and some nominal in the relative clause. The latter should be subsumed under those relative clauses derived by movement (see Shi 1992, also see Huang 1982 and Li 1990 for movement from an outer object position that bears an affected theta-role). The two types differ in the locality condition, just like the distinction between the two types of constructions discussed in the text. Because of the lack of space, we discuss these issues in a separate work.

(without any movement relation and without a corresponding gap), true relative clauses in Chinese are similar to those in English. They share the properties of long distance movement and island sensitivity.

Having discussed the derivations for Chinese relative clauses, let us turn to each of the generalizations presented in sections 2.1-2.4, which have been claimed to be manifestations of the structure in (6).

3.2. Relative pronoun --- null *wh*-operator

It, now, is clear that, even with the order of a relative clause preceding its head, it does not follow that a relative pronoun cannot exist. The data in (18)-(27) argue that at least some relative clauses in Chinese should be derived in the same way as their counterparts in English --- operator movement. If relative clauses in both languages can be derived by the same operator movement process, it casts doubt on the claim that a relative pronoun is possible in one language but impossible in the other. Indeed, the discussion in the previous section favors the existence of an operator, even though it is null. When the moved element corresponds to a *wh*-operator in English, the result of such a relativization is acceptable in Chinese; when the moved element corresponds to a *wh*-operator with a preposition in English (such as *this is the girl* ***with whom*** *I danced*), relativization is impossible in Chinese.[19]

There is further interesting evidence for the existence of a *wh*-operator and *wh*-operator movement, i.e, contrasts between topicalization and relativization in Chinese.

3.3. Operator movement --- comparison between topicalization and relativization

There are some important differences between topicalization and relativization in Chinese, as noted by Ning (1993). Recall that the sentences in (20a-f) indicate that any argument corresponding to *who, which* and any adjunct corresponding to *where, when, how* and *why* can be relativized. It is only when relativization involves more elements than a *wh*-operator (such as a preposition plus a *wh*-operator, *with whom, behind which, with which* exemplified in (21)-(22)) that relativization becomes unavailable. In contrast, topicalization is more limited. Although it is quite common for an argument to be topicalized (31a-b), topicalization of an adjunct corresponding to relativization of an adjunct *wh*-operator is not possible:[20]

[19] Alternatively, it is possible that argument relativization in Chinese is a process of raising of the relative head and only adjunct relativization involves operator movement. See Li (2001).

[20] Interestingly, similar differences between topicalization and relativization have also been noted to exist in Japanese. McCawley (1972, 209) notes that Muraki (1970) discusses such a difference: "Specifically, the particle *de* and the dative (as opposed to locative) occurrences of *ni* cannot be deleted befoe *wa*; nevertheless, corresponding relative clauses are possible." See

(31) a. *zhe chechang, ta bu xiu che.
this garage he not fix car
'This garage, he does not fix cars.'
cf.
a'. ta bu xiu che de chechang
he not fix car De garage
'the garage where he does not fix cars.'

b. *nage yuanyin, ta bu xiu che.
that reason he not fix car
'That reason, he does not fix cars.'
cf.
b'. ta bu xiu che de yuanyin
he not fix car De reason
'the reason he does not fix cars'

c. *nage fangfa, ta xiu hao le nabu che.
that way he fix well Asp that-Cl car
'That way, he fixed that car'
cf.
c'. ta xiu hao nabu che de fangfa
he fix well that-Cl car De way
'the way he fixed tha car'

Based on such contrasts, Ning (1993) argues that topicalization, in contrast to relativization, is not a process of *wh*-operator movement. Rather, it is direct movement of a constituent to the beginning of a sentence. Because it is movement of a constituent straightforwardly, an entire adjunct PP must be moved, not just the object of a P:[21]

(32) a. zai zhe chechang, ta xiu che.
at this garage he fix car
'At this garage, he fixed cars.'

b. wei na yuanyin, ta bu xiu che.
for that reason he not fix car
'For that reason, he does not fix cars.'

c. yong nage fangfa, ta xiu hao le nabu che.

McCawley (1972) for the relation between topicalization and relativization in Japanese.

[21] Chinese may use a verb in place of a P in such expressions.

use that way he fix well Asp that-Cl car
'In that way, he fixed that car'

Such a contrast between topicalilzation and relativization, in turn, lends support to the claim that relativization in Chinese can be generated by movement of a *wh*-operator.

3.4. Licensing by an "aboutness" condition --- topicalization vs. relativization

The contrast between the pairs of sentences in (31) further argues against resorting to an "aboutness" condition to license relative clauses. Recall that, according to the analysis discussed in the section 2, relative clauses are licensed by an "aboutness" condition, which also licenses topic structures. If both topicalization and relativization are licensed by an "aboutness" condition, it is not expected that differences exist between these two constructions. Nonetheless, we do find instances which are acceptable in topicalization and unacceptable in relativization structures; we also find instances the other way around. The examples that are acceptable in relativization but not topicalization are illustrated in (31). The other type of examples is shown below:

(33) a. yu, wo xihuan chi xian yu.
fish I like eat fresh fish
'Fish, I like to eat fresh fish.'

b.*wo xihuan chi xian yu de yu
I like eat fresh fish De fish
'the fish that I like to eat fresh fish'

Moreover, it is not clear how an analysis resorting to "aboutness" licensing of relativization can capture the subject-object asymmetry in sentences like (34a-b). On the other hand, the contrast is accommodated by an analysis of movement and existence of *pro* when movement is unavailable.[22]

[22] Such a subject-object asymmetry also exists in topicalization structures:

(i) a. nage ren, nu pengyou hen xihuan wo.
that-Cl person girl friend very like m
'That person, (his) girl friend likes me.'

b. *nage ren, wo hen xihuan nu pengyou.
that person I very like girl friend
'That person, I like (his) girl friend.'

This indicates that a vague "aboutness" condition is not sufficient to accommodate topicalization structures either. See Shi (1992), Ning (1993), Shyu (1994), for instance, for

(34) a. [[nu pengyou hen xihuan wo de] nage ren]
girl friend very like me De that-Cl person
'the person whose girl friend likes me'

b. *[[wo hen xihuan nu pengyou de] nage ren]
I very like girl friend De that person
'the person that I like (his) girl friend'

The occurrence of an overt pronoun makes (34b) acceptable:

(35) [[wo hen xihuan tade nu pengyou de] nage ren]
I like very his girl friend De that person
'the person that I like (his) girl friend.'

3.5. Complementizer and internally headed relative clause

Finally, let us consider the issue of relative complementizers and internally headed relative clauses. Given what have been presented concerning operators and operator movement in the above sections, it is not surprising to find that Chinese again seems to challenge the claims concerning complementizers in relative clauses and internally headed relative clauses in relation to word order in relative constructions. In Chinese, it is not clear that a complementizer does not exist in a relative clause. Some linguists have proposed that *de*, which always follows the relative clause, is a good candidate for a complementizer in a relative clause (see Li 1990 chapter 2 for relevant discussions). However, it is also possible to regard *de* as just a general modification marker, not bearing any special relation with a relative clause. We will therefore leave this issue for further research. On the other hand, there is more solid evidence against the existence of an internally headed relative clause in Chinese. Such a construction simply does not exist in this language. Indeed, Aoun and Li (1993) argue that the presence of such a construction in Japanese is related to the fact that a quantifier can be moved away from its host - quantifier floating (see Watanabe 1992). Chinese, in contrast, does not allow quantifier floating and does not have internally headed relative clauses. In other words, the possibility of an internally headed relative clause also is related to the possibility of movement (quantifier movement in this case).[23] Without elaboration, it

possible accounts.

[23] The contrast in the possibility of quantifier floating between the two languages is also manifested in other areas of their grammar such as the distribution of a question morpheme associated with a *wh*-element (see Li 1992, Aoun and Li 1993, Cheng 1997, Tsai 1994), or a number+classifier expression being moved from a position close to its related noun (Aoun and Li 1993), etc. For a list and discussion of the correlating properties, see Aoun and Li 1993.

suffices to state that internally headed relative clauses do not exist in Chinese.

4. DP projection and word order

We have shown in this work that, although Chinese and Japanese have identical word order concerning relative constructions (head-final), Chinese does not have any of the correlating properties discussed by Fukui and Takano for Japanese relative constructions. If word order and other correlated properties are taken to be evidence for the existence of a D projection and an N-to-D movement process in English, Chinese presents a dilemma: the facts concerning word order show that an N in Chinese cannot be raised to D. The consequences of lacking in a D projection and subsequent N-to-D raising, however, are not true in Chinese. Indeed, we showed in section 3 that Chinese relative constructions are not substantially different from their English counterparts with respect to derivational possibilities and conditions. They mainly differ in word order. In other words, despite the similarity in word order with Japanese relative constructions, Chinese relative constructions are not accommodated by an analysis according to which variations in the ordering of a relative clause and its head are to be traced to the difference between the structures in (4) and (6). The correlated properties derived from such a structural difference, thus, become suspicious. The fact that a relative clause precedes its head in Chinese, thus, cannot argue against the presence of N-to-D raising and cannot argue against the projection of a DP in Chinese.

In fact, we can show that Chinese does project a DP, considering the interpretation of relative constructions in different positions within a Chinese nominal expression. Recall that a DP is an individual-denoting expression and a D is the locus of reference. An N(P), in contrast, is a property-denoting expression. A DP-level modifier, therefore, should modify the reference (or further restrict the reference) and an NP-level modifier should modify the property (i.e., further describe the property). This seems to be the case in the relevant Chinese cases. As argued for in Li (1998, 1999b), demonstratives, which are individual-denoting expressions, are generated in D.[24] *Zhe yi-ge nuhai* 'this one-Cl girl' has the structure $[_{DP}$

[24] One may argue that demonstratives are the head of a demonstrative projection, which is different from a determiner projection. It is clear that there must be a projection above NP (and Classifier Phrase in Chinese, see Li 1998, 1999a,b and Cheng and Sybesma, 1999). The question is whether this projection is a demonstrative phrase or a determiner phrase. In languages like English where determiners and demonstratives are mutually exclusive. It makes sense to claim that a demonstrative phrase is also a determiner phrase. In a language like Chinese which does not have an overt determiner, it is simply a notational matter: whether the projection whose head denotes reference should be labeled as a demonstrative phrase or as a

zhe yi ge [$_{NP}$ *nuhai*]]. A modifier preceding a demonstrative is to restrict the reference and a modifier preceding the noun is to describe the property (see Lu 1998, cf. Chao 1068):

(36) a. zhe yi-shuang yishujia de shou
this one-Cl artist De hand
'this pair of artist hands'

b. yishujia de zhe yi-shuang shou
artist De this one-Cl hand
'this pair of hands of the artist'

(36a) describes the quality of the hands: they are hands that are artistic. (36b) restricts the reference: the hands belong to the artist, not other people. Huang (1982) notes the contrast between examples like (37a-b) and distinguishes the "restrictive" use of a relative clause preceding a demonstrative and the "non-restrictive" use of a relative clause following a demonstrative. The "non-restrictive" use is equivalent to our property-modification function.

(37) a. Niuyue, zhe-ge renren dou xihuan de chengshi
New York this-Cl everyone all like De city
'New York, the city that everyone likes'

b.??Niuyue, renren dou xihuan de zhe-ge chengshi
New York everyone all like De this-Cl city
'New York, the city that everyone likes'

In these examples, the speaker and the hearer know that the city they are discussing is New York. The expression 'that everyone likes' does not restrict the reference of the city. It simply describes the property of this city.[25]

determiner phrase.

In languages which allow demonstratives and determiners to co-occur, it is less clear whether there are two or just one projection. If a determiner is just an agreement marker on an element in D (a determiner being an expletive, see Vergnaud and Zubizarreta 1992), it is possible to maintain the existence of only one DP whose head is a demonstrative or a determiner or a demonstrative plus an agreement determiner. We leave this issue to further research.

[25] The contrast between (37a-b) is not shared by all speakers. This is not surprising. Even though New York should be known to everyone, the speaker may want to more clearly identify the city: New York, the city that I am referring to is the one that everyone likes. 'Everyone likes" restricts the reference of the city and 'the city that everyone likes' is in apposition to New York. The reference-restricting relative clause in (37b), thus, can be acceptable, just like (i)

The above discussion amounts to saying that a modifier (including a relative clause) can be freely adjoined to D(P) or N(P) and the interpretation varies with where the modifier is adjoined to.

If Li's proposal is correct that a DP is projected and that a definite bare N requires N-to-D raising in Chinese, we would expect a relative clause adjoined to a bare noun to be ambiguous. If a relative clause is adjoined to a bare noun which has been raised from N to D, it should have a restrictive function. If a relative clause is adjoined to a noun staying in N (N-to-D raising not taking place in the case of indefinite nouns), it should describe the property. This prediction seems to be true:

(38) a. wo xiang zhao (yi-ge) [[hui dazi de] mishu].
I want find (one-Cl) can type De secretary
'I want to look for a secretary that can type.'

b. [[hui dazi de] (na-ge) mishu] huilai le ma?
can type De (that-Cl) secretary return Asp Q
'Has the secretary that can type returned?'

The bracketed nominal is indefinite in (38a) and definite in (38b). The relative clause in (38a) is generally interpreted as describing the property of secretaries that I am looking for and the one in (38b), restricting the reference of 'secretary' to the one that can type. The contrast between (39a) and (39b) shows that, if a relative clause restricts the reference of the secretary, the nominal expression is definite (N-to-D raising has applied). If a nominal expression is interpreted as indefinite, the relative clause describes the property:

(39) a. wo xiang zhao dai shu lai de mishu. ---definite
I want find bring book come De secretary
'I want to look for the secretary that brought books here.'

b. wo xiang zhao dai-guo shu de mishu. ---indefinite
I want find bring-Asp book De secretary
'I want to look for secretaries that have brought books here.'

below, where the speaker identifies the relevant student by the relative clause. The restriction restricts the reference of 'student', not 'Zhangsan'.

(i) Zhangsan, renren dou xihuan de nage (xuesheng)
Zhangsan everyone all like De that-Cl student
'Zhangsan, the one (student) that everyone likes'

In (39a), the relative clause 'that brought books here' is used to identify the referent of *mishu* and the nominal expression is interpreted as definite. In (39b), the experiential aspect marker *guo* makes it easier for the relative clause to be interpreted as describing the property. The object in (39b) is interpreted as indefinite.

One further prediction of this proposal is that if a relative clause occurs with a quantity-denoting expression, which does not have a DP projection (see Li 1998), a modifier should modify an N, not a D. That is, we should expect the modifier to precede N immediately (modifying the N(P)). Again, this is born out by the contrast between the following expressions:

(40) a. liang-ge shou-xiao de xiaohai jiu gou le.
two-Cl thin-small De child then enough Par.
'Two thin and small children are enough.'

b. ??shouxiao de liang-ge xiaohai jiu gou le.
thin-small De two-Cl child then enough Par.
'Two thin and small children are enough.'

It is also not surprising that in contexts such as (38a) which prefers an indefinite interpretation of the object, it is much better to place the modifier right before the noun (modifying the noun):

(41) *wo xiang-zhao [[hui dazi de] yige mishu].
I want-find can type De one-Cl secretary
'I want to look for a secretary that can type.'

Summing up, we claim that a relative clause (and, more generally, a modifier) can be adjoined to a property-denoting N(P) or an individual-denoting D(P), generating different interpretations according to the structure. Note that the word order maintains to be [relative clause + relative head] in both cases. The ordering between a relative clause and its head does not give any indication of whether a DP is projected or whether N-ot-D raising has applied. It is interpretation that gives us an indication of the structure and derivation of nominal expressions with modifiers (including relatives). Because word order is not correlated with the derivation of relative constructions, it is not surprising that Chinese and English share many characteristics in the derivation of relative clauses, even though they differ in their ordering.

References

Abney, Steve. 1987. The English Noun Phrase and its Sentential Aspect. Doctoral dissertation, Cambridge, Mass: MIT.

Aoun Jopseph and Yen-hui Audrey Li. 1993. On Some Differences between Chinese and Japanese *wh*-elements. *Linguistic Inquiry* 24: 365-372.

Carstens, Vicki. 1991. *The Morphology and Syntax of Determiner Phrases in Kiswahili,* Doctoral dissertation, Los Angeles: University of California.

Chao, Yuen-Ren. 1968. *A Grammar of Spoken Chinese*. Berkeley, CA: University of California Press.

Cheng, Lisa. 1997. On the Typology of Wh-Questions. New York: Garland Publishing, Inc.

Cheng, Lisa and Ring Sybesma. 1999. Bare and Not-so-bare Nouns and the Structure of NP, *Linguistic Inquiry* 30: 509-542

Chierchia, Gennaro 1998. Reference to Kinds across Languages. *Natural Language Semantics* 6:339-405.

Chomsky, Noam. 1977. On *wh*-movement. in Peter Culicover, Thomas Wasow, Adrian Akmajian ed., *Formal Syntax*, Academic Press, New York, pp. 71-132.

Chomsky, Noam. 1986. *Barriers.* Cambridge, Mass: MIT Press.

Cole, Peter 1987. The Structure of Internally Headed Relative Clauses, *Natural Language and Linguistic Theory* 5: 277-302.

Diesing, Molly 1990. Verb Second in Yiddish and the Nature of the Subject Position. *Natural Language and Linguistic Theory* 8: 41-79.

Ernst, Thomas. to appear. *The syntax of adjuncts.* Cambridge University Press.

Fu, Jingqi. 1994. On Deriving Chinese Derived Nomimals: Evidence for V-to-N raising. Doctoral dissertation, University of Massachusetts, Amherst.

Fukui, Naoki and Yuji Takano. 1998. Symmetry in Syntax: Merge and Demerge. *Journal of East Asian Linguistics* 7: 27-86.

Fukui, Naoki and Yuji Takano. 2000. Nominal structure: an extension of the Symmetry Principle. In Peter Svenonius, ed., *The Derivation of VP and OV,* Amsterdam, Netherlands: John Benjamins Publishing Co., pp. 219-254.

Gasde, Horst-Dieter and Waltraud Paul. 1996. Functional Categories, Topic Prominence, and Complex Sentences in Mandarin Chinese, *Linguistics* 34: 263-294.

Hoji, Hajime. 1985. Logical form constraints and configurational structures in Japanese. Doctoral dissertation, University of Washington, Seattle.

Huang, C.-T. James. 1982. Logical relations in Chinese and the theory of grammar. Doctoral dissertation, MIT, Cambridge, Mass.

Kayne, Richard 1994. *The Antiasymmetry of Syntax*. Cambridge, Mass: MIT Press.

Kuno, Susumu. 1973. *The Structure of the Japanese Language.* Cambridge, Mass: MIT Press.

Li, Yen-hui Audrey. 1990. *Order and Constituency in Mandarin Chinese.* Dordrecht: Kluwer Academic Publishers

Li, Yen-hui Audrey. 1992. Indefinite *wh* in Mandarin Chinese. *Journal of East Asian Linguistics* 1: 125-156.

Li, Yen-hui Audrey. 1998. Argument Determiner Phrases and Number Phrases, *Linguistic Inquiry* 29: 693-702.

Li, Yen-hui Audrey. 1999a. Plurality in Classifier Languages. *Journal of East Asian Linguistics* 8: 75-99.

Li, Yen-hui Audrey. 1999b. Form and Function Correspondence: Structures and Interpretations of Nominal Expressions in Mandarin Chinese, in Takubo, Yukinori ed., *Comparative syntax of Japanese, Korean, Chinese and English,* Report of the International Scientific Research Program, Ministry of Education, Science and Culture, Japan, pp.147-186.

Li, Yen-hui Audrey. 2001. Head-final Relatives in One Family? a Comparative Study of Relativization in Chinese and Japanese, paper presented at IACL-10/NACCL-13 joint meeting at Irvine, California.

Longobardi, Guiseppe. 1994. Reference and Proper Names. *Linguistic Inquiry* 25: 609-666.

Lu, Bingfu. 1998. doctoral dissertation, University of Southern California, Los Angeles, California.

McCawley, James D. 1972. Japanese relative clauses. In Paul M. Peranteau, Judith N. Levi and Gloria C. Phares eds., *The Chicago Which Hunt: Papers from the Relative Clause Festival.* Chicago Linguistic Society, University of Chicago, pp. 205-214.

Muraki, Masatake. 1970. Presupposition, pseudo-clefting, and thematization. Doctoral dissertation, University of Texas, Austin.

Murasugi, Keiko. 1991. Noun phrases in Japanese and English: a Study in Syntax, Learnability, and Acquisition. Doctoral dissertation, University of Connecticut, Storrs, Connecticut.

Murasugi, Keiko. 2000. Antisymmetry analysis of Japanese relative clauses. The syntax of relative clauses, ed. by Artemis Alexiadou, Paul Law, Andre Meinunger and Chris Wilder. Amsterdam, Netherlands: John Benjamins Publishing Co., pp. 231-264.

Ritter, Elizabeth. 1991. Two Functional Categories in Noun Phrases: Evidence from Modern Hebrew, in Susan Rothstein. ed., *Syntax and Semantics* 25: *Perspectives on Phrase Structure*, New York: Academic Press, pp. 37-62.

Ritter, Elizabeth. 1995. On the Syntactic Category of Pronouns and Agreement, *Natural Language & Linguistic Theory* 13: 405-443.

Murasugi, Keiko. 1991. Noun phrases in Japanese and English: a Study in Syntax, Learnability, and Acquisition. Doctoral dissertation, University of

Connecticut, Storrs, Connecticut.

Ning, Chunyan. 1993. The Overt Syntax of Relativization and Topicalization in Chinese, Doctoral dissertation, University of California, Irvine.

Saito Mamoru. 1985. Some asymmetries in Japanese and their theoretical implications. Doctoral dissertation: MIT, Cambridge, Mass.

Schachter, Paul. 1973. Focus and Relativization. *Language* 49: 19-46.

Shi, Dingxu. 1992. The Nature of Topic Comment Constructions and Topic Chains, doctoral dissertation, University of Southern California, Los Angeles, California.

Shyu, Shuing. 1995. The Syntax of Focus and Topic in Mandarin Chinese. Doctoral dissertation: University of Southern California, Los Angeles.

Simpson, Andrew. 1997. On the Status of 'Modifying' DE and the Structure of the Chinese DP, ms, SOAS, London

Takano, Yuji. 1996. Movement and Parametric Variation in Syntax. Doctoral dissertation, University of California, Irvine.

Tang, C.-C. Jane. 1990. Chinese Phrase Structure and the Extended X'-theory. Doctoral dissertation, Cornell University, Ithaca.

Tsai, Wei-tien Dylan. 1994. On Economizng the Theory of A-bar Dependency. Doctoral dissertation, MIT, Cambridge, Mass.

Valois, Daniel. 1991. The Internal Syntax of DP and Adjective Placement in French and English. *NELS 21*, Proceedings of the 21st Conference of the Northeast Linguistic Society, Universite du Quebec a Montreal, 1991, pp.367-382.

Vergnaud, Jean-Roger. 1974. French Relative Clauses. Doctoral dissertation, MIT, Cambridge, Mass.

Watanabe, Akira 1992. Subjacency and S-structure Movement of *Wh*-in-situ, *Journal of East Asian Linguistics,* 1:255-291.

Vergnaud, Jean-Roger and Maria-Luisa Zubizarreta. 1992. The definite determiner and the inalienable constructions in French and in English. *Linguistic Inquiry* 23: 595-652.

On the Status of 'Modifying' DE and the Structure of the Chinese DP

ANDREW SIMPSON
*SOAS, University of London**

1. Introduction

This paper re-examines the status of so-called nominal 'modifying' *de* and the traditional head-final analysis of Chinese NPs/DPs and argues that NPs/DPs in Chinese are in fact uniformly head-initial with a fully regular underlying head-complement structure paralleling that in other languages. Surface distortion of this structure is suggested to be due to a property of *de* that it is an enclitic determiner of the type found in Romanian which attracts some XP element to its specifier position for phonological support, this triggering large-scale leftwards movement inside the DP. The paper also considers how definiteness may be encoded DP-internally both in Chinese and in other languages, and examines how determiners are used in a wide range languages to introduce modificational restrictions on nominal referents. Finally, it is shown that the analysis presented in combination with Fu's (1994) insights into the process/result distinction in Chinese

* Work for this paper was supported by DFG grant #GR 559/5-1

On the Formal Way to Chinese Languages.
Sze-Wing Tang and Chen-Sheng Luther Liu (eds.).

nominals is able to provide a simple account of a number of puzzles concerning the relative positioning of complements and adjuncts internal to the DP in Chinese.

2. Modifying *de*, Relative Clauses and Kayne (1994)

A primary goal of this paper is to develop a better understanding of the syntactic status and properties of the particle *de* found occurring in relative clauses, as a marker of possession, and with pre-nominal Adjectival-Phrases and PPs as illustrated in examples (1-4) below:[1]

(1) wo mai de shu
I buy DE book
'the book I bought'

(2) wo de shu
I DE book
'my book'

(3) hao de shu
good DE book
'good books'

(4) dui ta de xinren
to him DE trust
'trust in him'

Referred to variously as a relativizer, a genitive case-marker and sometimes just vaguely as a modifying particle, little consensus has been reached on the actual syntactic category of the element *de* and its status in the NP/DP is often simply ignored. In order to probe this issue further, I would like to focus first on the occurrence of *de* in relative clause structures and examine an interesting result which ensues from analyzing Chinese relative clauses in terms of Kayne's (1994) Antisymmetry of Syntax theory.

One important consequence of Kayne's general theory of word-order (the Linear Correspondence Axiom/LCA) is that rightward adjunction is not permitted, forcing the re-analysis of a number of constructions including relative clauses which have commonly been taken to involve such rightward adjunction. In order to avoid the assumption that a relative clause is rightwardly adjoined to the head noun/NP in languages like English, Kayne suggests the analysis sketched out in (5) below. The head noun/NP originates in the IP clause and undergoes raising to the specifier of a CP constituent which is selected as the *complement* of a determiner:

(5) [$_{DP}$ the [$_{CP}$ man$_i$ [$_{C)}$ that [$_{IP}$ I met t$_i$]]]]

---

[1] Note that the paper does not consider the use of the morphologically-related sentence-final *de*. For a discussion of the syntax of this element see Simpson & Wu (1999).

Considering languages in which the relative clause precedes the head-noun/NP, a number of patterns are found. In order to avoid the possibility of rightward-adjunction again, all such languages are essentially suggested to follow the derivation schematized in (5) above and then take this derivation further in a number of different ways. In Yoruba-type languages it is suggested that forms such as (5) will be transformed into structures such as (6) via raising of the entire CP following the head-noun in (5) to SpecDP, whereas in Amharic-type languages it is the IP constituent following the head-noun/NP which is argued to raise to SpecDP, resulting in the order in (7). The abstract examples (6) and (7) use English words for ease of exposition:

(6) [$_{DP}$ [$_{CP}$ man$_i$ [$_C$ that [$_{IP}$ I met t$_i$]]] [$_D$ the [t$_k$]] 'Yoruba'

(7) [$_{DP}$ [$_{IP}$ I met t$_i$]]$_k$ [$_D$ the [$_{CP}$ man$_i$ [t$_k$]] 'Amharic'

Certain languages having similar patterns to Amharic also seem to display a 'relative particle' sandwiched between the 'raised' relative clause and the determiner or head-noun/NP, resulting in a sequence such as (8):

(8) I met REL (the) man

Kayne argues that such elements cannot in fact be relativizers in a C^0 position as the analysis only allows that a C^0/Comp position could hypothetically occur either preceding the raised relative clause or following the head noun/NP, in the positions indicated in (9):

(9) # I met REL (the) man #

Kayne consequently suggests that such elements are actually Infl elements attached to the verb. Such a proposal is indeed potentially plausible as all of the languages identified as having 'raised' relative clauses are verb-final O-V languages and the 'relativizer' appears adjacent to the verb which is final in the relative clause - the 'relativizer' could then quite possibly be taken to be a verbal suffix. Chinese however causes an interesting problem for such an analysis - Chinese is a language with pre-nominal relative clauses and an element which looks like a relativizer (*de*) occurring between the relative clause and the head-noun, but Chinese is a language which is atypically *V-O* in its word order; consequently the 'relativizer' *de* does *not* necessarily occur adjacent to the verb and so cannot be analyzed as an inflectional suffix on the verb.[2] Consider the relative clause in (10) - for Kayne such a structure has to follow the lines of derivations already outlined - the head-noun/NP will be taken to raise to SpecCP from the underlying structure in (11) and then some IP-like clausal constituent following the head-noun will undergo further raising to an initial position, as in the schema in (12):

(10) [_ qu Beijing] de ren
go Beijing DE person
'the person who went to Beijing'

(11) [de $[_{CP}$ $\underline{ren_i}$ $[_{IP}$ t_i qu Beijing]]]

(12) $[[_{IP}$ $\underline{t_i \text{ qu Beijing}}$ $]_k$ [de $[_{CP}$ $\underline{ren_i}]$ t_k]]

The element *de* sandwiched between *qu Beijing* and *ren* cannot be analyzed as an inflectional suffix on the verb in the relative clause, nor can it be analyzed as a relativizer in a C^0 position, because Kayne's analysis does not allow for a C^0 node to occur in this position - the two potential C^0 positions are those indicated in (9), hence those signalled in (13) and not the position occupied by *de*:

(13) # qu Beijing <u>de</u> ren #

The only possible analysis for *de* following Kayne would seem to be that *de* in fact is a *determiner* occupying D^0, with the IP-RC raised to SpecDP

(14) $[_{DP}$ $[_{IP}$ t_i qu Beijing $]_k$ $[_D$ de $[_{CP}$ $ren_i]$ t_k]]

This clearly may be a rather unexpected result as *de* does not seem to display the behaviour and properties commonly associated with determiners. For example, *de* would first of all not seem to have any obvious *definiteness* value, which is generally taken to be a defining property of determiners. Secondly *de* may occur more than once in an NP/DP, as in (15), whereas DPs are regularly taken to be associated with a single D^0 position and hence a single occurrence of a determiner:

---

2 Relative clauses in Chinese are typologically extremely marked. In a study examining the word order patterns of 130 languages, Dryer (1992) reports that Chinese was the *only* language having both pre-nominal relative clauses and a basic verb-initial/V-O order; all other languages with the order relative clause - noun turned out to be uniformly O-V languages.

(15) wo-de zhu zai Beijing de hao pengyou
I DE live in Beijing DE good friend
'my good friend who lives in Beijing'

Thirdly, *de* can clearly co-occur with demonstratives which are otherwise commonly taken to instantiate and occur in D^0, suggesting that *de* itself is not in D^0 but is rather an element of a different type. The position occupied by the demonstrative in (16) might furthermore appear to be a quite regular determiner/D^0 position initial in the DP whereas *de* is never found to be DP-initial and always follows some other constituent:

(16) nei-ben [wo zuotian mai]-de shu
that CL I yesterday buy DE book
'that book I bought yesterday'

Instead, however, of immediately concluding that the Kaynean approach to relativization must necessarily be incorrect for Chinese because it leads one to what seems like an intuitively odd analysis of *de*, this paper will actually investigate the possibility that Chinese *de* may be a determiner, and will suggest that there is in fact much to be gained from understanding *de* as an instantiation of D^0. In what follows, the paper will first argue in section (3) that the reasons for rejecting *de* as a determiner noted above are not in fact well-grounded and that determiners cross-linguistically show a behaviour which is much more varied than that in languages such as English which have tended to shape our initial conceptions of the nature of determiners. Section (4) then continues with a comparison of determiners, demonstratives and quantifiers and a consideration of the notion of definiteness in DPs, and argues for a rather different analysis of the functional role of determiners. Finally section (5) attempts to show that an analysis of *de* as a determiner-element potentially allows for a more general analysis of DPs in Chinese in which such constituents need not be taken to be head-final as often assumed in the past, but can instead be shown to be very similar to descriptively head-initial DPs in other languages.

3. Multiple Determiners, Definiteness and Demonstratives

One of the properties of *de* mentioned in section 2 which might go against its analysis as a determiner is that one frequently finds more than a single occurrence of *de* in a DP and it is commonly assumed that there should only be a single D^0 position in any DP. Such an assumption may perhaps be largely based on our understanding of English and other west European languages where this restriction does indeed seem to hold. However, there are also a considerable number of languages where determiners do appear multiply within a single DP, as for example in Hebrew where (17) shows a determiner occurring both on the head noun and on the following adjective:[3]

(17) ha-bayit ha-gadol
the-house the-big
'the big house'

Albanian and Greek also show the same phenomena, in (18) and (19) respectively:

(18) djal-i i-mire
boy-the the-good
'the good boy'

(19) afto to oreo to vivlio
this the good the book
'this good book'

Consequently the fact that *de* may occur multiply within the NP/DP in Chinese is not necessarily a good reason for rejecting *de*'s status as a determiner - the multiple occurrence of determiners in a single DP is cross-linguistically not unusual and the additional occurrence of determiners marking *adjectival modification* relations is actually well-attested.

A second potential argument against a determiner analysis of *de* noted in section 2 was that *de* would not seem to have any inherent definiteness value, and such a property is often taken to be a crucial identifying property of determiners. However, here again it can be shown that there are many cases of determiners occurring without any contribution to the definiteness of a DP and that an element need *not* necessarily mark (in-)definiteness on a DP in order to qualify as a determiner. There are, for example, clear uses of the so-called 'definite' determiner as an expletive place-holder element occurring with names in Italian, German and many other languages (as seen in (20/21) below). In such combinations it is critically the presence of the name in the DP which results in the DP being interpreted as definite, and the determiner itself has no strong contribution to the DP in terms of definiteness. Longobardi (1994) discusses the patterning in (21) and suggests that the definiteness of the DP is formally established by N-to-D movement of the name; this may take place overtly as in (21b), but if it does not do so, an expletive determiner must instead be inserted as a place-holder in D^0, and the name is then suggested to raise to D^0 at LF. Noting that failure to insert the dummy determiner will result in ungrammaticality (as in 21c), the important contribution of the determiner is then not one of

[3] Examples here are taken from Giusti (1997).

supplying definiteness but simply that of filling a position, similar to the occurrence of expletive subjects used to satisfy the EPP in clauses:

(20) der Karl
the Karl

(21) a. il mio Gianni
the my Gianni
b. $Gianni_i$ mio t_i
c. *mio Gianni

Albanian (22) additionally shows that the necessary insertion of a 'definite' determiner with an adjective in fact has no relation to the ensuing definiteness of the DP, and is reported in Guasti (1997) to be triggered solely by properties of the adjectival stem - in (22) a 'definite' determiner occurs with the adjective but the whole DP is actually indefinite:

(22) nje djale i mire
a boy the good
'a good boy'

It can also be noted that the 'definite' determiner in English may in certain cases be used without giving rise to any necessary interpretation of definiteness/familiarity as illustrated in examples (23) and (24):

(23) I bet you'll never find <u>the</u> secretary of a deputy who's willing to testify against him.[4]

(24) The Crow and the Fox (as a book/story title)[5]

The referents represented by the DPs marked with definite determiners in (23) and (24) may be fully novel to the hearer/reader and so need not necessarily be interpreted as definite.

Finally, French uses the 'definite' determiner in instances of inalienable possession where English would use an indefinite determiner, hence again an instance where the 'definiteness' specification of a determiner is far from clear:

(25) Olga a <u>le</u> bras enflé.
Olga has the arm swollen
'Olga has <u>a</u> swollen arm.' (Tellier 1994)

---

[4] This example again comes from Guasti (1997).

[5] Interestingly, the Miao language of Weining as reported by Bisang (1997) has two different types of classifier which are associated with definiteness and indefiniteness and would here in (24) select the *indefinite* novel classifier for a similar story title.

Consequently it can be argued that it is not possible to suggest that determiners must always have necessary inherent definiteness properties and accordingly reject the analysis of *de* as a determiner because it appears to lack such a definiteness specification. Clear determiners in other languages frequently do not seem to make any contribution to the definiteness of a DP and may appear to have instead some other kind of purely expletive function.

The third initial reason given for possibly rejecting an analysis of *de* as a determiner was that *de* is found to co-occur with demonstratives which traditionally have been taken to instantiate D^0. Such an assumption is in large part based on the observation that determiners and demonstratives may not co-occur in languages such as English, as in (26):

(26) *the that book *that the book

However, here again there is now abundant cross-linguistic evidence that determiners frequently may co-occur with demonstratives and hence that they do not always compete for the same D^0 position. Greek as already illustrated in (19), Spanish, Romanian, Hungarian and Irish are just a few of the many languages where determiners and demonstratives are found together in the same DP. Spanish and Irish in fact show that when the demonstrative occurs after the noun a determiner is actually forced to co-occur with the demonstrative, as seen in (27). In Spanish such an order alternates with one in which the demonstrative occurs intially and suggests that the determiner is simply an expletive place-holder for the demonstrative which is itself responsible for the definiteness specification of the DP:

(27) a. el hombre este
the man this
'this man'

b. *hombre este

c. $este_i$ hombre t_i

d. *(an) fear seo (Irish)
the man this
'This man'

Grosu (1988) also convincingly suggests that a wide variety of complex patterns found in Romanian DPs may be neatly explained if one assumes that demonstratives are in fact inserted as XPs in lower DP-internal *specifier* positions rather than head positions. In (28a) it can be seen that N-to-D head movement licitly takes place over a demonstrative; here it is argued that this movement is not blocked by the Head Movement Constraint/HMC precisely because the demonstrative is not in an intervening head-position. Movement of an AdjP to SpecDP is however blocked when a demonstrative is present below the determiner, as in (28b), because the latter is (suggested to be) an XP closer to SpecDP and so the demonstrative should itself raise to this position due to Relativized Minimality/the Shortest Move Condition, as indeed in (28c): [6]

(28) a. baiat$_i$-ul acesta frumos t_i
boy - the this nice
'this nice boy'

b. *frumos$_i$-ul acesta t_I baiat
nice – the this boy

c. acest$_I$ t_I frumos baiat
this nice boy

Giusti (1997) furthermore shows that Spanish, Greek and Irish all provide evidence that demonstratives may be base-generated in low positions inside DPs. For example, it is noted that the demonstrative in Spanish appears to occur as the lowest modifer of N, preceding all PPs but following all adjectives including thematic ones, as in (29):

(29) la reaccion (*esa) alemana (esa) a las criticas
the reaction that German that to the criticisms
'that/the German reaction to the criticisms.'

The order reported for Irish is schematically as indicated in (30) below, with demonstratives similarly occurring in a low position following determiners, numerals and adjectives:

(30) Det NumP N AP* <u>Dem</u> RC

Giusti (1997) suggests that one should therefore assume that demonstratives are perhaps universally base-generated in relatively low Spec positions rather than directly in D^0 and that when they do occur initially, this should be taken to be the result of movement from the lower base-generated position.

Turning to Chinese, it is found that demonstratives can occur both in an initial position in a DP and also in a lower position as in Irish, Spanish and Greek, as shown in (31). Following Giusti's analysis of the latter langauges, it can therefore be suggested that the variability in positioning of

---

6 Note that movement of the AdjP to SpecDP is otherwise well-formed and satisfies the enclitic requirements of the determiner if the demonstrative is not present, as presently illustrated in example (34).

demonstratives in Chinese may be due to such elements being base-generated either in a lower DP-internal position or in a second higher/DP-initial position:

(31) (nei-suo) zai da-shan de (nei-suo) xin fangzi
Dem-CL in big-mountain DE Dem-CL new house
'that new house in the mountains'

Consequently, given the wider patterning of demonstratives and determiners observed above, it can be argued that *de*'s potential to co-occur with a demonstrative is in fact not a strong reason for rejecting an analysis of *de* as a determiner – cross-linguistically it is found that determiners do indeed very frequently co-occur with demonstratives, and Chinese may well be similar to Spanish, Romanian and other languages in simply allowing for demonstratives to be base-generated either low in the DP or in a more canonical DP-initial position.[7]

3.1 Further objections

By considering a wider range of determiner behaviour in slightly less familiar languages it is consequently possible to provide good counter-arguments to all of the initial objections raised against analyzing *de* as a determiner. There are however various other obvious questions which any analysis of *de* as a determiner also needs to answer - first of all, importantly if *de* is in D^0, why is it that it never appears in an initial position in the DP? Here the relevant generalization would seem to be that *de* is always closely associated with some XP to its immediate left, this being clearly evidenced by the pause intonation patterns which can be made *after* but never directly *before de*. Pursuing the hypothesis that *de* is a determiner element, it can now be suggested that this tight linking of *de* with the XP which immediately precedes it may be explained if one takes *de* to be a determiner of the same basic type as found in Romanian and argued by Grosu (1988) to be an enclitic requiring leftward phonological support. This property of the definite determiner in Romanian clearly triggers raising of some other element to a position immediately preceding the determiner - a noun in (33), an adjective in (34) or a demonstrative as in (28c) above - and shows a clear contrast with DPs headed by the *indefinite* determiner which is not an enclitic and so does not cause any parallel raising to take place (35). Example (32) shows that DPs headed by the definite determiner *–ul* are ill-

[7] It may of course also be possible to assume that the demonstrative-classifier unit is regularly base-generated in the lower position and then sometimes optionally raised to the higher DP-initial position.

formed if no raising of another DP-internal element takes place to the left of *–ul*:

(32) *-ul potret unei fete
the portrait a.Gen girl

(33) potret$_i$-ul t_i unei fete
portrait-the a.Gen.girl
'the portrait of a girl'

(34) frumos$_i$-ul t_i baiat
nice - the boy
'the nice boy'

(35) un portet al unei fete
a portrait of-the one girl
'a portrait of the girl'

In Chinese DPs headed by *de* I would therefore like to suggest that an XP-element is attracted to SpecDP by *de* in D^0 for entirely parallel reasons, to support *de* as an enclitic.[8] Such an assumption, supported by the clear phonological phrasing of *de* with the XP to its left, will quite simply account for the regular non-initial positioning of *de*, as illustrated again in (36) and (37) below:

(36) [$_{IP}$ wo zuotian mai]$_i$-de nei-ben [$_{CP}$ shu [t_i]]
I yesterday buy DE that-CL book
'the book I bought yesterday'

(37) [wo]$_i$ de t_i nei-ben-shu
I DE that-CL book
'that book of mine'

Such an analysis also has the advantage that it accounts for the unexpected pre-nominal positioning of relative clauses in Chinese in terms of the special properties of a single lexical item, i.e. the enclitic requirements of the D^0 element *de*, rather attributing it to a general parameter of the language. As pointed out in footnote 2, Dryer (1992) observes that Chinese is essentially unique in being the only language attested anywhere with a basic V-O word order and also *pre-nominal* relative clauses, RC-N structures elsewhere being found to occur only in very regular O-V, (descriptively) head-final languages. This exceptional

[8] Note, incidentally, that the homophonous potential and adverbial markers *de* have also frequently been analyzed as clitics.

fact about Chinese clearly must have some explanation, and it would seem most appropriate to assume that it relates to the exceptional properties of a single lexical element rather than being the outcome of the general typological nature of Chinese, whose overall V-O head-initial character would clearly lead one to expect only post-nominal relative clauses to occur.

An analysis along such lines however also raises a question about certain other elements which can potentially precede relative clauses in fully DP-initial positions, as shown in (38). If relative clauses do indeed occur (raised) in SpecDP, one needs to ask what positions these other DP-initial elements might be occurring in:

(38) hen-duo/liang-ben/mei-ben [$_{DP}$ [$_{IP}$ wo zuotian mai]$_i$-de [$_{CP}$ shu [t_i]]]
very-many/2-CL/every-CL I yesterday buy DE book
'very many books/two books/every book that I bought yesterday'

(39) nei-ben [$_{DP}$ [$_{IP}$ wo zuotian mai]$_i$-de [$_{CP}$ shu [t_i]]]
Dem-CL I yesterday buy DE book
'that book I bought yesterday'

Concerning the DP-initial pre-relative clause elements in (38), it is often assumed that certain quantifiers and quantificational elements may actually select DP as their complement, as in English (40) and other languages:

(40) [$_{QP}$ [$_{Q}$ all [$_{DP}$ the books]]]

Giusti (1997) shows that certain of these quantifiers may also be positionally quite ambiguous in various languages and occur either high in a Q^0 position or lower down in some adjectival specifier. Romanian in particular has the interesting example of an element meaning 'both' which takes on morphologically different shapes when used initially in Q^0 and when occurring as a pure adjective lower down in the DP:

(41) [$_{QP}$ amindoi [$_{DP}$ baieti$_i$ -i t_I]] (amindoi=Q^0)
both children-the
'both the children'

(42) [$_{DP}$ ambi$_i$-i t_i baieti (ambi=Adj raised from regular
both-the children lower Adj position)
'the two/both children'

I would consequently like to suggest that the DP-initial, pre-relative clause quantifiers in Chinese examples such as (38) are occupying a pre-DP Q^0 or SpecQP position parallel to that in other languages (and like quantifiers in Romanian may also alternatively occur in a lower DP-internal position).

Regarding the pre-relative clause position of the demonstrative in (39), I would like to suggest that this element may occur positioned in the specifier of a functional projection dominating DP which specifically encodes the deictic location/orientation of a DP. In his thorough investigation of the internal functional structure of clauses, Cinque (1999) notes that the highest functional projections of a clause would seem to relate the clause directly to the speaker in terms of his/her attitude to its truth, and the origin of a piece of information with respect to the speaker (evidential marking). Interpreting this as a semi-deictic/metaphorical siting of the proposition relative to the speaker, and making the common assumption that DPs and clauses have essentially similar structures, it can be suggested that DPs may also have an equivalent origin-focused deictic functional projection high in their structure relating the reference of the DP to the speaker/hearer in a way which parallels the origin-related high functional structure present in clausal constituents. Assuming this tentatively to be so, pre-relative clause demonstratives such as that in (39) can be suggested to be base-generated in (or perhaps undergo raising to) the specifier of such a deictic projection.[9]

If the patterns found in (38) and (39) can thus be given a reasonable explanation, a second more testing question about the *de*-as-enclitic determiner hypothesis is now the following. If *de* is indeed to be analyzed as a determiner, why is it then not possible to have just simple sequences of *de*-noun or noun-*de* as in (43) below?

(43) a. *de ren b. *ren-de
DE person person-DE
intended: 'the person'

(43a) is ruled out because it has been suggested that *de* requires some element in its specifier to provide it with phonological support, but nothing so far explains why (43b) should not be possible with the noun/NP *ren* raised to SpecDP. This particular problem I will actually set aside just for the present and return to it later on in section 4.1. For now it can be noted that the underlying intuition which needs to be captured is that *de* only ever occurs when there is some modification relation. In section 4.1 it will be shown that there are in fact *many* other instances cross-linguistically where determiners or determiner-like elements similarly seem to require the presence of some other modifying phrase in order to legitimately occur in syntactic structure, and hence the requirement that the putative Mandarin

[9] In support of such proposals, it can be noted that Huang (1982) suggests that a demonstrative in a position preceding a relative clause results in a clearly stronger deictic interpretation than one following a relative clause, hence that different interpretations are associated with demonstratives in the pre- and post-relative clause positions.

determiner *de* be accompanied by some other modifying phrase is really just one instantiation of a more general pattern which possibly calls for a wider reassessment of the functional role of determiners.

4. Definiteness, Demonstratives and Szabolcsi (1994)

In this section I would first like to return to *de* and the *definiteness issue* - the traditional assumption that the definiteness of a DP is a direct result of the definiteness specification of a DP's determiner. Essentially I will propose adopting a version of a rather different approach towards the locus of definiteness in the DP put forward in Szabolcsi (1996), investigating the structure of the DP in Hungarian.

Szabolcsi makes the interesting observation that a determiner in Hungarian may co-occur with a low demonstrative or other low quantifier such as *minden* 'every' only if some other element such as a reduced relative clause or a possessor phrase intervenes between these elements, as e.g in (44) and (45):

(44)	a	*(tol-ed	kapott)	valemennyi	level
	the	from-2sg	received	each	letter
	'the letter I/we received from you'				

(45)	az	*(en)	minden	allitas-om
	the	I	every	book
	'my every book'			

If a determiner does not occur in forms such as (44), then the Demonstrative/Quantifier is forced to raise to the initial D^0 position, as in (46):

(46)	valamennyi$_i$	tol-ed	kapott	t$_i$	level
	each	from-2sg	received		letter

(47)	*tol-ed	kapott	valamennyi	level
	from-2sg	received	each	letter

Suggesting that this raising is triggered by a simple need to fill the D^0 position with some overt element, Szabolcsi then notes that the interpretation of (44) with the determiner and (46) without the determiner is exactly the same and concludes that the determiner does not make any special contribution towards interpretation in (44). Szabolsci goes on to argue that if the definiteness interpretation in (46) results from the presence of the quantifier alone, it should likewise also result from just the quantifier in (44) where the determiner is in fact present. Interpretations of definiteness are consequently suggested not to come from determiners in Hungarian and it is argued that such elements must therefore have some other function in the DP. Drawing a parallel with CP complementizers, Szabolsci proposes that the primary function of both determiners and complementizers is to act as *subordinators* and formally enable a CP proposition or a DP to refer as an argument. She then notes that complementizers cross-linguistically might in fact seem to have two regular functions - sometimes acting simply as pure embedders/subordinators and elsewhere also ‘typing’ clauses in the sense evoked by Cheng (1997). In some languages these two functions may possibly be performed by separate lexical items, as for example in Japanese where the element *to* is a pure clausal embedder and *ka* is an interrogative clause typer, however it is suggested that other languages might be found to employ a single lexical element for both functions, as for example in English with the C^0 'that' functioning being as an embedder and as a (declarative clause) typer. Parallel to this and in the domain of the DP, Szabolcsi speculates that the English determiner 'the' might similarly fulfill both functions of subordination *and* providing a definiteness specification (an equivalent ‘typing’ function), this potentially allowing for an explanation of why determiners do not co-occur with demonstratives in English - the determiner alone is able to fulfill both roles of subordinating and typing). In Hungarian Szabolcsi takes the determiner to be a pure subordinator, while the definiteness specification of the DP is assumed to *always* come from some other element - an overt demonstrative or quantifier if one is present, as in (44/45/46), *or* some covert null variant of such elements which is suggested to occur when only the determiner is overtly present, as in (48):

(48) a ∅ level
      the ∅ letter

Finally, Szabolcsi suggests that although definiteness may in fact be the result of the (definiteness) specification of a low position hosting demonstratives and certain quantifiers in all languages (rather than come from a purely subordinating determiner element in D^0), there may also be some kind of definiteness ‘concord’ process whereby a higher subordinating determiner has to agree in definiteness specification with a lower demonstrative. Such a definiteness agreement process would then require the use of the 'definite' determiner in Hungarian (44/45) rather than an indefinite equivalent.[10]

I would now like to assume, following Szabolcsi's insights above, that the definiteness specification of a DP may indeed be a direct function of a position where demonstratives and indefinite quantifiers potentially can occur, lower than the initial D-position, and that definiteness may not be directly or even necessarily a function of D^0. In Chinese it can be seen that the overall definiteness of a DP would often seem to relate to elements which appear lower than the initial (D-)position, as illustrated in examples (49) and (50):

(49) wo de nei-ben shu
I DE that-CL book
'that book of mine' DEFINITE

(50) wo de liang-ben shu
I DE 2-CL book
'two books of mine' INDEFINITE

Concerning the definiteness concord which is in other languages assumed to exist and be manifested between a lower demonstrative and a higher D^0 position (in Szabolcsi's approach), here it can be suggested that this has only a covert, abstract representation in Chinese and no overt morphological reflex, as the single lexical element *de* occurs in D^0 in both definite and indefinite DPs such as (49/50). In regard to such a suggestion, note first of all that if the essential definiteness of the DP is indeed a function of low demonstratives or (possibly indefinite) quantifers, then there clearly is no absolute necessity for the definiteness value to be repeated overtly elsewhere in D^0, hence D^0 elements should not necessarily be expected to overtly encode (in)definiteness. Secondly, if a language were to possess only one instantiation of D^0 (i.e. have just a single embedding determiner element), neutral with regard to any overt definiteness specification, this will have the effect that overt definiteness concord will simply just not be visible in the language, in the same way that a language with a single subordinating complementizer/C^0 will not show any overt finiteness agreement/concord with an embedded T^0-head. This then is essentially what I would like to suggest is the case in Chinese, that the element *de* is simply a determiner now under-specified for and neutral with regard to definiteness, so that *overt* definiteness concord does not occur in

[10] Szabolcsi likens this concord/agreement to that obtaining between a complementizer and a lower T^0-head - a complementizer may have to 'agree' in terms of finiteness with T^0, as in English where that is a finite-C and for a non-finite C.

Chinese, unlike in Hungarian/Spanish etc.[11] The issue that *de* is claimed to be a determiner yet appears to have no inherent definiteness specification can consequently be given a reasoned explanation, and the suggested covert nature of the representation of DP-internal definiteness concord in Chinese can be taken to be just a further example of the frequent overt/covert alternation of agreement phenomena assumed in natural language.

4.1 The Function of *de*

Here the paper now returns to a question raised earlier in section 2 and speculates that the actual function of the determiner *de* in Chinese (and possibly determiners in certain other languages) may perhaps be somewhat different from Szabolcsi's idea of a pure subordinating function. The important question put aside in section 2 was why it is not possible to have just the element *de* and a bare head-noun/NP as in (51):

(51) *ren$_i$ -de t$_i$
person DE

As briefly noted in section 2, the idea which needs to be captured is that *de* only occurs when there is some other modifying element present. This section will now try and show that there are in fact many instances where determiners or determiner-like elements require some other modifying element to be present, and that broadly this might indeed be a pre-condition on determiners of certain types, possibly that the primary function of these determiners precisely is to enable a modification relation to be effected; the determiners themselves might then perhaps be taken to instantiate syntactic

[11] Note that the present lack of overt definiteness specification in *de* may well not have been true of the morpheme *de* in the past. As noted in Simpson 2001, it is widely speculated that the element *de* developed from the earlier classical Chinese element *zhi* which had a distribution largely parallel with modern Chinese *de*. Here it can be noted that in addition to functions similar to modern Chinese *de*, *zhi* was significantly also used as a clear demonstrative, as illustrated in (i) below:

(i) zhi er chong you he zhi
these two worm again what know
'And what do these two worms know?' (Zhuangzi 1.10)

Modern-day *de* consequently may have developed from an early demonstrative and so at an earlier time have had a positive definiteness specification just like other demonstrative elements. See here Simpson 2001 for much further discussion of the issue of definiteness agreement and its gradual loss over time. Given furthermore the common observation (e.g. Vincent 1997) that determiners are elements which develop out of earlier demonstratives, the fact that *de* most probably developed from a demonstrative is also further good support for the suggestion that *de* is now a determiner/an element of category D^0.

variables allowing the modifying element to enter into some kind of a non-canonical predication relation with the noun.

A first illustration of the wider connection between determiners and noun modification was actually present in the preceding section. There it was shown that the sequence the...every in Hungarian is only licit if some additional modifying expression is included in the sequence, either a possessor or a reduced relative clause as schematized in (52), hence that the determiner may only co-occur with a demonstrative if there is some other noun modifier present:[12]

(52) the *(poss-NP/RC) that/every N

A second example of essentially the same phenomenon can be given from Vietnamese. Bisang (1997) argues that classifiers are not always necessary for counting in Vietnamese and that it is therefore possible to have a numeral with a noun without a classifier as in (53):

(53) trong nha-hat kia co muoi-bay ghe
in cinema this are 17 chairs
'There are 17 chairs in this cinema.'

However, if a further modifying expression is added in to (53), use of the classifier interestingly becomes obligatory, as illustrated in (54). Therefore a clear link obtains between the occurrence of a modifying expression and that of a determiner-like element, classifiers in many languages having clear determiner-like properties - see here Cheng & Sybesma (1996) on Cantonese, Daley (1995) on Vietnamese, also Simpson (2001):

(54) trong nha-hat kia co muoi-bay *(cai) ghe lam bang cay tot
in cinema this are 17 CL chairs made of wood good
'There are 17 chairs made of good wood in this cinema.'

Further examples can actually be given from English. Whereas sequences of determiners and quantifiers such as the every boy are not normally licensed (as in Hungarian), when an additional modifying possessor phrase is added on, this can have the effect of making such sequences quite acceptable and licensing the determiner to appear with the quantifier:

(55) *the every whim
(56) the every whim [of Margaret Thatcher]

---

[12] Note too the suggestive fact that both these types of modifiers are elements which occur marked by *de* in Chinese.

(57-59) below show a similar patterning, this time with a relative clause. Whereas (57) is grammatical with a demonstrative, if the demonstrative is replaced with a determiner, the sequence immediately becomes unacceptable (58). This illicit presence of the determiner can then however be licensed by the addition of a modifying relative clause, so again the presence of the determiner is dependent on that of the relative clause:

(57) that sweater of John's (is expensive)

(58) *the sweater of John's (is expensive)

(59) the sweater of John's [that you showed me last night]

Another quite similar case is noted in Kayne (1994) - in English, names can only be accompanied by determiners if there is also an additional modifying relative clause, as shown by the contrast in (60) and (61):

(60) *the Rome

(61) the Rome [that I love]

Through all of these cases we see then that the presence of the determiner depends on the presence of a second modifying element, which is exactly what is also found with *de* in Mandarin. As certain determiner elements consequently seem to be intrinsically bound up with (the presence of) restrictive modification, it can be suggested that the introduction of a predication relation may indeed be a critical, primary function of such elements. Here we may also reflect back on earlier examples from Romanian, Albanian and other languages where it was shown that adjectives introducing properties of the head noun are all marked with a determiner, this in addition to the presence of a determiner on the head noun, as for example in (17) repeated here:

(17) ha-bayit ha-gadol
the-house the-big
'the big house'

Generally then it actually seems to be quite common for restrictive predication on a noun to be introduced by means of a determiner. Given such an observation, it is possible to understand the determiner in these instances as providing something like a visible externalized variable allowing an unsaturated predicate to be interpreted as modifying some other nominal, and this is how I would here like to propose analyzing Chinese *de* -

as an element of this same determiner class specifically used to introduce a predicative restriction on some second nominal expression. This function of *de* parallel to that of clear determiners in other environments may then be held directly responsible for the fact that sequences such as **ren-de* in (51) critically do not occur - *de* obligatorily introduces a restriction on the head noun but none is present in such sequences.[13] [14]

---

[13] An alternative (though perhaps less revealing) way to capture the fact that *de* co-occurs not just with a bare noun but necessarily also with some kind of modifier is to suggest that this is simply due to the syntactic sub-categorization requirements which *de* has - if *de* specifically selects for a CP complement rather then an NP complement (as indeed suggested here), then in addition to the head-noun following *de* there will clearly also always be a clausal modifier present (raised to SpecDP after relativization of the head-noun to SpecCP).

[14] In connection with the '*ren-de'-problem, a reviewer of the paper asks why it is that an intermediate form such as (i) cannot give rise to a surface form (ii) via raising to SpecDP of the NP rather than the IP:

(i) [de [[$_{NP}$ shu]$_i$ [$_{IP}$ wo mai t_i]]

(ii) *[[$_{NP}$ shu]$_i$ [de [t_i [$_{IP}$ wo mai t_i]]]

(iii) [[$_{IP}$ wo mai t_i]$_k$ de [[$_{NP}$ shu]$_i$ t_k]

If movement of the IP to SpecDP is triggered by a need to provide phonological support for *de*, one might wonder why the NP could not be raised to SpecDP to provide this phonological support instead of the IP. This, I believe, can arguably be ascribed to the selective nature that clitics are cross-linguistically observed to show and the fact that clitics vary quite considerably with regard to their tolerance of different phonological hosts. Whereas certain clitics may allow attachment to a wide variety of hosts, others appear to be rather intolerant and target only a single specific type of host (as e.g. the pronominal clitics in Romance languages). Chinese *de* can therefore be suggested to be highly selective in this latter way and only target/attract a clausal IP constituent, not NPs or any other type of element; in the Minimalist model of syntax this may be achieved by assuming that *de* is base-generated with strong *v*-(or T-)features which are satisfied when a clause headed by an element with *v*-features is attracted to the Specifier of DP (it can also be noted that movement of the full IP rather than just the I^0/V^0 carrying the *v*-features may be forced by the Head Movement Constraint - head-movement of I^0/V^0 alone might well be impossible across the intervening C^0 head.

This answer to the question of why (ii) is not permitted will in fact also provide an alternative solution to the '*ren-de' problem (as the same reviewer suggests) - if *de* will only tolerate (can only attract) an IP to its Spec for phonological support, then the non-occurrence of '*ren-de' forms will be straightforwardly ruled out - <u>ren</u> as an NP will simply fail to satisfy the highly selective enclitic requirements projected by *de*. Note that possessor structures such as (iv) which might appear to pose a problem for such a view are analyzed in Simpson (1998) as relative clause-type structures containing a null verb of predication. Consequently the constituent to the left of *de* is (suggested to be) an IP out of which the head-noun <u>shu</u> has been relativized and the IP-requirement imposed by *de* is indeed uniformly maintained:

(iv) [$_{IP}$ wo t_i]$_k$ de [[shu]$_i$ t_k]
I DE book
'my book'

5. DP Structure, Complements and Adjuncts

Having argued for the analysis of *de* as a determiner in the preceding sections, I would now like to try to show how such an analysis allows for a somewhat different view of DP structure in Chinese which accounts for the apparent head-final character of NPs/DPs and suggests that the NP/DP is instead a fully regular head-initial phrasal-type. The traditional assumption that DPs/NPs are head-final in Chinese can be suggested to be otherwise rather problematic, first of all for the purely theory-internal reason that head-final categories are argued not to exist in approaches such as Kayne (1994) and more generally because Chinese elsewhere seems to be regularly head-initial in all its other major categories - in PPs, VPs, IPs (with auxiliary verbs preceding the VP), and in CP (with elements such as *ruguo* and *yaoshi* 'if' etc occurring in C^0 and preceding IP).[15] The NP/DP might then seem to be rather exceptional if it were to really be head-final.

To begin with, we can briefly review what has been proposed along the way in sections 2-4. Basically, it has been suggested that the structure of the DP is as in (62):

(62) DeicticP Q $D_{\underline{(de)}}$ Poss Dem Num N

Such a structure also coincides with what is found in many other languages and so would seem to receive cross-linguistic support if DPs are assumed to exhibit a universal type of hierarchical organization.[16]

Turning now to other elements which occur DP-internally, Lin (1994) and Tang (1990) both suggest that there is actually no structural distinction in Chinese DPs between complements and adjuncts because adjuncts regularly occur separating complement-type elements from the nouns which select them, as in (53) where the PP *dui Lisi* is the complement of the head noun *piping* but the adjunct *yanli (de)* separates these two elements:

(63) Zhangsan [dui Lisi] yanli de piping
Zhangsan towards Lisi severe DE criticism
'Zhangsan's severe criticism of Lisi'

---

[15] See also Simpson & Wu (to appear) for evidence that the clause-final positioning of certain sentential particles is not a good indication of the underlying location of C^0 relative to its IP complement.

[16] Supposing one analyzes English (i) below as being derived via the movement indicated, in order to account for the otherwise odd final position of the possessor following the head noun (basically as in Kayne 1994), then English can also be argued to have the underlying order in (62) with demonstratives and numerals being base-generated below D and Poss:
(i) [those three books]$_k$ of John's t_k .

Tsao (1997) however shows that ordering restrictions which do seem to reflect a complement/adjunct distinction within DPs are to be found when both elements are clausal, as seen in examples (64) and (65) which show that a clausal complement must occur adjacent to the selecting noun and an adjunct clause may not intervene:

(64) [wo zuotian tingdao]-de [Deng Xiao-ping shishi]-de xiaoxi
I yesterday hear DE Deng Xiao-ping die DE news
'the news that Deng Xiao-ping had died which I heard yesterday'

(65) *[Deng Xiao-ping shishi]-de [wo zuotian tingdao]-de xiaoxi
Deng Xiao-ping die DE I yesterday hear DE news
'the news that Deng Xiao-ping had died which I heard yesterday'

Assuming this to be a valid indication that there is indeed a DP-internal complement/adjunct distinction, it suggests that the complement PP *dui Lisi* in (63) separated from its selecting N-head by the adjunct *yanli (de)* should then be analyzed as having been repositioned away from its base-generated complement position. Now, if the complement PP has indeed undergone repositioning, there is no compelling reason to assume that it has been moved from a position *preceding* the noun rather than from a position following the noun - i.e. there is no strong reason for believing that Chinese is underlyingly N-final rather than N-initial as the complement of a noun might always seems to be forced to undergo some kind of movement away from its base-generated position, and hence it may never be possible to be exactly sure where the original base position of the complement actually is.

Continuing on, Fu (1994) provides convincing arguments that elements occurring with *process* nominals in Chinese really are arguments and contrast in their behaviour with similar elements occurring with result nominals and other non-verbal nouns which appear more genuinely adjunct-like. Process nominals are distinguished from result nominal equivalents by occurring with special classifiers (*ci*, *bian* and *hui*) and the process light verb *jinxing*, and by being compatible with 'time-how-long' adverbs rather than 'time-when' adverbs. Using such diagnostics, Fu shows first of all that the complement of a process nominal must indeed be present, as illustrated in (66):

(66) ta ??(dui zaiqing) de baodao jinxing-le san-ge-xiaoshi
he towards disaster DE report last Asp 3-CL-hours
'His reporting of the disaster lasted three hours.'

Secondly it is shown that only a single instance of the element *de* occurs with process nominals; in contrast to result nominals neither the subject argument nor a PP may be marked with an additional *de* in process nominal structures, such as (67) and (68):

(67) [Lisi (*de) dui zhei-ge anjian de diaocha] jinxing-le yi-ge-xiaoshi
Lisi DE to this CL case DE investigation last Asp 1-CL-hour
'Lisi's investigation of this case lasted an hour.'

(68) [ta zai zher (*de) dui zhei-ge anjian de diaocha] jinxing-le yi-ge-xiaoshi
he at here DE to this CL case DE investigation last-Asp 1-CL-hour
'His investigation of this case here lasted an hour.'

Fu then suggests that process nominals are syntactically derived from underlying VPs, pointing out that the linear sequence of all elements associated with a process nominal precisely follows that found in VPs with complements realized as PPs and contrasts with the more varied order of the same elements in non-process nominals. Fu proposes that the V^0 head of the posited underlying VP raises rightwards past *de* to a head-final N^0 resulting in a deverbal derived nominal with many of the properties of VPs, abstractly as indicated in (69):

(69)

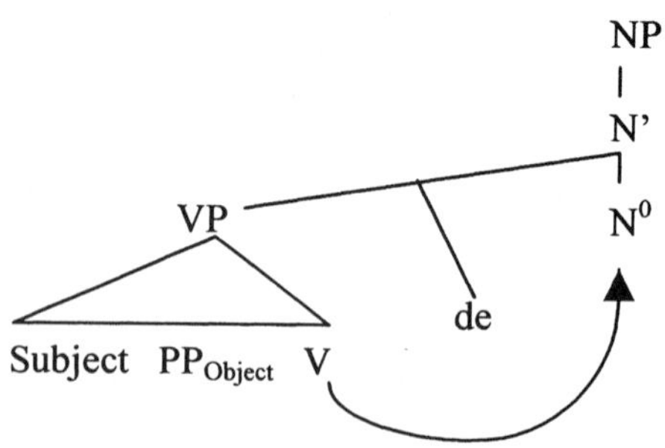

While agreeing with much of the argumentation in Fu, I would like to suggest that the derivation actually procedes in a different linear direction. One potential shortcoming of the analysis given by Fu is that it is not clear what position *de* occurs in, and why as an X^0 category it does not block head-movement of the verb and give rise to a Head Movement Constraint/HMC violation. Here I would consequently like to propose that the relevant structure underlying process nominals is not in fact head-final but a fully regular head-initial structure, that the verb does raise to N^0 as Fu suggests but in a leftward movement as in (70), followed by raising of the remnant VP higher to SpecDP (as in 71, with *de* in D^0). In such a derivation there will be no HMC violation as the verb does not raise over *de* to a higher head position, and no new assumptions are needed to account for the structure:

(70)

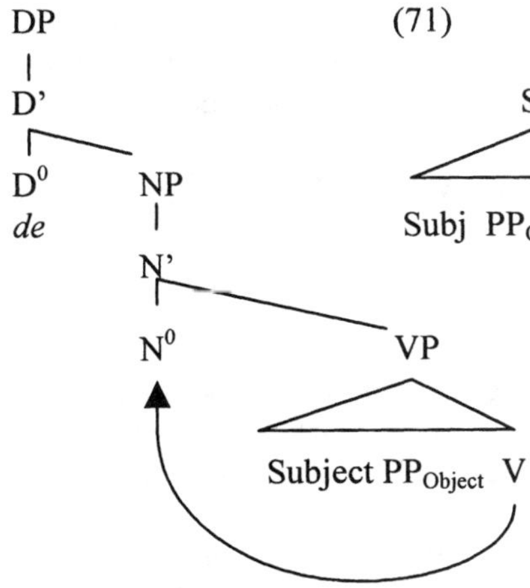

(71)

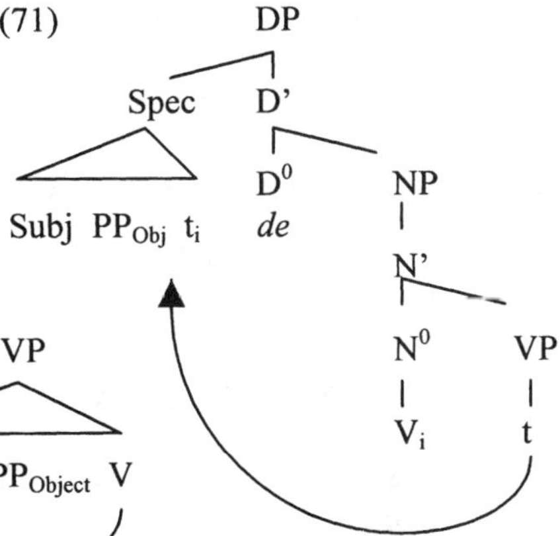

In this fairly straightforward way it can easily be seen how an NP may come to have the appearance of being strongly head-final on the surface yet in fact relate to an underlying structure which is fully head-initial. To illustrate the derivation with a concrete example, sentence (63) will have a regular head-initial underlying form (72) which subsequently gets converted into the surface form via two applications of movement - first V-to-N movement in (73) and then VP-remnant movement to SpecDP as in (74):

(72) $[_{DP}$ de $[_{NP}$ $[_{VP}$ Zhangsan dui Lisi yanli piping]

(73) $[_{DP}$ de $[_{NP}$ $[_{N}$ piping$_i$ $[_{VP}$ Zhangsan dui Lisi yanli t_i]

(74) $[_{DP}$ $[_{VP}$ <u>Zhangsan dui Lisi yanli t_i</u> $]_k$ de $[_{NP}$ $[_{N}$ piping$_i$ t_k]]]

Note that it is no longer particularly problematic that *dui Lisi* the PP complement of the head noun is not adjacent to the noun, appearing to be separated from the N^0 by the adjunct *yanli* - essentially the position of *yanli* between *dui Lisi* and *piping* is fully due to its adverbial-type position in the corresponding VP. A single *de* occurs in D^0 and the VP is attracted to SpecDP for the same reasons as in other cases, to support the clitic-like D^0-element *de*. In short, a simple explanation of the word order facts can be provided in a principled way which is fully in line with Kayne's assumption that languages are uniformly head-initial

One might then ask what happens when there are in fact two occurrences of *de*, and how one might account for the ordering restrictions found in examples (64) and (65). (64) will be generated in the following way. The DP object to the verb *tingdao* 'the news that Deng Xiao-ping died' will first have to be formed and then inserted into the larger structure (as object to *tingdao*). Consequently the derivation begins with the structure in (75):

(75) [$_{DP}$ de [$_{NP}$ xiaoxi [Deng Xiao-ping shishi]]

(75) is then converted into (76) for the normal reasons, and inserted as the object of *tingdao* in (77):

(76) [$_{DP}$ [Deng Xiao-ping shishi]$_{i}$ [$_{D}$ de [$_{NP}$ xiaoxi t_{i}]]]

(77) wo zuotian tingdao [$_{DP}$ Deng Xiao-ping shishi de xiaoxi]

(77) is subsequently converted into a relative clause structure where *de* selects a CP and the relativized element is attracted to SpecCP as in (78):

(78) [$_{DP}$ de [$_{CP}$[$_{DP}$ D-X-P shishi de xiaoxi] [$_{IP}$wo zuotian tingdao t_{m}]]]

Finally the IP is attracted to SpecDP as in all regular relative clauses, resulting in the attested surface form:

(79) [$_{DP}$[$_{IP}$ wo zuotian tingdao t_{m}]$_{p}$ [$_{D}$ de[$_{CP}$[$_{DP}$ D-X-P shishi de xiaoxi] t_{p}]]

The reverse derivation should not be available, where the relative clause would be created first and then the complement clause is built in afterwards, i.e. it should not be possible to first create a DP *wo zuotian tingdao de xiaoxi* 'yesterday' and then somehow add in an extra initial determiner and follow this by building in the complement to the head noun *xiaoxi* in such a way that it could be attracted up to the initial SpecDP resulting in a form such as (78).[17] Consequently the proposed account of *de* as a determiner combined with Kayne's approach to relative clauses provides an explanation of the ordering restrictions noted by Tsao, and generally the analysis is able to make sense of the apparent surface head-final nature of Chinese NPs without the need for any radical new assumptions. Chinese can therefore be argued to be underlyingly head-initial and fully regular in

17 Such a derivation would be clearly counter-cyclic, building in a complement after the noun is embedded in higher structure.

its DP structure with an internal hierarchical organization clearly parallel to that in other languages. What causes significant surface distortion of this regularity can in large part be suggested to be simply the enclitic attractor-like properties of the element *de* when analyzed as a determiner.

6. Concluding Remarks

Concluding now with some brief summarizing remarks, this paper began by showing that the typologically odd combination of basic V-O order and N-final relative clauses together with Kayne's analysis of relativization leads to the initially surprising result that *de* in Chinese should be analyzed as a determiner. Rather than immediately rejecting this conclusion however, the paper showed that a broad investigation of the patterning of determiners across languages provides evidence that the obvious initial objections to an analysis of *de* as a determiner are not in fact well-grounded. Following ideas in Szabolcsi (1994), it was suggested that while elements in D^0 may often show overt morphological definiteness concord with lower demonstratives and quantifiers which properly encode the definiteness value of a DP, in Chinese such definiteness agreement is simply not overtly instantiated, and *de* therefore has no outwardly identifiable definiteness specification. The paper then considered further the function of determiners and *de* and it was shown that determiners may frequently only appear when there is some modification relation present, and hence that determiners might well have modification as a primary function in a number of languages, possibly providing an external variable in an unsaturated open predication. Finally the paper re-examined the general architecture of the Chinese DP and attempted to show that the analysis of *de* as a clitic-like determiner attracting some element to its Spec along with Kayne's theory of relativization and Fu's insights into process nominals ultimately leads to a view of the underlying structure of DPs in Chinese which is both highly regular and resolves the theoretical problem that Chinese DPs/NPs might appear to be exceptionally head-final in their surface word-ordering patterns.

References

Bisang, Walter. 1997. Classifiers and Southeast Asian languages. Counting and beyond. Paper presented at ALT II, Eugene Oregon.

Cheng, Lisa L-S. 1997. *On the typology of wh-questions*. New York: Garland.

Cheng, Lisa & Rint Sybesma 1996. A theoretical perspective on classifiers and DP in Chinese. Paper presented at the 1996 Conference on Sino-Tibetan Languages, Beijing.

Cinque, G. 1999. *Adverbs and functional heads: a cross-linguistic perspective.* New York: Oxford University Press.

Daley, Karen. 1995. The use of classifiers in Vietnamese narrative texts. Doctoral dissertation, University of Texas

Dryer, Matthew. 1992. The Greenbergian word order correlations. *Language* 68/1, 81-138.

Fu, Jingqi. 1994. On deriving Chinese derived nominals: evidence for V-to-N raising. Doctoral dissertation, University of Massachusetts, Amherst.

Giusti, Giuliana. 1997. The categorial status of determiners. In *The New Comparative Syntax* ed: L. Haegeman, 95-123. New York: Longman.

Grosu, Alex. 1988. On the distribution of genitive phrases in Roumanian. *Linguistics* 26:931-49.

Huang, C.-T. James. 1982. Logical relations in Chinese and the theory of grammar. Doctoral dissertation, MIT.

Kayne, Richard. 1994. *The antisymmetry of syntax.* Cambridge, MA: MIT Press.

Li, Yen-hui Audrey. 1997. Structures and Interpretations of Nominal Expressions. Paper presented at the 1997 North American Conference on Chinese Linguistics, Victoria.

Lin, Jo-wang. 1994. Noun phrase structure in Mandarin Chinese: DP or NP. Paper presented at the Third International Conference on Linguistics and Language in China, Hsinchu.

Longobardi, Giuseppe. 1994. Reference and proper names: a theory of N-movement in syntax and Logical Form. *Linguistic Inquiry* 25:609-66.

Simpson, Andrew. 2001. Definiteness agreement and the Chinese DP. *Language and Linguistics* 2:125-156.

Simpson, Andrew. & Xiu-Zhi Zoe Wu. 1999. The syntax and interpretation of sentence-final DE. In Proceedings of the 1998 North American Conference on Chinese Linguistics. GLSA, USC.

Simpson, Andrew & Zoe Wu. IP-raising, tone sandhi and the creation of particles: evidence for cyclic spell-out. To appear in the *Journal of East Asian linguistics.*

Szabolcsi, Anna. 1994. The Noun Phrase. In *Syntax and semantics 27: the structure of Hungarian,* ed. F. Kiefer & K. Kiss, 179-274. San Diego, California: Academic press.

Tang, Chih-chen Jane. 1990. Chinese phrase structure and the extended X'-theory. Doctoral dissertation, Cornell.

Tellier, Christine. 1994. The HAVE/BE alternation: attributes in French and English. *Probus* 6, 235-262.

Tsao, Feng-fu. 1997. Complement and adjunct distribution and the two-place nominal in Chinese. Paper presented at the 1997 North American Conference on Chinese Linguistics, Victoria.

Vincent, Nigel. 1997. The emergence of the D-system in Romance. *Parameters of morpho-syntactic change*, ed. by Ans van Kemenade and Nigel Vincent, 149-169. Cambridge: Cambridge University Press.

Zhuangzi, cited according to Zhuangzi yinde (A concordance to Chuang Tzu), Harvard-Yenching Institute Sinological Index Series, Supplement No. 20. Peiping: Yenching University Press, 1947.

The Parametric Theory of Verb Movement and Its Consequences*

SZE-WING TANG

The Hong Kong Polytechnic University

1. An overview

Building on the insights of Emonds (1978), Pollock (1989) proposes that V moves to T in French whereas V does not move to T in English. Suppose that adverbs are adjoined to VP. Given that V does not move out of VP in English, postverbal adverbs are not allowed in English. The contrast between English and French with respect to adverb placement, such as (1) and (2), is thus explained. A similar analysis is also adopted by Chomsky (1991).

* Some of the ideas presented in this paper were originally inspired by a series of lectures by Richard Kayne and a talk by Jim Huang at the 1997 LSA Summer Institute held at Cornell University. Some materials of this paper were presented at the 'On the Formal Way to Chinese Languages' held at University of California, Irvine (December 1997) and incorporated into my dissertation. Some ideas of this paper were further developed and presented at Western Conference on Linguistics held at University of Texas at El Paso (October 1999), the Linguistic Society of Hong Kong Annual Research Forum held at the Chinese University of Hong Kong (December 1999), and the 9th International Conference on Chinese Linguistics held in Singapore (June 2000). I would like to thank Brian Agbayani, Naoki Fukui, Naomi Harada, Jim Huang, Richard Kayne, Hilda Koopman, Audrey Li, Luther Liu, Kazue Takeda, Akira Watanabe, and Ed Zoerner for helpful discussion on various occasions. Thanks also go to the two anonymous reviewers for comments on earlier version of this paper. The input from the participants at the conferences mentioned above has been invaluable. All errors remain my own. The research was partially funded by the Hong Kong Polytechnic University Central Research Grant G-T971.

On the Formal Way to Chinese Languages.
Sze-Wing Tang and Chen-Sheng Luther Liu (eds.).

(1) John (often) kisses (*often) Mary.
(2) Jean (*souvent) embrasse (souvent) Marie.

Along the lines in Emonds-Pollock, Chomsky (1993, 1995) proposes that V moves to T in both English and French. According to Chomsky, the only difference is that V-to-T movement is overt in French whereas V-to-T movement is covert in English. The difference between the derivation in the overt component and the derivation in the covert component in English can be illustrated in (3a) and (3b), respectively.

(3) a. ...$[_{TP}$ T $[_{VP}$ V (Spell-Out)
b. ...$[_{TP}$ V-T $[_{VP}$ t_V (LF)

Under the influence of the theory of verb movement advocated by Pollock (1989) and Chomsky (1991, 1993, 1995), it has been assumed in the literature that verbs do not move to T in the overt component in Chinese, á la English. Cheng (1989) proposes that V-to-T movement only takes place in the covert component in both Chinese and English. If aspect markers are overt realizations of T (or its equivalence), one possibility to derive the right word order in Chinese is to assume that the aspect marker undergoes downward movement from T to V, á la the analysis of affix hopping in English, and then V moves to T along with the aspect marker in the covert component (Cheng 1989), as illustrated in (4). We may call this approach the 'yo-yo movement approach'.

(4) a. ...[t_{Asp} $[_{VP}$ V-Asp (Spell-Out)
b. ...[V-Asp $[_{VP}$ $t_{V\text{-}Asp}$ (LF)

Another possibility is to assume with the lexicalist approach that the aspect marker and the verb already form a verbal complex in the lexicon (Gu 1995). Under this approach, the verbal complex moves to T only in the covert component and there is no verb movement in the overt component in Chinese. An implication of this approach is that V moves to T in the covert component in both Chinese and English. In any event, Chinese and English would look identical at Spell-Out with respect to verb movement.

An alternative view is that verb movement in Chinese is shorter than that in English in the covert component, which can be called the 'covert asymmetry approach' for the ease of presentation. To account for the contrast between (5) and (6) with respect to the possibility of the occurrence of indefinite subjects, Tsai (1994 et seq) argues that covert V-to-T movement is possible only in English but not in Chinese. (7a) is the LF representation of (5). After V moves to T, the scope of the existential closure is extended to T' and the trace of the subject is within its scope. Hence, the indefinite subject is licensed. (7b) is the LF representation of (6). As V does not move out of *v*P at LF in Chinese, the trace of the subject is beyond the scope of the existential closure. Hence, indefinite subject in Chinese is not allowed.[1]

(5) A child laughed.

(6) *Yi-ge xiaohaizi xiao-le.
  one-Cl child laugh-Perf
  'A child laughed.'

(7) a. $\ldots[_{TP}\ \text{Subj}\ [_{T'}\ \exists\text{-}[_{T'}\ \text{V-T}\ [_{vP}\ t_{Subj} \ldots [\ t_V$ (English)
  b. $\ldots[_{TP}\ \text{Subj}\ [_{T'}\ \text{T}\ [_{vP}\ t_{Subj}\ \exists\text{-}[_{v'}\ \text{V-}v \ldots$ (Chinese)

I have introduced three different views of verb movement in Chinese, namely the yo-yo movement approach, the lexicalist approach, and the covert asymmetry approach. As we can see, these three approaches would have the same prediction that the landing site of V at Spell-Out in Chinese and English would be the same.

Let us scrutinize these three approaches under the Minimalist Program (Chomsky 1993 et seq). Notice that the yo-yo movement approach heavily relies on downward movement. The first problem is that the derivation is global in nature, which leads to the problem of computational complexity though downward movement seems compatible with the Attract F analysis.[2] For example, suppose that both α and β are possible candidates for checking off the feature in the γ position in (8).

(8)

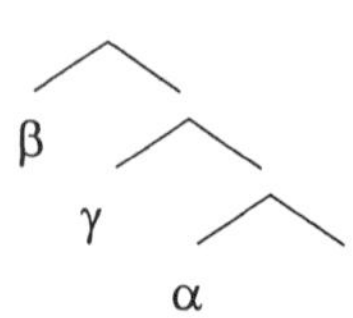

In principle, either α or β can be attracted to γ since both α or β are considered to be the 'closest features' that enter into the checking domain of γ. If economy considerations are strictly local, γ should attract α instead of β when γ is merged with α in the derivation. Hence, the downward movement of the V-Asp complex in (4a) is not motivated.

---

[1] X. Li (1997) follows the covert asymmetry approach to account for the lack of distributivity in Chinese.

[2] Attract F is defined as the following: 'K *attracts* F if F is the closest feature that can enter into a checking relation with a sublabel of K.' (Chomsky 1995: 297).

Another problem of the yo-yo movement approach is that it violates a fundamental claim of the nature of Move in the Minimalist Program that a chain CH = (α, $t(\alpha)$) formed by Move must meet the C-Command Condition on movement: α must c-command its trace (Chomsky 1995: 253). However, Chomsky (1995: 255) points out that overt operations might not meet the C-Command Condition due to the ordering requirement being irrelevant for LF convergence, assuming that c-command plays a role in determining linear order (Kayne 1994). Takeda (1997) argues the C-Command Condition also holds in the covert component, according to which Attract is divided into two sub-parts: a searching down process Search and a moving up process Move. In other words, Move is always raising regardless of whether it takes place overtly or covertly. Consequently, there cannot be an operation that allows lowering. In this vein, the yo-yo movement approach should be eliminated.

An analysis that all these three approaches share is that there is covert movement. However, whether covert movement exists is dubious. Covert verb movement should not be driven by interface conditions imposed by sensorimotor systems assuming that there is no connection between the LF interface and the PF interface.[3] Let us assume that covert verb movement is driven by semantics. It is not clear why V must move to T in the covert component in English but not in Chinese if the covert asymmetry approach is correct. Obviously, under the covert asymmetry approach, parametric variation between Chinese and English is not deduced from detectable and visible properties, which departs from the fundamental assumption in the Minimalist Program.[4]

To maintain the mechanism of covert verb movement, one may assume with the lexicalist approach that V moves to T in the covert component in both Chinese and English. However, some typological variations between these two languages as noted by Tsai (1994) cannot be explained under the lexicalist approach.

Besides these three approaches we have examined so far, an alternative view of verb movement that seems to be compatible with the spirit of the Minimalist Program is that the path of verb movement in Chinese is shorter than that in English in overt syntax, which was originally suggested by Huang (1997) and adopted by Fukui and Takano (1998). For the ease of presentation, let us call this approach the 'overt asymmetry approach'.

Following Kayne (1998), Huang (1997) argues that in English V moves higher than in Chinese to account for the fact that Chinese does not have

[3] The term 'interface conditions' is used in Chomsky 2001b. It is also known as 'bare output conditions' in Chomsky 1995 and 'legibility conditions' in Chomsky 2000, 2001a.

[4] Chomsky (2000, 2001a) even speculates that head movement is not part of the narrow syntax but rather an operation of the phonological component. If he is right, there should not be any covert verb movement. See also fn 19.

postverbal *no*-phrases. In English, V moves beyond Neg. As a result, Neg and the *any*-phrase are adjacent and a postverbal *no*-phrase is derived, as in (9b), assuming that *no*-phrases are formed by negation + *any*-phrase under adjacency (Klima 1964).[5] As V never moves beyond Neg in Chinese, postverbal *no*-phrases are banned, as in (10b).

(9) a. Nobody saw me.
    b. I saw nobody.

(10) a. Meiyouren kanjian wo.
        nobody see I
        'Nobody saw me.'
     b. *Wo kanjian meiyouren.
        I see nobody
        'I saw nobody.'

In this paper, I provide independent evidence to support the overt asymmetry approach that V moves out of *v*P in English whereas V moves only to *v* in Chinese, assuming that there is *v*P between TP and VP in the clausal structure (Hale and Keyser 1993, Chomsky 1995).[6] It will be shown that some interesting consequences can be derived from the theory advocated in this paper. In section 2, I argue that V moves out of *v*P in English but not in Chinese by using the data from the distribution of focus adverbs.

2. Distribution of Focus Elements

2.1. Basic Data

The restrictive focus element *only* essentially can occur in the postverbal position in English, as illustrated in (11).

(11) John (only) kisses (only) Mary (only).

Interestingly, unlike English, the distribution of the restrictive focus element *zhi* 'only' is very restricted, which is always preverbal in Chinese. The focus element *zhi* 'only' never occurs in a postverbal position, as exemplified by (12).

---

[5] Kayne (1998) assumes that *no*-phrases are derived by VP pied-piping, as in (i). Following Kayne's analysis, Huang (1997) proposes that verbs do not move in Chinese.

(i) I [[$_{VP}$ saw $t_{anybody}$] [Neg [anybody [t_{VP}

[6] For the claim that V moves out of *v*P overtly in English, see Johnson 1991, Koizumi 1995, Kural 1998, and Tang 1998.

(12) Zhangsan (zhi) kanjian (*zhi) Lisi (*zhi)
Zhangsan only see only Lisi only
'Zhangsan (only) saw (only) Lisi.'

The additive focus element *even* can occur either in a preverbal position or in a postverbal position in English whereas the additive focus element *shenzhi* 'even' must be preverbal in Chinese. The contrast can be seen in (13) and (14). Notice that unlike *only*, the additive focus element *even* cannot follow an object in English.

(13) John (even) loves (even) Mary (*even).

(14) Zhangsan (shenzhi) xihuan (*shenzhi) na ge shagua (*shenzhi).
Zhangsan even like even that Cl idiot even
'(Even) Zhangsan (even) likes that idiot.'

In the case of the distribution of focus element *also*, there is also the same difference between Chinese and English as what we have seen in other focus elements. The focus element *ye* 'also' is always preverbal in Chinese.

(15) a. John (also) invited (also) his wife's cousin Jane (also).
b. ?He invited also Jane.

(16) Zhangsan (ye) yaoqing-le (*ye) Lisi (*ye).
Zhangsan also invite-Perf also Lisi also
'Zhangsan also invited Lisi.'

As noted by Taglicht (1984:83), the object following *also* must be heavy, such as *his wife's cousin Jane* in (15a). If the object is phonologically light, such as *Jane* in (15b), the judgment is degraded. Essentially the focus element *ye* 'also' in Chinese is preverbal.

In sum, the descriptive generalization can be summarized as in (17).

(17) The focus elements could be either preverbal or postverbal in English whereas they must be preverbal in Chinese.

Since the distribution of all these focus elements is quite similar, in what follows, my attention will be restricted mainly to *only* and *zhi* 'only'.

2.2. Are the focus elements adverbs?

Can we provide a theoretical analysis to account for the generalization in (17)? One possibility is to assume that there is a 'Quantificational Force Parameter' proposed by Lin (1997), à la Tsai (1994), that quantificational force can be realized at different syntactic levels. In English quantificational force may be realized on nominals whereas in Chinese quantificational force is realized at the sentential level only. Lin suggests that focus elements in Chinese, such as *zhi* 'only', are adverbs realized at the sentence level whereas those in English could be adjoined to DP. Hence, focus elements can serve as sentential adverbs only and postverbal focus elements are prohibited in Chinese.

The claim that focus elements, such as *zhi* 'only', are adverbs in Chinese is not controversial. The focus elements in English, such as *only*, *even*, and *also*, are also treated as adverbs by grammarians (Quirk et al 1972:§8). Some pieces of evidence suggest that the focus element and the nominal do not form a syntactic constituent. Examples (18), (19), and (22) are from Rooth (1985:93). The ungrammaticality of (18) and (19) shows that '*only* + nominal' cannot be the complement of a preposition. (20) and (21) further suggest that the focus element and the nominal do not form a syntactic constituent.[7]

(18) *The library is closed on only Sunday.
(19) *The children play in only the common.
(20) ?*I saw John and even the student.
(21) *John and even the student came.
(22) *The entrance only to the Santa Monica freeway was blocked off.

Interestingly, if the two conjoined elements are verbal projections, such as (23), the judgment improves.[8] (23) shows that in principle the focus element *even* can enter the coordinate construction. The contrast between (20) and (21) on one hand and (23) on the other hand suggests that the focus element and the nominal do not form a syntactic constituent.

(23) John hugged Bill and even kissed Peter on the lips.

Though in some cases the focus elements may follow a preposition, they are not counterexamples.

---

[7] The judgment of (20) and (21) may improve if there is a pause before *and*. (i) and (ii) could be formed by conjunction reduction. If this is correct, it is clauses that are conjoined, instead of nominals.
(i) I saw John, and even the student.
(ii) John, and even the student came.
The grammaticality of (iii) may show that *only* and *Sunday* form a constituent. I suspect that (iii) is derived from (iv) in which *on* is deleted. Thanks to Jim Huang for pointing out (iii).
(iii) It is closed on Sunday, and only Sunday.
(iv) It is closed on Sunday, and only on Sunday.
Furthermore, I do not know how (v) is derived and leave it open in the discussion.
(v) the only entrance to the Santa Monica freeway

[8] Thanks to Kazue Takeda (personal communication) for drawing my attention to verbal coordination and to Ed Zoerner (personal communication) for constructing the example in (23).

(24) John wrote about only linguistics.

Those prepositions in (18) and (19) belong to temporal prepositions. Notice that the status of the preposition in (24) and those in (18) and (19) should be different. For example, *about* allows preposition stranding whereas temporal prepositions do not. Consider the contrast between (25) and (26).[9]

(25) What did you write about?
(26) *What time did John arrive at?

I assume with Hornstein and Weinberg (1981) that the verb and the preposition may be reanalyzed as a verb. For example, the verb *write* and the preposition *about* in (24) and (25) undergo reanalysis. It is a complex verb that the focus element *only* and the *wh*-word follow. The temporal prepositions cannot undergo reanalysis and thus remain their original status.

However, there seem to be some examples that suggest that the focus element and the nominal form a constituent.[10] Rooth (1985:90-91) cites the following examples from Taglicht (1994) to show that (27) is ambiguous while the scope in (28) is fixed. These examples imply that *only* and the nominal form a constituent which can be assigned scope at LF.

(27) I knew he had learnt only Spanish. (I knew he hadn't learnt any other language/I didn't know he had learnt any other language.)
(28) I knew he had only learnt Spanish.

Based on the observation of Jackendoff (1972), Rooth (1985:91-92) points out that the postverbal *even* and the nominal must form a constituent because *even* in (30) can associate only with the nominal that follows it, unlike the preverbal *even* in (29)

(29) a. JOHN even gave his daughter a new bicycle.
b. John even GAVE his daughter a new bicycle.
c. John even gave HIS daughter a new bicycle.
d. John even gave his DAUGHTER a new bicycle.
e. John even gave his daughter a NEW bicycle.

---

[9] As pointed out to me by an anonymous reviewer, the contrast between *about* and temporal prepositions can also be shown by pseudopassivization as in the following examples.
(i) This was talked about.
(ii) *Today was closed on.

[10] See Bayer 1996 for a constituency test for German to show that the focus element and the nominal form a constituent.

	f.	John even gave his daughter a new BICYCLE.
(30)	a.	*JOHN gave even his daughter a new bicycle.
	b.	*John GAVE even his daughter a new bicycle.
	c.	John gave even HIS daughter a new bicycle.
	d.	John gave even his DAUGHTER a new bicycle.
	e.	*John gave even his daughter a NEW bicycle.
	f.	*John gave even his daughter a new BICYCLE.

As pointed out by Jim Huang (personal communication), (31) may suggest that *only* and the nominal form a syntactic constituent.

(31) It is only linguistics that John wrote about.

Are postverbal focus elements in English adverbs? Do the focus element and the nominal form a constituent? I will try to solve the above dilemma in the next subsection.

2.3. Analysis

Travis (1988) argues that adverbs are 'defective' categories and related to some feature of a verbal head. Horvath (1995) argues that focus features are associated with functional categories. Based on these two ideas, I conclude that the following generalization holds in every language.

(32) Focus adverbs must be adjoined to a verbal functional category.

According to (32), focus adverbs can merge with *v*P, TP, and CP, which are regarded as the extended projections of the verbal category V. Adjunction of the focus adverbs to VP and DP is prohibited in both of these languages by (32) because the former is not functional and the latter is not verbal.

Ting (1995) and Huang (1999) argue that the complement of *get* in the short passive is a bare VP. The ungrammaticality of (33a) supports the generalization in (32). (33b) is grammatical because there are some additional functional projections in the long passive.

(33)	a.	John (only) got (*only) blamed.	(short passive)
	b.	John (only) was (only) blamed.	(long passive)

Based on the generalization stated in (32), to derive the word order 'Subj + V + *only* + Obj' in English, the focus adverb *only* is adjoined to *v*P and V moves out of *v*P, as in (34).[11]

(34)

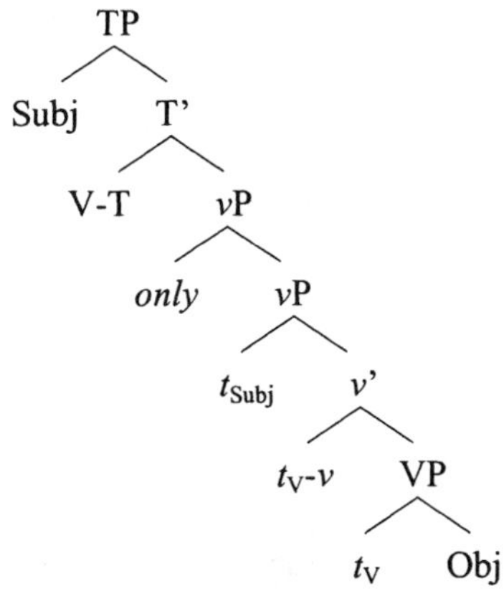

To derive the word order 'Subj + V + Obj + *only*', I assume that an affix feature [-DP] is assigned to *v*.[12] Movement of the focalized object to *v*P is triggered by the affix feature [-DP] of *v*, which is driven by focalization or prosody. The affix feature [-DP] could be 'activated' when the focus adverb is adjoined to *v*P.[13] Given that verbs move out of *v*P overtly in English, the focalized object is always in a postverbal position, as indicated in (35).

---

[11] Kayne (1998) has a similar analysis of *only*. According to him, *only* is a head which bears a feature [+w] (mnemonic for word order) that must be checked by another head. *Criticized only Bill* has the following derivation. However, the nature of the feature [+w] and the head that *only* moves to are not clear. Also, he does not explain how *criticized Bill only* is derived.

(i) ...only [criticized Bill] ⇒ (attraction by *only*)
...Bill only [criticized t_{Bill}] ⇒ (raising of *only*)
...only Bill t_{only} [criticized t_{Bill}] ⇒ (VP-preposing)
...[criticized t_{Bill}] only Bill t_{only} t_{VP}

In addition, V may have some additional extended projections between *v*P and TP in English. They could be AspP (aspect phrase), ReltP (relative tense phrase), etc. when auxiliaries are realized. See Solà 1996 and Cinque 1999.

[12] The affix feature [-DP] of *v* can be regarded as the 'P-feature' or the 'EPP-feature' of *v*, as what proposed by Chomsky (2000).

[13] The condition of 'activation' seems to vary. The discussion here suggests that the element that is in the checking domain of a head H may 'activate' a feature of H. Zhang (1997) proposes that a feature of H may be 'activated' by some feature in the complement domain of H. Takeda (1997) and X. Li (1997) propose that a feature of H may be 'activated' by feature movement. I leave all these interesting consequences open here.

(35)

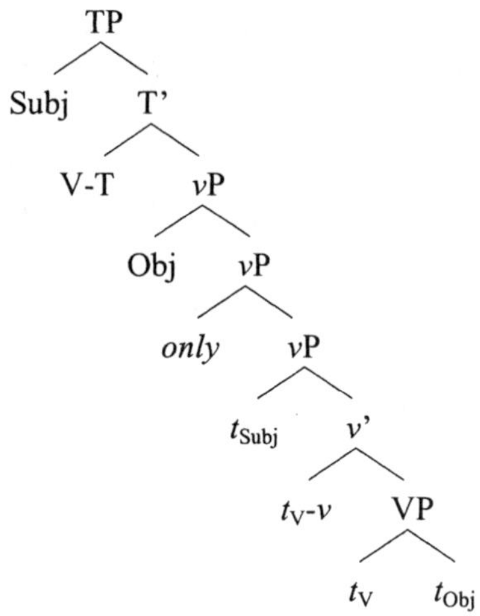

Traces are semantically defective. I have suggested in Tang 1998 that adverbs cannot be licensed by a trace at LF. Let us take (36) to be correct.

(36) *Adverb Licensing*
Adverbs cannot be licensed by a trace at the LF interface level. (Tang 1998:32)

In principle, (34) and (35) would be ungrammatical because *only* is licensed by a trace of V (or a trace of V-*v*). To avoid the problem, English may allow the focus adverb and the nominal to 'reanalyze' as one constituent at Spell-Out, as (37a) and (37b). In other words, the postverbal focus elements are adverbs underlyingly but they become part of the nominal at Spell-Out after reanalysis.[14] Hence, the dilemma of the constituency test of the focus elements we have seen previously is solved.

(37) a. … [$_{TP}$ V-T [$_{vP}$ *v* [$_{DP}$ *only* DP]] (cf. (34))
b. … [$_{TP}$ V-T [$_{vP}$ [$_{DP}$ DP *only*][$_{vP}$ *v* [$_{VP}$ t_V t_{DP}]]]] (cf. (35))

Consider the following examples, in which the focus adverb *only* is focusing on the head of the object *a picture* instead of the *wh*-word. Extraction of the *wh*-word *who* out of the focalized object is acceptable in (38) and (39). I propose to explain the contrast in the following way. The focalized object in

[14] Thanks to Jim Huang (personal communication) for the suggestion of reanalysis. Reanalysis of the focus adverbs is reminiscent of the derivation of *no*-phrases along the lines in Klima 1964. The formation of *no*-phrases in English seems to be in parallel fashion.

(38) and (39) does not move to *v*P and it remains *in-situ*. To derive the word order in (40), the focalized object moves to *v*P triggered by the affix feature [-DP] of *v*. The judgment of the extraction of the *wh*-word from the moved object is degraded, which exhibits the CED effects. Though *a picture of* and *only* may reanalyze as one constituent, i.e. [a picture of *t* only], at Spell-Out, extraction of the *wh*-word is still ungrammatical because the object is still adjoined to *v*P. Reanalysis does not change the syntactic position of the object.

(38) Who did John only draw [a picture of *t*]?
(39) Who did John draw only [a picture of *t*]?
(40) ?*Who did John draw [a picture of *t*] only?

The analysis in Chinese seems straightforward. Suppose that the focus adverb *zhi* 'only' is adjoined to *v*P. As V does not move out of *v*P, *zhi* 'only' is always in the preverbal position, as shown in (41).

(41)

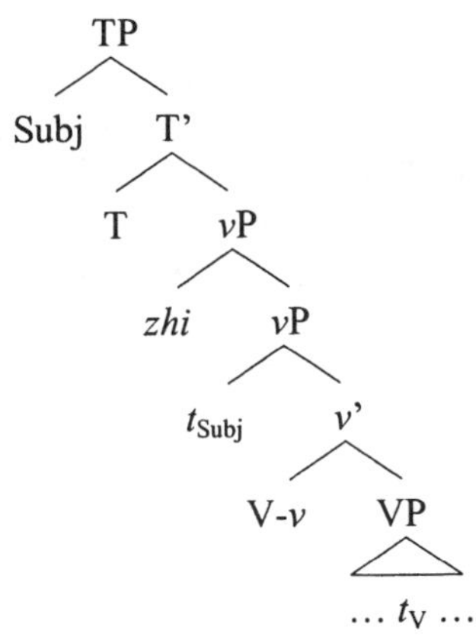

In addition, because of the generalization stated in (32) which requires that focus adverbs be adjoined to a functional verbal category, the focus adverb *zhi* 'only' cannot be adjoined to the lexical projection VP. Hence, Chinese never allows postverbal focus adverbs.

2.4. Adjacency Condition and the distribution of adverbs

The fact that Chinese does not allow postverbal focus adverbs could be associated with a more general property of this language that postverbal adverbs are banned in Chinese. Postverbal adverbs are not allowed in Chinese, as exemplified in (42).

(42) Wo (hen kuaide) xie-le (*hen kuaide) zhe pian lunwen.
I very fast write-Perf very fast this Cl thesis
'I wrote this thesis very fast.'

To rule out the postverbal adverbs in Chinese, one possibility is to assume that the postverbal object in (42) is precluded by the Adjacency Condition (Li 1990, à la Stowell 1981). Regarding the analysis of the Adjacency Condition, if the word order 'V + Adv + Obj' in Chinese is ruled out by Case theory, it is not clear why (43) is still ungrammatical, given that the PP *gei wo* 'to me' is not assigned Case. The English counterpart, as shown in the translation, is perfectly acceptable.

(43) *Ta song-le yi-zhang zhaopian <u>toutoude</u> gei wo.
he give-Perf one-Cl photo secretly to I
'He gave a picture secretly to me.'

If a manner adverb is adjoined to VP, after V moves to *v*, the adverb will be licensed by the trace of the verb, as in (44), in which the subject trace is omitted. Adverb Licensing (=(36)) is violated and thus adverbs cannot be adjoined to VP in Chinese, regardless of whether XP in (44) is DP or PP. As a result, adverbs must be adjoined to *v*P and the projections above *v*P in Chinese (C.-C. J. Tang 1990). The fact that Chinese does not have postverbal adverbs is derived.

(44)

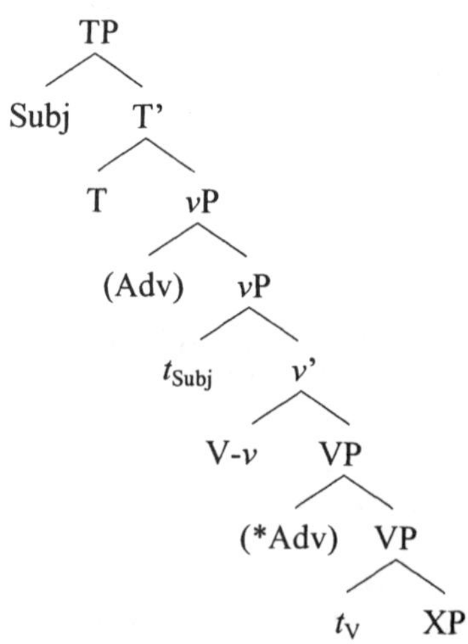

English allows the word order 'V + Obj + Adv + PP' because the object moves to *v*P overtly. P has already incorporated into *v* to license the adverb.[15] After V moves out of *v*P, the word order 'V + Obj + Adv + PP' is derived. However, given that V never moves out of *v*P in Chinese, the adverb always stays in the preverbal position and thus (43) is ungrammatical. The analysis of (42) and (43) is compatible with the overt asymmetry approach defended in this paper.

Apparently, some adverbial elements, such as duration phrases, may occur in a postverbal position, as in (45). Would (45) be a counterexample?

(45) Wo lai Meiguo wu nian le.
I come America five year Part
'I have been in America for five years.'

Li (1987) argues that the duration phrase *wu nian* 'five years' is an indefinite NP which is the complement of the verb. As the position of the duration phrases is different from that of adverbs in Chinese, (45) should not be a counterexample to the claim that V does not raise out of *v*P in Chinese. The structure of (45) could be represented in (46), in which the duration phrase is the complement of V.[16]

(46)

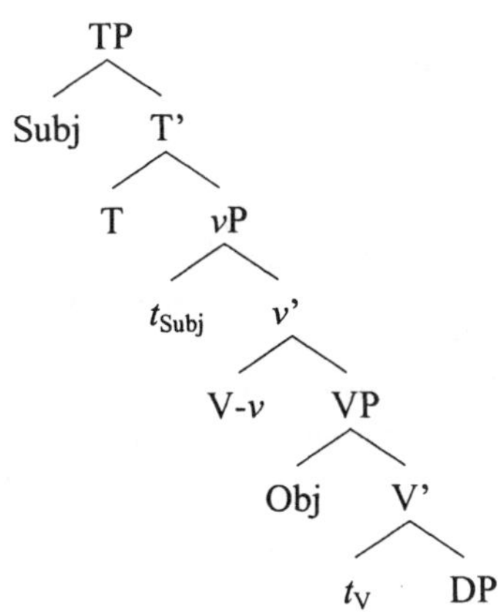

[15] The preposition in the English translation in (43) may be treated as a particle so that V and P may form a complex verb in the first place and then the verbal complex undergoes movement to a higher functional head, à la Johnson (1991).

[16] (i) will have a different structure. According to Huang (1991 et seq), the duration phrase and the direct object form a gerund.

(i) Ta piping-le liang nian Zhangsan.
he criticize-Perf two year Zhangsan
'He criticized Zhangsan for two years.'

Notice that there is another possibility to derive the postverbal adverb in (47a) in English without violating Adverb Licensing. Let us assume that the manner adverb *secretly* is adjoined to TP or some functional category higher than TP. The Spell-Out as well as LF representation for sentence (47a) will be (47b). As the adverb is not licensed by a trace at LF, the derivation converges at LF. To derive the right word order, we may assume that TP undergoes remnant movement, à la Cinque (1999), as represented in (47c). The adverb is not located in the sentence final position. I assume that such remnant movement in English takes place in the phonological component. Even though the adverb is licensed by the trace of TP in (47c), the derivation still converges because the Adverb Licensing does not hold at the PF interface level.

(47) a. John wrote his dissertation secretly.
b. ... [$_{XP}$ Adv [$_{TP}$ V-T ... DP]]]
c. ... [$_{XP}$ [$_{TP}$ V-T ... DP]][$_{XP}$ Adv t_{TP} ...

TP remnant movement in English is considered to be a stylistic rule, subject to some phonological constraints. The motivation for TP remnant movement is purely for PF convergence. (48) shows that Chinese does not have a counterpart of (47a).

(48) *Ta xie-hao ta-de lunwen toutoude.
he write-finish his thesis secretly.
'He wrote his thesis secretly.'

To explain the ungrammaticality of (48), we may assume that such a stylistic rule does not hold in Chinese. In terms of the theory of feature checking, the affix feature that triggers TP remnant movement in the phonological component is missing in Chinese. Parametric variation between these two languages is attributed to parametrization of affix features, conforming to the Overt Parametrization Hypothesis (Tang 1998), according to which features that may play a role from the lexical array (or 'numeration') to the PF interface level, such as categorial features, affix features, and phonetic features, are subject to parametric variation.

3. Some residues

3.1. Remnant VP movement vs. V movement

To derive the word order of the sentence in (49), Kayne (1998) proposes the following derivations in (50).[17] According to him, (50a) is the basic structure. First of all, *Bill* is attracted by *only*, as in (50b). The focus element *only* is a head which bears a feature [+w] (mnemonic for word order) that must be checked by another head. In (50c), *only* moves to a head to check off the feature [+w]. Finally, VP undergoes remnant movement along with the trace of *Bill*, as in (50d).

(49) ...criticized only Bill.

(50)
a. only [criticized Bill] ⇨
b. Bill only [criticized t_{Bill}] (attraction by *only*) ⇨
c. only Bill t_{only} [criticized t_{Bill}] (raising of *only*) ⇨
d. [criticized t_{Bill}] only Bill t_{only} (VP-preposing)

Though Kayne's analysis of the focus element *only* can also account for the word order in English, his analysis faces some questions that will not arise in my proposal.

Firstly, the nature of the feature [+w] and the head that *only* moves to are not clear. The postulate of the unmotivated category and feature seems ad hoc.

Secondly, he does not explain how *only criticized Bill* is derived. One possibility is to assume that *only* moves to a head that is higher than the landing site of VP remnant movement structurally. Needless to say, the nature of such a head that triggers movement of *only* needs further justifications.

Thirdly, Kayne does not discuss how (51) is derived. Suppose that the attraction of *Bill* by *only* is due to focalization. Presumably, to derive (51), he would assume that *Bill* first moves to *only* and then VP undergoes remnant movement. The feature [+w] would be missing and thus *only* would remain *in-situ*. If this is the derivation of (51), the contrast between (49) and (51) with respect to *wh*-movement (see the discussion of (39) and (40)) cannot be explained.

(51) ...criticized Bill only.

In my proposal, what moves out of *v*P in English is V instead of VP. My analysis not only derives the word order correctly without positing any ad hoc

---

[17] See also footnote 5 for a similar analysis of *no*-phrases.

functional categories but also avoids the problems that Kayne's analysis has, which should be a desirable move.

3.2. Movement and morphology of verbs

In this paper, I have argued that V moves to T overtly in English, contra the Emonds-Pollock-Chomsky's approach. To capture the differences between English and French with respect to adverb placement (see (1) and (2)), I propose that where movement takes place is determined by morphology.

(52) Movement of morphologically 'rich' elements takes place in the phonological component whereas movement of morphologically 'impoverished' elements takes place in the overt component. (Tang 1998: 27)

The rationale for (52) is that where affix features are assigned is subject to parametric variation. If an affix feature is assigned to a word as it is selected for the lexical array, the word becomes 'inflected' and has 'rich' morphology when it is introduced into the derivation. Basically it has the relevant inflectional features when it is introduced into the derivation and can be interpreted at the interface levels, particularly, at the LF interface, without moving anywhere. If the word moves, movement should be triggered by phonological properties.

On the other hand, if an affix feature is combined with a word in the derivation, the word is morphologically 'impoverished' and semantically 'defective' when it is introduced into the derivation. The morphologically 'impoverished' word has to move to pick up relevant features (inflectional affix features) before Spell-Out for LF convergence.

Lasnik (1995) convincingly argues that English verbs are morphologically 'impoverished' and French verbs are morphologically 'rich' when they are introduced in the derivation. The relevant inflectional affix feature is assigned to T in English and thus V moves to T in English overtly.[18] The motivation for moving V to T in English is to check off the inflectional affix feature of T that needs V to support.

Why can't V move to T in Chinese? I suspect that this is due to the morphological requirement of the affix features of T. To be more specific, I propose that the affix feature of T in Chinese is checked off by Merge instead of Move. In Chinese, it is the sentence final particles that check off the affix feature of T.

---

[18] To account for the linguistic variation between English and French with respect to adverb placement, I further argue that French verbs move to T in the phonological component, according to (52). See Tang 1998 for details.

Sentence final particles in Chinese can be classified into two types: outer particles and inner particles (Tang 1998 and references cited therein). The former mainly consists of mood particles, such as the interrogative particles *ma* and *ne*, and the latter includes temporal particles, such as *le* in (53) and *laizhe* (54). These two types of sentence final particles are overt realizations of T and C in Chinese, respectively. The temporal particle *le* signals a 'current relevant state' (Li and Thompson 1981) and the temporal particle *laizhe* refers to an event in the 'recent past' (Chao 1968).

(53) Ta chu qu mai dongxi le.
he exit go buy thing Part
'He's gone shopping.'

(54) Xia yu laizhe.
fall rain Part
'It just rained.'

To derive the right word order in Chinese, T moves to C followed by TP remnant movement to the specifier of CP, assuming that 'specifier-head-complement' is the universal word order (Kayne 1994). The representation is shown in (55). My analysis can also explain why the inner particle is always preceding the outer particle, as shown in (56).

(55)

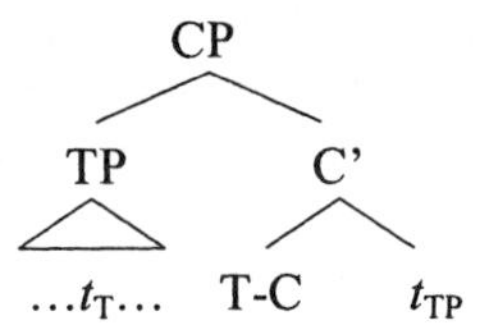

(56) a. Ta chi-le fan le ma?
he eat-Perf rice Part Q
'Has he eaten?'

b. *Ta chi-le fan ma le?
he eat-Perf rice Q Part

Let us assume that my analysis is correct. If the relevant feature of T has already been checked off by the sentence final particles in Chinese, V-to-T movement becomes unnecessary and should be banned.

Though Chinese and English differ with respect to V-to-T movement, a characteristic that these two languages share is that the affix feature of T needs a verbal element to check off. Historically, the sentence final particles *le* and *laizhe* were verbs in Chinese. The particle *le* was derived from the verb *liao* 'finish' whereas *laizhe* was derived from the verb *lai* 'come'. It seems natural to assume that sentence final particles are still verbal in modern Chinese. If this is correct, the affix feature of T in Chinese is also checked off by a verbal element, on a par with the case in English.

Based on the facts from Chinese and English, I speculate that the inflectional affix feature of T must be checked off by a verbal element cross-linguistically. Simply speaking, tense features need a verbal element to support. Along these lines, I assume that (57) should be a universal generalization.[19]

(57) The inflectional affix feature of T that is associated with tense must be checked off by a verbal element.

How to derive the generalization in (57)?

Let us consider the classification of categorial features seriously. In his feature system, Chomsky (1970, 1981) points out that the distinction between the two primitive categorial features [+N] and [+V] is that the former is substantive whereas the latter is predicative. The claim that the inflectional affix feature of T associated with tense must be checked off by a [+V] element implies that tense features need to be attached to a host that is predicative. The universal generalization in (57) could be a semantic requirement imposed on the LF interface. Let us pursue this possibility.

Stowell (1996) argues that tense is predicative. Tense features, which belong to semantic features, do not have any categorial features. Along these lines, I suspect that tense features must be attached to a predicative host in order to be interpreted as a predicative entity in the clausal structure at LF. In terms of syntax, such a relation is ensured by means of feature checking. If this is correct, the generalization in (57) is thus derived.

Let us consider the ungrammatical example in (58a).

(58) a. *The little baby lovely-*ed*.
b. *… A-X [$_{AP}$ t_A …

Suppose that there is an extended projection X of A that bears the inflectional affix feature (tense feature) [-V]. If there is no copula in the structure, the adjective *lovely* will move to X directly in order to check off the inflectional affix feature of X. Let us assume with Tang (1998) that the categorial feature of adjectives in English is [+N]. In other words, the derivation crashes in (58b) at both interface levels: it crashes at PF because adjectives in English cannot check off the inflectional affix feature [-V]; it

---

19 If verb movement is a possible strategy to satisfy (57), head movement should not be completely excluded from the narrow syntax, contra Chomsky (2000, 2001a) (see fn 4). In any event, what is compatible with Chomsky's (2000, 2001a) speculation in the present discussion is that head movement is triggered by phonetically affixal elements and must be overt.

crashes at LF because the tense feature cannot be attached to a predicative host, i.e. a [+V] element. The ungrammaticality of (58a) is thus accounted for.

Notice that the choice of the verbal element that can check off the inflectional affix feature of T associated with tense is arbitrary. It happens that the inflectional affix feature of T is checked by sentence final particles in Chinese and by verb movement in English. Whether sentence final particles should be present in a language is a language-particular rule. Universal Grammar has nothing with it.

Though Universal Grammar cannot tell us whether sentence final particles should exist in a particular language, what it can do seems to be the selection of optimal candidates. From a global economy consideration, if the operation Merge alone is able check off the affix feature in a language, a more complex operation, such as Move (=Copy + Merge + Delete + Form Chain), should be banned. The idea is that (i) Merge is cheaper than Move and (ii) at any point in a derivation where both Merge and Move are applicable, the cheaper operation is chosen. Such an idea is also known as 'Merge over Move' or 'MOM' (Chomsky 1995, 2000, 2001a).[20]

If sentence final particles exist in a language, verb movement would not be an optimal strategy to check off the inflectional affix feature of T. In other words, verb movement is a 'last resort' option to check off the affix feature [-V] of T. The above discussion is summarized as the following conjecture.

(59) The availability of sentence final particles that have a temporal interpretation correlates with the lack of V-to-T movement in the overt component.

Informally speaking, we may say that Chinese employs a more 'economical' strategy to check off the inflectional affix feature of T. As English does not have sentence final particles, it can only choose a more 'costly' strategy to satisfy the requirement.

The conjecture in (59) should not be isolated. It seems to be reminiscent of the correlation between the existence of question particles and overt *wh*-movement and the correlation between the existence of classifiers and overt noun movement. It is a well-known fact that Chinese lacks overt *wh*-movement that English has. Cheng (1991) points out that if question particles are available to type a clause as a *wh*-question, overt *wh*-movement should be banned. I have argued elsewhere that the existence of classifiers blocks noun movement in Chinese and some southeast Asian languages (Tang 1999). If the above observations are correct, movement is not the optimal strategy in the

---

[20] If MOM is correct, movement should not be a free operation, contra Chomsky (2001b).

clausal and nominal domains in Chinese. Perhaps Chinese can be regarded as a typical 'MOM language'.

Notice that (59) should not be understood that the lack of V-to-T movement in the overt component in a language necessarily implies the existence of sentence final particles. For example, French verbs are morphologically 'rich'. According to (52), V undergoes movement to T only in the phonological component in French (Tang 1998). However, French is not a language that has sentence final particles. The lack of overt V-to-T movement in French is mainly due to the fact that the inflectional affix feature (tense feature) has been combined with the verb in the lexical array. (57) is satisfied in the numeration: the tense feature has a verbal element as its host. As a result, V-to-T movement in French is purely phonological, not for LF convergence.

In any event, it turns out that the fundamental difference between Chinese and English with respect to V-to-T movement is related to the existence of sentence final particles. Though it is very difficult to explain why Chinese has sentence final particles that English lacks, the conjecture in (59) could tell us something about the deep properties of Chinese as well as the nature of natural languages. Falsifying (59) awaits future research.

4. Summary

In this paper, I have argued that the lack of the pastverbal focus adverbs in Chinese is due to the fact that V never moves out of *v*P in Chinese. On the other hand, as English verbs move to T overtly, postverbal focus adverbs exist. I have also argued that so-called Adjacency Condition can be captured under the proposed parametric theory of verb movement. I have also suggested that the availability of sentence final particles correlates with the lack of V-to-T movement in the overt component. The findings in this paper are relevant to our deeper understanding of possible parameters permitted by Universal Grammar.

Due to limitation of space, I cannot provide an extensive analysis on all linguistic variations between Chinese and English under the parametric theory of verb movement proposed in this paper. Many interesting consequences should await future research. I hope that my proposal outlined here may open up a new way of looking at the typological differences between Chinese and English in terms of the principles-and-parameters approach.

References

Bayer, Josef. 1996. *Directionality and logical form: on the scope of focusing particles and wh-in-situ*. Dordrecht: Kluwer Academic Publishers.

Chao, Yuen-Ren. 1968. *A grammar of spoken Chinese*. Berkeley and Los Angeles: University of California Press.

Cheng, Lisa Lai-Shen. 1989. Aspectual Licensing of pro in Mandarin Chinese. Ms., MIT.

Chomsky, Noam. 1970. Remarks on nominalization. In R. Jacobs and P. Rosenbaum, eds., *Readings in English transformational grammar*. Waltham, Mass.: Ginn.

Chomsky, Noam. 1981. *Lectures on Government and Binding*. Dordrecht: Foris Publications.

Chomsky, Noam. 1991. Some notes on economy of derivation and representation. In Robert Freidin, ed., *Principles and parameters in comparative grammar*, 417-454. Cambridge, Mass.: The MIT Press.

Chomsky, Noam. 1993. A minimalist program for linguistic theory. In Kenneth Hale and Samuel Jay Keyser, eds., *The view from Building 20: essays in linguistics in honor of Sylvain Bromberger*, 1-52. Cambridge, Mass.: The MIT Press.

Chomsky, Noam. 1995. Categories and transformation. In *The Minimalist Program*. 219-394. Cambridge, Mass.: The MIT Press.

Chomsky, Noam. 2000. Minimalist inquiries: the framework. In Roger Martin, David Michaels, and Juan Uriagereka, eds., *Step by step: essays on minimalist syntax in honor of Howard Lasnik*, 89-155. Cambridge, Mass.: The MIT Press.

Chomsky, Noam. 2001a. Derivation by phase. In *Michael Kenstowicz ed., Ken Hale: a life in language*, 1-52. Cambridge, Mass.: The MIT Press.

Chomsky, Noam. 2001b. Beyond explanatory adequacy. *MIT Occasional Papers in Linguistics 20*. Cambridge, Mass.: MITWPL.

Cinque, Guglielmo. 1999. *Adverbs and functional heads: a cross-linguistic perspective*. New York and Oxford: Oxford University Press.

Emonds, Joseph. 1978. The verbal complex V'-V in French. *Linguistic Inquiry* 9: 151-175.

Fukui, Naoki, and Yuji Takano. 1998. Symmetry in syntax: merge and demerge. *Journal of East Asian Linguistics* 7: 27-86.

Gu, Yang. 1995. Aspect licensing, verb movement and feature checking. *Cahiers de Linguistique Asie Orientale* 24(1), 49-83.

Hale, Kenneth, and Samuel Jay Keyser. 1993. On argument structure and the lexical representation of syntactic relations. In Kenneth Hale and Samuel Jay Keyser, eds., *The view from Building 20: essays in linguistics in honor of Sylvain Bromberger*, 53-109. Cambridge, Mass.: The MIT Press.

Hornstein, Norbert, and Amy Weinberg. 1981. Case theory and preposition stranding. *Linguistic Inquiry* 12: 55-91.

Horvath, Julia. 1995. Structural focus, structural Case, and the notion of feature-assignment. In Katalin É. Kiss, ed., *Discourse Configurational Languages*, 28-64. New York and Oxford: Oxford University Press.

Huang, C.-T. James. 1991. verb movement, (in)definiteness, and the thematic hierarchy. In Paul Jen-Kuei Li, Chu-Ren Huang, and Ying-Chin Lin, eds., *Proceedings of the Second International Symposium on Chinese Languages and Linguistics*, 481-498. Taipei: Academia Sinica.

Huang, C.-T. James. 1997. Japan cannot say 'No-'. Handout of talk given at Workshop on Japanese Syntax in a Comparative Context, LSA Linguistic Institute, Cornell University.

Huang, C.-T. James. 1999. Chinese passives in comparative perspective. Ms., University of California, Irvine. (To appear in *Tsing Hua Journal of Chinese Studies*.)

Jackendoff, Ray S. 1972. *Semantic interpretation in generative grammar.* Cambridge, Mass.: The MIT Press.

Johnson, Kyle. 1991. Object position. *Natural Language and Linguistic Theory* 9, 577-636.

Kayne, Richard S. 1994. *The antisymmetry of syntax.* Cambridge, Mass.: The MIT Press.

Kayne, Richard S. 1998. Overt vs. covert movement. *Syntax* 1, 128-191.

Koizumi, Masatoshi. 1995. Phrase structure in minimalist syntax. Doctoral dissertation, MIT.

Klima, Edward S. 1964. Negation in English. In J. Fodor and J. Katz, eds., *The structure of language*, 246-323. Englewood Cliffs: Prentice-Hall.

Kural, Murat. 1998. verb movement in English and morphological transparency. *UCI Working Papers in Linguistics 4*, 105-140. Irvine, Irvine Linguistics Students Association.

Lasnik, Howard. 1995. Verbal morphology: *Syntactic Structures* meets the Minimalist Program. In Héctor Campos and Paula Kempchinsky, eds., *Evolution and revolution in linguistic theory*, 251-275. Washington, D.C.: Georgetown University Press.

Li, Charles N., and Sandra A. Thompson. 1981. *Mandarin Chinese: a functional reference grammar.* Berkeley and Los Angeles: University of California Press.

Li, Yen-hui Audrey. 1987. Duration phrases: distributions and interpretations. *Journal of the Chinese Language Teachers Association* 22(3): 27-56.

Li, Yen-hui Audrey. 1990. *Order and Constituency in Mandarin Chinese.* Dordrecht: Kluwer Academic Publishers.

Li, Xiaoguang. 1997. Deriving distributivity in Mandarin Chinese. Doctoral dissertation, University of California, Irvine.

Lin, Jonah Tzong-Hong. 1997. Quantificational Force Parameter and the determiner *ge* in Chinese. Paper presented at Interface Strategies in Chinese: Syntax and Semantics of Noun Phrases, Cornell University.

Pollock, Jean-Yves. 1989. verb movement, Universal Grammar, and the structure of IP. *Linguistic Inquiry* 20: 365-424.

Quirk, Randolph, Sudney Greenbaum, Geoffrey Leech, and Jan Svartvik. 1972 *A grammar of contemporary English*. London: Longman.

Rooth, Mats Edward. 1985. Association with focus. Doctoral dissertation, University of Massachusetts, Amherst.

Solà, Jaume. 1996. Morphology and word order in Germanic languages. In Werner Abraham, Samuel David Epstein, Höskuldur Thráinsson, and C. Jan-Wouter Zwart, eds., *Minimal ideas*, 217-251. Amsterdam: John Benjamins Publishing Company.

Stowell, Timonthy. 1981. Origins of phrase structure. Doctoral dissertation, MIT.

Stowell, Tim. 1996. The phrase structure of tense. In Johan Rooryck and Laurie Zaring, eds., *Phrase structure and the lexicon*, 271-286. Dordrecht: Kluwer Academic Publishers.

Taglicht, Josef. 1984. *Message and emphasis*. London and New York: Longman.

Takeda, Kazue. 1997. Attract and locality of movement. Ms., University of California, Irvine.

Tang, Chih-Chen Jane. 1990. Chinese phrase structure and the extended X'-theory. Doctoral dissertation, Cornell University.

Tang, Sze-Wing. 1998. Parametrization of features in syntax. Doctoral dissertation, University of California, Irvine.

Tang, Sze-Wing. 1999. Some speculations about the syntax of noun phrases. *UCI working papers in linguistics 5*, 135-154. Irvine: Irvine Linguistics Students Association.

Ting, Jen. 1995. A non-uniform analysis of the passive construction in Mandarin Chinese. Doctoral dissertation, University of Rochester.

Travis, Lisa. 1988. The syntax of adverbs. In *McGill working papers in linguistics: special issue on comparative Germanic syntax*.

Tsai, Wei-Tien. 1994. On economizing the theory of A-bar dependencies. Doctoral dissertation, MIT.

Zhang, Ning. 1997. Syntactic dependencies in Mandarin Chinese. Doctoral dissertation, University of Toronto.

Predemonstrative Modifiers

ALEXANDER WILLIAMS
University of Pennsylvania

1 Introduction[1]

The Mandarin demonstrative phrases (1) and (2) differ minimally in string order. The modifier *huang-de* 'yellow' follows the demonstrative determiner in (1) and precedes it in (2).

(1) nei-zhi huang-de gou
DEM-CLS yellow-DE dog
'that yellow dog'

(2) huang-de nei-zhi gou
yellow-DE DEM-CLS dog
'the yellow dog'

Yet the phrases differ significantly in their presuppositions. (2) presupposes that the domain of discourse contains only one yellow dog (Chao 1968, Wu 1994), as I show in Section 3. (1), on the other hand, may be felicitous given

[1] Thanks go to Robin Clark for his patient help; to Tony Kroch, Ellen Prince and Audrey Li for early comments; to Xiao Yuan, Liang Minmin, Chiou Fudong, Sun Yuan and again Audrey Li, for judgments.

On the Formal Way to Chinese Languages.
Sze-Wing Tang and Chen-Sheng Luther Liu (eds.).

a domain of many yellow dogs, providing that the speaker manages to direct attention to a subset in which there is only one—by pointing, for example. I reflect this difference in the choice of English glosses. The construction exemplified by (2) carries the domain-general uniqueness presupposition of the English definite. The cardinality presupposition of noun phrases like (1) is relativized by context, as is typical of demonstratives.

My purpose in this paper is to explain how these differences in meaning arise compositionally from those in string order, without attributing to phrases like (2) any semantic or pragmatic characteristics not evidenced in natural data. I argue in Section 4 that previous interpretations of the contrast between (1) and (2) (Chao 1968, Huang 1983, Wu 1994, and others) have failed in this. Section 5 derives an explanation from a simple observation: demonstratives have a characteristic sensitivity to context. Evidently the demonstrative determiner denotes a function not saturated by the common noun phrase (N-BAR) to its right alone. Hence it includes a variable not instantiated by N-BAR, typically left open to context. I demonstrate that when there is a predemonstrative modifier, it saturates exactly this variable. Phrases like (2) are thereby shut off to context, and acquire a broad uniqueness presupposition. The resultant theory is attractively minimal: it invokes no machinery not forced by the semantics of demonstratives generally, and is straightforwardly compositional. It also has promising extensions. In Section 6, I sketch a projection of the theory to certain sentential topic constructions, unifying our understanding of nominal and clausal grammar in Mandarin.

2 Descriptive Conventions

The canonical Mandarin demonstrative phrase has the form DEM + NUMERAL + CLASSIFIER + N-BAR. N-BAR terminates with the head noun at the right edge, and may include a sequence of modifiers preceding the head. The category of modifier includes adjectives, relative clauses, and prepositional phrases, as well as possessive and locative noun phrases. NUMERAL is sometimes omitted, but only when its understood value is 1. I will refer to the sequence DEM + NUMERAL + CLASSIFIER simply as DEM_n, where n=NUMERAL. (1) is a typical demonstrative phrase. Such phrases, where no modifier precedes the determiner, I will call *DemPs*.

(2) exemplifies a variant type of demonstrative phrase, wherein a modifier does precede the determiner. Schematically: MOD + DEM + NUMERAL + CLASSIFIER + N-BAR. In this structure as in the canonical structure, N-BAR may still include further modifiers, but I will only designate a predemonstra-

tive modifier as MOD. Demonstrative phrases with an initial modifier, like (2), I will call *MDemPs*.[2]

I now motivate my glosses of (1) and (2).

3 Describing the Differences between (1) and (2)

3.1 MDemPs Have a Universal Cardinality Presupposition

Let U_S be the domain with respect to which a simple sentence S is evaluated.[3] An MDemP in S refers felicitously only if U_S contains exactly NUMERAL (=n) things satisfying MOD and N-BAR. That is:

(3) An MDemP in S is felicitous only if, in U_S:

$$| \|\text{MOD}\| \cap \|\text{N-BAR}\| | = \text{NUMERAL}.$$ [4]

Call this a *universal* cardinality presupposition. In example (2), NUMERAL=1, MOD='yellow', and N-BAR='dog'. (2) refers successfully only if, in U_S, $| |yellow| \cap |dog| | = 1$; in other words, only if U_S contains exactly one yellow dog. I take this to follow from the infelicity of (4) and (5).

(4)# huang-de nei-zhi gou he huang-de nei-zhi gou dou tai ke'ai le
yellow-DE DEM_1 dog and yellow-DE DEM_1 dog both too cute LE
'The yellow dog and the yellow dog are just too cute.'

(5)# huang-de nei-zhi gou he nei-zhi huang-de gou dou tai ke'ai le
yellow-DE DEM_1 dog and DEM_1 yellow-DE dog both too cute LE
'The yellow dog and that yellow dog are just too cute.'

The first conjunct in (4) and (5), namely the MDemP (2), refers to a yellow dog. In neither case can it be followed, without perversity, by a noun phrase referring to a second yellow dog. If MDemPs carry the presupposition given in (3), then (2) presupposes a unique yellow dog in U_S, and therefore cannot innocently be followed by mention of a second yellow dog. I conclude that

---

[2] One basic semantical assumption should be mentioned. In this paper, I take predemonstrative MOD, like N-BAR, to denote uniformly in <e,t>. Non-intersective modifiers will pose the standard problems, but this is not the place to discuss them.

[3] The domain can be affected as evaluation proceeds, but, certainly within a single sentence, and probably over longer stretches as well, only monotonically. The reader should appreciate that, within the bounds of monotonicity, U_S may be significantly different from earlier U_{S-n}.

[4] $|X|$ will mean the semantic evaluation of X with respect to the model. $|yellow|$ is the set of yellow things in U_S. I will not distinguish orthographically between X and the function which translates X in the formalism, often written X′. Hence, *yellow* stands for either an English word, or the function $\lambda x.yellow(x)$. Context should disambiguate.

(3) is correct. MDemPs have the broad cardinality presupposition characteristic of definite descriptions. (See Williams 1998 for further discussion.) When NUMERAL=1, the MDemP has a universal uniqueness presupposition.[5]

Prosodic emphasis on the determiner will not cancel this presupposition. When either or both of the medial determiners in (4) are stressed, speakers still judge the sentence infelicitous. Things may improve somewhat if the second NP is a very strongly stressed DemP. In Mandarin as in English, to follow mention of a presupposedly unique yellow dog with emphatic deictic reference to a second yellow dog is odd, but not always terribly so. (6) is (5) with stress on the second conjunct.

(6) ?? huang-de nei-zhi gou he NEI-zhi huang-de gou dou tai ke'ai le
yellow-DE DEM_1 dog and DEM_1 yellow-DE dog both too cute LE
?? 'The yellow dog and *THAT* yellow dog are just too cute.'

That (6), in either language, is not atrocious does not mean that *huang-de nei-zhi gou* and *the yellow dog* do not presuppose a unique yellow dog. It simply shows that listeners are willing to accommodate updates to and corrections of what had been presupposed. What the emphatic stress signals here is precisely an update of—specifically, an addition to—the domain, at that point in the discourse. The fact that the domain has two yellow dogs at that point does not mean that it may felicitously have two earlier, when the MDemP is used. The mitigated infelicity of (6) consequently offers no evidence against (3), any more than it destroys the received understanding of English definite descriptions.

(4) and (5) cannot be redeemed by accompanying the MDemPs with the sort of ostensive gestures canonically associated with demonstrative reference either. The judgments are delicate, but my informants still consider (4) and (5) very odd, even when the speaker (e.g.) points in different directions, towards different dogs, as she utters each conjunct. Again, emphatic stress on the second NP would have, at best, the flavor of an update or correction. These judgments further corroborate (3). Singular MDemPs presuppose uniqueness with respect to the entirety of U_S, not just with respect to some contextually defined subset thereof.

3.2 DemPs Have a Relative Cardinality Presupposition

Contrast plain DemPs, like (1). These exhibit the sensitivity to context characteristic of demonstrative phrases. Demonstrative phrases range only over a subset (generally proper) of U_S, where restriction to that subset is effected

[5] One significant difference between MDemPs and English definites is that the former—like typical demonstrative phrases—permit only non-attributive (rigid, non-intensional) readings.

by some feature of context (Kaplan 1977). Paradigmatic examples show the domain restricted by a pointing finger, a directed gaze, or a topic-changing expression like 'as for the yellow ones…'. Call the contextually-defined subset of U_S over which a demonstrative phrase D ranges U_S/D. Restriction to U_S/D can be strictly local to D: two demonstrative phrases in a single sentence may range over different subsets of U_S. For example, uttering (7), I may point towards the tree as I utter the first DemP (D_1) and towards the fountain as I utter the second (D_2), thereby designating distinct local domains U_S/D_1 ($\{x$: x is by the tree$\}$) and U_S/D_2 ($\{y$: y is by the fountain$\}$) with respect to which each is evaluated.

(7) nei-zhi huang-de gou he nei-zhi huang-de gou dou tai ke'ai le
DEM$_1$ yellow-DE dog and DEM$_1$ yellow-DE dog both too cute LE
(pointing towards the tree) (pointing towards the fountain)
'That dog and that dog are just too cute.'

In this way, demonstrative phrases differ from definite descriptions, which, like MDemPs, range over all of U_S.

Modulo this difference, however, the presuppositions of demonstrative phrases and definite descriptions are similar. Demonstrative phrases do have a cardinality presupposition, but it is *relative* to the local domain supplied at utterance. A demonstrative phrase with NUMERAL=1 is felicitous only if it denotes a unique individual in U_S/D. There must be exactly one yellow dog by the tree, and exactly one by the fountain, for (7) to work out. So two identical DemPs can cooccur felicitously, but only if they have distinct local domains, $U_S/D_1 \neq U_S/D_2$. The felicity condition on the use of DemPs is consequently that, in $U_S/D \subseteq U_S$, the cardinality of ‖N-BAR‖ must be NUMERAL:

(8) A DemP in S is felicitous only if, *in* U_S/D:

$$| \|\text{N-BAR}\| | = \text{NUMERAL}.$$

In the case of (1), this means that, in U_S/D: $| \|\textit{yellow dog}\| | = 1$.

3.3 The Discourse-Pragmatics of MDemPs

Williams (1997) gives a foundation for an objective pragmatic theory of MDemPs. The purpose of this study was to determine the discourse conditions in which MDemPs are used, and to compare these to those of determiner-less bare N-BAR definites (BNDs), like *huang-de gou* 'the yellow dog.'[6] The comparison was to BNDs, not DemPs, since BNDs carry a universal cardinality presupposition, and so are minimally different from MDemPs. Given this, the question arises, in what situations is an MDemP used, rather than the semantically very similar BND?

Roughly four hours of free conversation, text and sound, between (twenty-three) pairs of native Mandarin speakers were studied. The source was the Linguistic Data Consortium's *Callhome Mandarin* corpus. MDemP and BND tokens were coded in accord with a taxonomy of "information status" adapted from Prince (1992). Relevant here is whether a token referred to an entity that: (a) had been mentioned already in the discourse; or (b) had not been mentioned already, but whose existence was plausibly inferable from the existence of other entities in the discourse model; or (c) had not been mentioned before, and was not inferable. Let's call tokens referring to entities with property (a) *D-Old*, with property (b) *Inferable*, and with property (c) *D-New*. I was strict with what counted as *Inferable*. Schools generally have principals, and babies have mothers, but much more elaborate guesswork did not constitute a plausible inference.

The study shows that MDemPs are nearly always make the first explicit mention of the referent (90.5%), and are D-New fully 71.4% of the time (Table 1). In extreme contrast, only 13.3% of BNDs are D-New. The remainder is split almost equally between D-Old and Inferable. The discourse functions of these noun phrase types thus differ massively, despite their very similar semantics.

Discourse Status	MDemPs		BNDs	
D-Old	9.5 %	(8/84)	40.8 %	(104/255)
Inferable	19.1	(16/84)	45.9	(117/255)
D-New	71.4	(60/84)	13.3	(34/255)

Table 1.

This discovery, that MDemPs canonically introduce novel referents, allows us to reduce our reliance on vague intuitions about when MDemPs are appropriately used. I suggest below that it may also explain why these have often been felt to be contrastive constructions.

The scope of the study did not include DemPs. In doing the research, however, it was apparent that DemPs were D-Old far more often than MDemPs were. DemPs seem to require a higher degree of salience in their

6 In some contexts, a bare N-BAR string is indefinite or generic. The study was not concerned with such uses.

referents—roughly as English demonstrative phrases require a more salient referent than definite descriptions (Gundel et al. 1993). Like its gloss, (9) can be used felicitously even if the hearer had no idea that my neighbors had a dog, as long as he finds the presupposition easy to accommodate.

(9) gebi-de nei-zhi gou
neighboring-DE DEM_1 dog
'The dog next door' (from Gundel et al. 1993)

The DemP counterpart of (9), however—*gebi-de nei-zhi gou*, which I would gloss as 'that dog next door'—is not felicitous in the same conditions. It requires antecedent knowledge of that particular dog.

4 Previous Accounts

4.1 Predemonstrative Modifiers as Contrastive

Chao (1968: 286) proposes that predemonstrative placement has the same semantic effect as contrastive stress. Thus (2) is alleged to have the same "sense" as (1) with contrastive stress on *huang-de* 'yellow'. Endorsing this analogy, Wu (1994) sees a possible explanation for the universal cardinality presupposition of MDemPs. Contrastively stressing a modifier, she argues, effects the implication that no individual in the relevant context but the intended referent has the property expressed by that modifier. (10), both in Mandarin and in the English gloss, is unacceptable for this reason, even with stress on the determiner of the second conjunct.

(10)# nei-zhi HUANG-de gou he NEI-zhi huang-de gou dou tai ke'ai le
DEM_1 yellow-DE dog DEM_1 yellow-DE dog both too cute LE
'That YELLOW dog and THAT yellow dog are just too cute.'

Thus, were MDemPs inherently contrastive constructions, we might have an explanation of the uniqueness effect.[7]

That they are not even typically contrastive is clear both from careful consideration of example sentences, and from examination of naturally occurring data. Consider (9) from above, and (11) below.

[7] Certainly, having a uniqueness presupposition does not itself entail being rhetorically contrastive, in any obvious sense. English definite descriptions, for example, are not generally used for contrastive effect.

(11) shangci shuicao huaile, ba ta xiuhao-de nei-ge jiahuo
last-time sink broke BA it fix-DE DEM_1 fellow
'The guy who fixed my sink last time it broke'

These phrases do not generally evoke a rhetorical contrast with the dogs who don't live next door or the guys who did not fix my sink last time. Contrast with non-dog things next door or with guys who fixed a non-sink last time (and so on) is no more likely. Such interpretations require special circumstances, and thus contrast is not an inherent feature of the MDemP. It is consequently not surprising that, of the 84 unambiguous MDemP tokens I gathered from nearly four hours of Mandarin phone conversations, only five could even be argued to be rhetorically contrastive, and only two were convincingly so (Williams 1997).[8] Plainly, MDemPs are not necessarily, or even usually used for contrastive effect. Thus Wu's proposed explanation will not work.

Why then is the feeling that MDemPs are contrastive so common? I would like to suggest that its source is exactly the fact that MDemPs are typically D-New (see Section 3.3). Out of context, a form generally used to introduce novel referents perhaps invites the imagination of a context against which the referent has maximal novelty.

4.2 Predemonstrative Modifiers as Specially Restrictive

Chao (1968: 286) also suggested that predemonstrative relative clauses are "restrictive," while those following the determiner are "descriptive." Chao's glosses of noun phrases with postdemonstrative modifiers show that he understood "descriptive" to entail nonrestrictive, and those who have followed Chao's suggestion have explicitly made this connection (C.T.J. Huang 1983, C.R. Huang 1988, among others).

Even if true, this claim will not explain the universal cardinality presupposition of MDemPs, as Wu (1994) also points out. Restrictive modification does not miraculously produce uniqueness presuppositions. In fact, nonrestrictively modified definites will generally have even broader uniqueness presuppositions than their restrictively modified counterparts, since the set denoted by the restrictively modified NP complement to the determiner will generally be smaller. The contrast Chao proposes is therefore useless for current purposes.

In any case, there are convincing reasons to think that postdemonstrative modifiers *are* restrictive. (Predemonstrative modifiers are uncontroversially restrictive.) Here, I will only just briefly mention these.

[8] I cannot include the corroborating data here, since it consists of long segments of discourse, which make their point only in large numbers.

First, modification of a non-specific indefinite (of the free-choice sort) is perforce restrictive, on pain of absurdity; yet modifiers happily follow the determiner of a Mandarin indefinite with narrow-scope in an intensional context. Plausibly, if internal modifiers are restrictive under indefinite determiners, they are restrictive under demonstrative determiners as well. Second, (1) would be a natural thing to say facing a scrum of playful puppies, not expecting the hearer could identify his intended referent without the information that it is yellow. So, while a rich context might always render the content of any noun phrase unnecessary or redundant, a post-demonstrative modifier can be quite significant in establishing reference. Therefore postdemonstrative modifiers must be restrictive.

4.3 Lexical Ambiguity

Li and Thompson propose that "the demonstrative *nei* 'that' ... is beginning to function as 'the' if it is not stressed. For example: *Ni renshi bu renshi* [$_{\text{DemP}}$ *nei-ge ren*], 'Do you know that/the person?'" (1981: 131). Assuming this claim should entail its practical contrapositive—that stress will force the pure demonstrative reading of *nei*—it cannot be perfectly correct. Were it, we should be baffled by the fact that (12), a version of (4) in which all the internal *nei*'s are stressed, is still infelicitous.

(12)# huang-de NEI-zhi gou he huang-de NEI-zhi gou dou tai ke'ai le
yellow-DE DEM$_1$ dog and yellow-DE DEM$_1$ dog both too cute LE
'The (*that) yellow dog and the (*that) yellow dog are just too cute.'

Thus the claim cannot be entirely right, at least with respect to the determiner in MDemPs, and so cannot be used to explain the definite-description semantics of these constructions.

Annear (1965, cited in Wu 1994) suggests that the demonstrative determiner itself changes its meaning, between 'the' and 'that,' depending on position vis-à-vis the modifiers. I submit without argument that this is a sort of lexical ambiguity better avoided. An account that can explain the meaning differences of the demonstrative phrases compositionally, without positing ambiguity, is to be preferred.

4.4 Coreference

One last conceivable account of the facts posits a relation of anaphoric coreference between DEM$_n$+N-BAR and the preceding MOD. Mandarin permits headless DPs of the form "modifier + *de*", which refer to those contextually relevant things (one or more) that satisfy the modifier. One might then speculate that in (2), *huang-de* ('yellow-DE') is a headless DP denoting a group of contextually relevant yellow things, and the subsequent string *nei-zhi gou* ('DEM_1 dog') refers back that group. Yet that group will in general be much too large, and thus the speculation fails. Often enough, far too many things will be in the set of yellow things, even the contextually relevant ones, for 'that dog' to be coreferent with it. Were only doghood contextually relevant, of course, the set might shrink to the right size (namely NUMERAL). But natural data show quite clearly that the property expressed by the head noun of the demonstrative phrase is quite often not salient in antecedent discourse (Williams 1997). Thus the local anaphora theory is irredeemable. The mistake it makes is to regard DEM_n+N-BAR as referring *to* the set denoted by the predemonstrative modifier. I argue in the next section that it is correctly taken to referring *in* that set.[9]

5 MOD Saturates the Demonstrative Context Variable

I claim that predemonstrative modifiers are explicit and syntactically encoded realizations of the local restriction from U_S to U_S/D characteristically associated with demonstrative phrases. MDemPs are simply DemPs where the local domain-restriction is explicit, and given within the scope of the demonstrative phrase itself, rather than supplied by context. I will say that the interpretation of a demonstrative phrase contains a variable instantiated either by MOD or by MOD_{CXT} (where $\|\text{MOD}_{\text{CXT}}\|=U_S/D$, as specified by context at utterance). This analysis follows from the data in Section 3.

5.1 MOD is in Complementary Distribution with MOD_{CXT}

Often the sensitivity of a certain function to context is expressed in the semantics by the addition of a variable, a context variable, to be instantiated by information from outside the scope of that function (see e.g. Chierchia 1995 and Westerståhl 1989). That N-BAR does not complete the content of a DemP is therefore also plausibly encoded by adding a variable to the function DEM_n. Call this variable M. For a DemP, N-BAR will instantiate one variable in DEM_n, but M will remain open, leaving the phrase indexical. Let us use the term 'MOD_{CXT}' as a variable over those aspects of context which effect local restriction of the domain for a demonstrative, such that MOD_{CXT} denotes U_S/D. At the tokening of a DemP, then, M is specified as MOD_{CXT}. Now recall the observations in Section 3.

---

[9] Two other problems with the coreference idea are that it would require unprecedented binding mechanisms to assure the strict locality of anaphora, and that, incorrectly, it would allow MOD and the following determiner to constitute distinct intonational phrases.

There I described DemPs as carrying a relativized cardinality presupposition. The denotation of N-BAR must have cardinality NUMERAL, in the contextually given local subdomain U_S/D (=|MOD_{CXT}|). Repeating (8):

(13) A DemP in S is felicitous only if, in U_S/D:

$$| \|\text{N-BAR}\| | = \text{NUMERAL} .$$

The cardinality presupposition of MDemPs, I called universal. The intersection of the predicates overt in the phrase must denote only NUMERAL things in the entire domain, U_S. Repeating (3):

(14) An MDemP in S is felicitous only if, in U_S:

$$| \|\text{MOD}\| \cap \|\text{N-BAR}\| | = \text{NUMERAL}.$$

But of course conditions (13) and (14) can both be subsumed under the schema in (15).

(15) A DemP or an MDemP in S is felicitous only if, in U_S:

$$| \text{ X } \cap \|\text{N-BAR}\| | = \text{NUMERAL}$$

where X=$\|$MOD$\|$ for MDemPs, and X=$\|MOD_{CXT}\|$ for DemPs.

And this generalization prompts a simple explanation of the contrast between (1) and (2).

According to (15), predemonstrative MOD is semantically in complementary distribution with MOD_{CXT}, as the data in (4–7) show. Context may restrict the domain if, (7), and only if, (4–6), no modifier precedes DEM. This is explained directly if MOD and MOD_{CXT} compete for the same variable in the semantic representation. By hypothesis, MOD_{CXT} instantiates the context variable M. Thus I put forward (16) as the central thesis of this paper, and correspondingly restate (15) as (17).

(16) a. A modifier preceding DEM_n instantiates the variable M in the denotation of DEM_n.

b. When no modifier precedes DEM_n, M is left unspecified until use, when it is specified by context as MOD_{CXT}.

(17) A Mandarin demonstrative phrase in S is felicitous only if, in U_S:
$$|\ \|M\| \cap \|\text{N-BAR}\|\ | = \text{NUMERAL}$$

In other words, predemonstrative position is a syntactic reification of the so-called context variable in the semantics of DEM_n.

(16) and (17) derive the data straightforwardly. In (1), where N-BAR is *huang-de gou* 'yellow dog', no modifier precedes DEM_1. Hence by (16b), M is left unspecified. And consequently, (1) presupposes only that there is one yellow dog in some subset of the domain—the exact subset to be specified by MOD_{CXT} at tokening. In (2), where N-BAR is *gou* 'dog', the modifier *huang-de* 'yellow' precedes DEM_1. Hence by (16a), *huang-de* saturates M, preempting any contribution of context. The presupposition of (2) is therefore determined fully by its lexical content alone. Whenever it is used, the entire domain must include just one yellow dog.

(18) defines one possible formal interpretation for DEM_n consonant with these conclusions, and treating DEM_n as a generalized quantifier.[10,11] (18a) translates DEM_n as a lambda expression, and (18b) gives its truth-conditions. The variable names are mnemonic. M is to be instantiated by $\text{MOD}_{(\text{CXT})}$, N by N-BAR, and P by the clausal predicate (remember, DEM_n is here being treated as a quantifier). I assume that, when no overt modifier precedes DEM_n, M is filled by a silent indexical element, which will take the value MOD_{CXT} at use. As usual, '#' means that a presupposition is violated, and so the expression lacks an uncontroversial truth-value.

(18) a. $\lambda M \lambda N \lambda P.\text{DEM}_n'(M,N,P)$

b.
$$\begin{aligned} \|\text{DEM}_n'(M, N, P)\| &= 1, \text{ iff } && |\ \|M\| \cap \|N\|\ | = n \\ & \text{ and } && \|M\| \cap \|N\| \subseteq \|P\|. \\ &= \#, \text{ if } && |\ \|M\| \cap \|N\|\ | \neq n. \\ &= 0, \text{ only if } && \|M\| \cap \|N\| \not\subseteq \|P\|. \end{aligned}$$

Before proceeding to discuss the syntax implied by (18a), I want to point out a claim of some theoretical interest associated with (16). According to this thesis, the so-called context variable conventionally deployed in the semantic representation of demonstratives is a syntactically real argument in Mandarin, within DP. If true, this not only substantiates the use of

[10] The basic orientation of (18) comes from Keenan & Stavi 1986.

[11] By treating DEM_n as a quantifier, I pass over the fact (noted in footnote 5) that demonstratives are generally directly referring expressions. I do this for simplicity's sake, as the question of how to formalize direct reference is a complex one (see Kaplan 1977, for starters). I hope the reader dissatisfied by this very partial formalization has no difficulty adapting it to a more adequate one.

such variables (see Williams 1998), but also discovers a generally unobserved possibility in the mapping between the syntax and semantics of natural language. English does not realize the context variable syntactically. When the local domain of a demonstrative is restricted verbally in English, that restriction is (in the less technical sense) periphrastic—e.g., 'as for the area by the fountain…'. Mandarin, on the other hand, has the option of a restricting predicate occurring bare, in a fixed, non-appositive syntactic position, as a real argument. Below, in Section 6, I correlate this property with those of a certain Mandarin topic constructions. (16) will thereby prove to be an interesting step towards a unified understanding of syntax/semantics relations in Mandarin.

5.2 Constituency and Composition

(18a) entails the following composition for (2), our example MDemP.

(19)

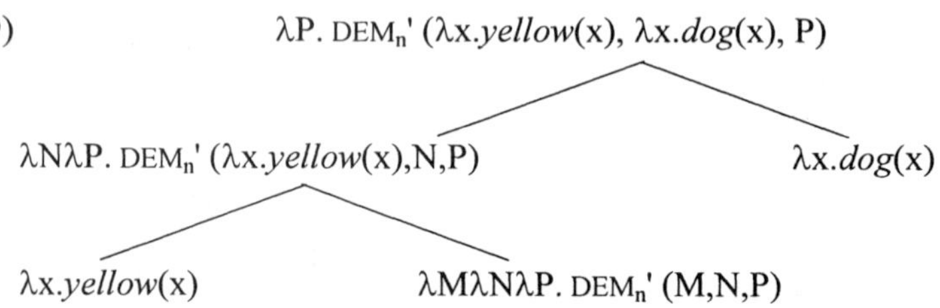

That DEM_n should apply first to MOD, and then the result to N-BAR, is conveniently left-to-right, and perhaps accords impressionistically with the idea of MOD as a DP-local domain restriction. But it is not necessitated by the truth-conditional semantics. Reversing the order of λM and λN in (18a) yields the truth-conditionally equivalent (20).

(20)

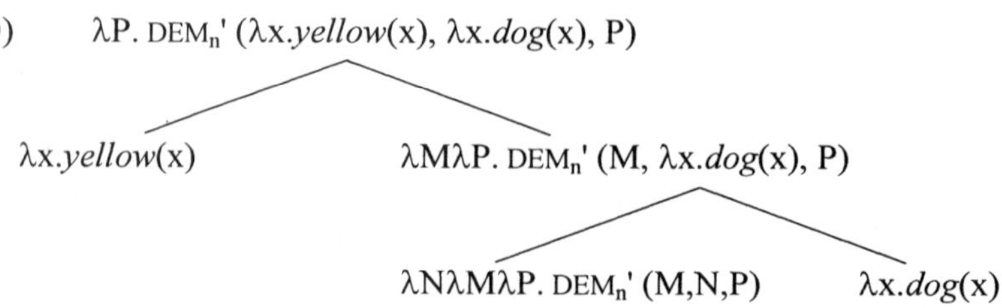

The coordination facts, however, prefer the structure in (19). MOD and DEM_n can coordinate, as in (21) below, independently of N-BAR. (Native speakers accept (21), even if they might not write it in a formal essay.) This is evidence that MOD and DEM_n form a constituent—something we might also have expected from the fact that they invariably form one intonational phrase. DEM_n and N-BAR, on the other hand, cannot coordinate under a predemonstrative modifier. This is shown by (22), which is completely unacceptable as bracketed here.

(21) [huang-de nei-zhi he hei-de nei-zhi] gou
yellow-DE DEM_1 and black DEM_1 dog
'The yellow and the black dog' (one of each)

(22)* huang-de [nei-zhi gou he nei-tiao yu]
yellow-DE DEM_1 dog and DEM_1 fish
* on the reading: 'The yellow dog and the (yellow) fish'

On a different parse, the string in (22) could mean 'the yellow dog and that fish,' where what is coordinated would be two full DPs. But it cannot have the reading given, which assumes the distribution of the modifier over both conjuncts. This argues that, in an MDemP, DEM_n and N-BAR do not form a constituent independent of MOD. Hence we have support for the tree in (19), and for the order of lambdas in (18a).

Of course, (20), but not (19), looks isomorphic to the uniformly right-branching X-bar structure customarily assigned to Mandarin DPs (Huang 1983, Tang 1996). If the composition tree should be isomorphic to the syntactic tree, and the purely right-branching tree in fact gives the correct syntax, then we should have to prefer (20), the appeal of (19) notwithstanding. I leave open the question of whether any further facts—in particular, binding facts—decide the choice.

Independent of this issue, there is one significant syntactic (or compositional) advantage to my analysis. I avoid having to posit any special mechanisms to interpret predemonstrative modifiers as restrictive.

As discussed in Section 4.2, modifiers preceding DEM are restrictive, contributing an essential condition on the reference of the phrase. Other theories have taken this to mean that MOD modifies N-BAR, with DEM_n taking the result as its argument. Presuming that modification obtains only under sisterhood, this will require that MOD be related to a position adjacent to N-BAR—by movement, let's suppose. But such movement has no syntactic motivation here. Nor could it by itself explain the meaning difference between (1) and (2). Worse, it would threaten to conflate their meanings altogether.

Compare the present analysis. It produces the effect of restrictive modification, but through the semantics of DEM_n, rather than by combining MOD and N-BAR directly. The two predicates instantiate distinct variables in DEM_n; but it happens that DEM_n's meaning invokes their intersection (see (18b)). And since DEM_n is adjacent to both, functional application (the only interpretive rule needed here) can proceed directly, over contiguous terms. Importantly, the valence of DEM_n is not increased just to avoid transformations or special rules of construal. The extra variable M is needed to encode the sensitivity of demonstratives to context—more specifically, to encode the fact DEM_n is never saturated by N-BAR alone.[12] The insight of this paper is that this variable allows us to explain the presuppositional contrast between (1) and (2), given the observed complementarity between MOD and MOD_{CXT}. Thus we manage to solve the semantic and the syntactic problems posed by predemonstrative modifiers in one simple stroke.

6 Extension to Topics "Chinese-style"

(16) claims that Mandarin, unlike English, has a non-periphrastic means of explicitly restricting the local domain for a demonstrative. The restricting expression behaves syntactically like an argument, with no need of an introductory preposition or conjunction. Comparison to "topics Chinese-style" (Chafe 1976), or "double subject" constructions (Li & Thompson 1981), is irresistible. These topics, exemplified in (23–24), are clause-initial phrases that, while not semantic arguments of the verb, are somehow closely related to the clausal proposition or its subject.

(23) nei-xie shu shushen da
DEM-CLS tree trunk big
'Those trees, the trunks are big.' (Chafe 1976)

(24) jiaju jiu-de hao
furniture old-DE good
'Furniture, old is good.' (Li & Thompson 1981)

(25) zhei-ban xuesheng ta zui congming
DEM-CLS students s/he most intelligent
'[In] this class of students, s/he is the most intelligent.' (ibid)

A distinguishing feature of such topics is, again, that they are non-periphrastic. They occur bare, without the Mandarin equivalents of 'as

12 The problem of how to interpret predemonstrative MOD restrictively is, in the abstract, equivalent to the problem of how to interpret relative clauses restrictively within a so-called NP-S analysis (see Partee 1975). Bach & Cooper (1979) propose to solve the latter problem by (optionally) increasing the valence of determiner meanings—almost as I solve the former problem here. Yet Bach & Cooper's use of this device is ad hoc in comparison, since their extra variables are introduced only to produce a non-transformational NP-S theory that is compositional at surface structure. The variable I introduce is non-optional and independently motivated.

for...' or 'speaking of...', and seem like syntactic arguments of the clause as such. But it is clear that their similarity to predemonstrative modifiers (as I have described them) does not end with their syntactic parsimony. Chafe (1976) writes that: "What the topics [Chinese-style] appear to do is limit the applicability of the main predication to a certain restricted domain. The bigness of trunks [(23)] applies within the domain of those trees." According to Li & Thompson (1981): "[T]he topic is the *whole* of which the subject is a *part*. [In (23)], the subject is *possessed* by the topic, while in [(24) and (25)], the topic names a class and the subject names a *subset* of that class." I propose to generalize these analyses by saying that the topic restricts the domain of discourse to just the set it denotes, and the subsequent subject is evaluated in that set. That is, I claim that the apparatus I have developed for predemonstrative modifiers can be used to handle topics of the "double subject" type. (We might then call MOD a DP topic.) This would be a welcome result, as it would minimize the amount of special machinery needed to explain the distinctive characteristics of Mandarin syntax, and its relation with semantics.

7 Conclusion

The present analysis of predemonstrative modifiers in Mandarin is simple, compositional, and consonant with the facts of actual usage. Recognizing the distinctive context-sensitivity of demonstratives, I expand the valence of the function DEM_n, introducing a variable to be instantiated by context. This is standard. What I add is the empirical thesis that, when there is a predemonstrative modifier, it instantiates exactly this variable, closing the demonstrative function to context, and thereby keeping its cardinality presupposition from being relativized to a smaller domain. The data support this thesis convincingly. Two string-identical MDemPs—like two identical DemPs accompanied by coextensional deictic gestures—cannot felicitously cooccur, ever. Hence predemonstrative modifiers must fill the context variable. To inscribe this conclusion in the syntax, the context variable is realized in the predemonstrative position. The semantics of MDemPs thus falls compositionally out of the semantics of demonstratives generally. What special tools the theory does use are themselves stimulating. If Mandarin realizes the demonstrative context variable syntactically, then we have both an interesting fact about natural language semantics, and a promising lead on how to handle other constructions that seem to involve fixing local domains of evaluation, like "Chinese-style" sentence topics. Most importantly, the theory delivers an explanation of the basic contrast between the presuppositions of (1) and (2), without claiming that predemonstrative modifiers have some special interpretation, not born out by natural data.

References

Annear, S.S. 1965. English and Mandarin Chinese: Definite and indefinite determiners and modifying clause structures. Mimeograph.

Bach, E. and R. Cooper. 1978. The NP-S Analysis of Relative Clauses and Compositional Semantics. *Linguistics and Philosophy* 2. 145-50.

Chafe, W. 1976. Givenness, Contrastiveness, Definiteness, Subjects, Topics, and Point of View. *Subject and Topic*, ed. C. Li. 25-55. New York: Academic Press.

Chierchia, G. 1995. *Dynamics of Meaning*. Chicago: The Chicago University Press.

Chao, Y.-R. 1968. *A Grammar of Spoken Chinese*. Los Angeles: University of California Press.

Gundel, J., N. Hedberg, and R. Zacharski. 1993. Cognitive Status and the Form of Referring Expressions in Discourse. *Language* 69: 274-307.

Huang, C.-T. J. 1983. On the Representation of Scope in Chinese. *Journal of Chinese Linguistics* 11: 36-91.

Huang, C.-R. 1987. *Mandarin Chinese NP de: A Comparative Study of Current Grammatical Theories*. Doctoral dissertation, Cornell University.

Kaplan, D. 1977. Demonstratives: An Essay on the Semantics, Logic, Metaphysics, Epistemology of Demonstratives and Other Indexicals. *Themes from Kaplan*, eds. J. Almog, J. Perry, and H. Wettstein. Oxford: Oxford University Press.

Keenan, E. A and J. Stavi. 1986. A Semantic Characterization of Natural Language Determiners. *Linguistics and Philosophy* 9: 253-326.

Li, C. and S. Thompson. 1981. *Mandarin Chinese: A Functional Reference Grammar*. Los Angeles: University of California Press.

Linguistic Data Consortium. *Callhome Mandarin*. http://www.ldc.upenn.edu

Partee, B. 1975. Montague Grammar and Transformational Grammar. *Linguistic Inquiry* 6: 203-300.

Prince, E. F. 1992. The ZPG letter: Subjects, Definiteness, and Information Status. *Discourse Description: Diverse analyses of a Fund Raising Text*, eds. S. Thompson and W. Mann. Philadelphia: John Benjamins Publishers.

Tang, C.-C. J. 1996. *Ta mai-le bi shizhi* and Chinese Phrase Structure, in *The Bulletin of the Institute of History and Philology, Academica Sinica*, vol. 67, part 3. Taipei: Academica Sinica.

Westerståhl, D. 1989. Quantifiers in Formal and Natural Languages. *Handbook of Philosophical Logic*, eds. D. Gabbay and F. Guenther. Dordrecht: Kluwer.

Williams, A. 1997. Mandarin Predemonstrative Modifiers and Discourse Status. Manuscript, University of Pennsylvania.

Williams, A. 1998. Context Variables and Mandarin Demonstratives. *CLS 34: The Main Session*. 407-20.

Wu, M. A. 1994. Demonstratives, Focus, and the Interpretation of Complex NPs in Mandarin Chinese. *Studies in the Linguistic Sciences* 24: 473-85.

Serial Verb Construction and Verbal Compounding

CHING-HUEI TERESA WU
McGill University

1. Introduction

This paper is an investigation of two types of constructions, Consecutive Constructions (so-called Serial Verb Constructions, henceforth SVC) and Resultative Constructions, in Mandarin Chinese. A comparison between Mandarin and Edo, a Kwa language spoken in Nigeria, West Africa, will be discussed from the perspective of parametric typology. Consecutive Constructions show Subject-V1-Object-V2 order in both Mandarin and Edo, as shwon in (1) and (2) respectively. Unlike Edo's Resultative Construction (4) which remains the same SVC on the surface, Mandarin presents obligatory V1-V2 Compounding (henceforth VVC) with the order of Subject-V1-V2-Object in Resultative Constructions, as shown in (3):

Consecutive Constructions

(1) Libai **mai** shu **kan** MANDARIN (Subject-**V1**-Object-**V2**)
Libai bought book read
"Libai bought a book to read."

(2) Òzó **lé** èmiówó **khién** EDO (Subject-**V1**-Object-**V2**)
Ozo cook meat sell
"Ozo cooked the meat and sold it."

On the Formal Way to Chinese Languages.
Sze-Wing Tang and Chen-Sheng Luther Liu (eds.).

Resultative Constructions

(3) Libai **tang-ping**-le chenshan MANDARIN (Subject-**V1-V2**-Object)
Libai iron-flat-Perf shirt
"Libai ironed the shirt flat."

(4) Òzó **gbé** émá!tón **pèrhé** EDO (Subject-**V1**-Object-**V2**)
Ozo pound metal flat
"Ozo pounded the metal flat."

Traditionally sentence patterns like (1) are noted as IRREALIS DESCRIPTIVE CLAUSES (Li & Thompson (1981)), whereas those like (3) as RESULTATIVE COMPLEMENT CONSTRUCTIONS. The VVC patterns like (3) are proposed as the result of verb movement by the syntactic approach (Sybesma (1992), Stewart (1998), among others)[1]. I propose that V2s in Mandarin like (3) are Achievements, rather than Statives like Edo (4). The different category of V2s is responsible for the VVC order presented in Mandarin since, I argue, Mandarin V2s contain certain aspectual feature which Edo lacks. This aspectual feature is the factor that triggers V2-movement for feature checking purpose and renders the occurrence of VVCs. On the other hand, although Consecutive Constructions in Mandarin and Edo have the same SVC order on the surface, these two languages, I suggest, have different syntactic structures in which an adjunct CP clause is involved in Mandarin.

2. Resultative Constructions

Resultative Constructions treated as Causative Constructions in Levin & Rappaport Hovav (1995). Causative Constructions consist of two events: CAUSE and RESULT. The first events in Resultative Constructions thus are NON-STATE events denoted by an "action" as *da* "strike" in (5), or an "emotional action", as *qi* "anger" in (6), whereas the second events are STATE events expressing a "result" or a "change of state" of the preceding actions, such as *shang* "injured" in (5) and *huen* "unconscious" in (6):

(5) Libai **da-shang**-le Dufu
Libai strike-injured-Perf Dufu
"(lit.) Libai struck Dufu injured."

(6) Libai **qi-huen**-le Dufu
Libai anger-unconscious-Perf Dufu
"(lit.) Libai angered Dufu unconscious."

[1] I propose in this paper that VVCs in Mandarin are constructed in Syntax through verb movement in a VP shell structure and I further claim that the derivation of VVCs in Mandarin is triggered by certain aspectual feature in Syntax. The possibility that VVCs in Mandarin are formed in Lexicon by lexical incorporation is not totally excluded. Some linguists (Li (1990), Cheng & Huang (1994) and Cheng, Huang, Li & Tang (1997), among others) have suggested that resultative VVCs in Mandarin take place at the lexical level instead of the syntactic level.

Baker & Stewart (1996) state that these two events are represented by two verbs, V1s are NON-STATE, which are Activities but never be Statives, Achievements or Accomplishments, while Statives (or Unaccusatives) (V2s) are STATE. Following Baker & Stewart (1996), V1s in Mandarin are characterized as Activity verbs. However, differing from Baker & Stewart (1996), I argue that V2s in Mandarin are Achievements rather than Statives.

2.1 Telicity Features

In the spirit of Levin & Rappaport Hovav (1995), Resultative Constructions do not only just contain "action" and "change of state", but a causal relation is also involved. The causal relation follows from the interpretation of the eventuality as an Accomplishment. Accomplishments, according to Smith (1991), consist of a "process" and a "change of state". The change is the "completion" of the process. Smith (1991) maintains that different situation types are characterized with different features, TELIC and ATELIC. Events are categorized as TELIC [+telic] or ATELIC [−telic] by Smith (1991). TELIC events are directed toward a temporal "endpoint" whereas ATELIC events are simply "processes". Hence, Accomplishments and Achievements, for instance, contain "final endpoints" and are [+telic]; Activities simply denote "processes", so they are [−telic]. In contrast, Statives do not take time, that is, temporal telicity is irrelevant to Statives. Telicity value is not applicable for Statives. The value of telicity is shown in (7):

(7) Features of situation types (Smith (1991:30))

Situations	Static	Telic
States	[+]	N/A
Activity	[−]	[−]
Accomplishment	[−]	[+]
Achievement	[−]	[+]

Since the causal relation in Resultative Constructions follows from the interpretation of the eventuality as an Accomplishment, I propose, adopting Larson's (1988) VP shell structure, Smith's (1991) conception of temporal telicity, the idea of decomposition in Hale & Keyser (1993) among others and Travis' (1997, forthcoming) proposal of Inner Aspect, that there is an inner aspectual projection α in Resultative Constructions which is generated between the CAUSE verb/light verb and V1, and functionally α contains a [+telic] feature and structurally it is selected by CAUSE. A resultative event can be viewed as a pair consisting of an ACTION and a RESULT expressed by V1 and V2 respectively. V1 and V2 project as VP1 and VP2 where VP1 is the complement of α which requires the ACTION-RESULT event to achieve a property of "completion". On the semantic version of a Larsonian structure, as noted in Baker (1997), the Agent NP is generated in the higher VP shell since it is the argument of the CAUSE verb. The Theme is affected by the ACTION of V1 and obtains the RESULT of V2[2]. The structure of a Resultative Construction is illustrated like (8):

(8)

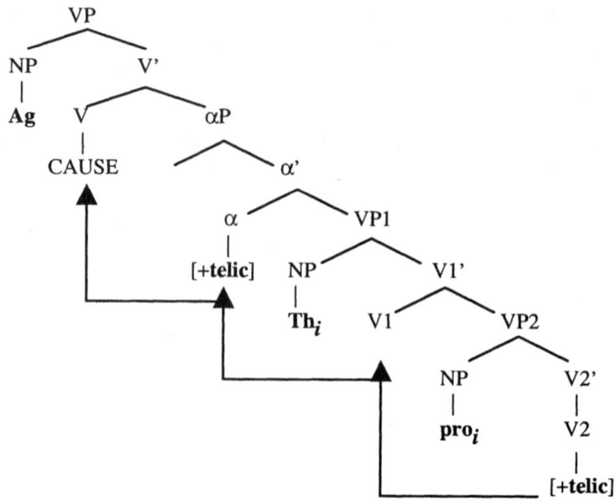

I argue that V2s in Mandarin Resultative Constructions, differing from the V2s in SVC languages, exceptionally contain [+telic] feature. The [+telic] feature of α thus is a crucial parametric factor that triggers Mandarin V2s to move up to check their [+telic] feature. Mandarin VVCs are then formed through verb movement. The parameter of VVCs which is defined in (9):

---

[2] In Mandarin Resultative Constructions the Theme of V1 is not necessarily the NP which obtains the RESULT of V2. The RESULT *sheng* "win" in (i) is predicated of the Agent *Libai* of V1 *da* "hit/do" rather than the Theme *Dufu*, whereas *shoupa* "handkerchief" in (ii) is not an argument of the Unergative V1 *ku* "cry" but the affected NP of the RESULT V2 *shi* "wet":

(i) Libai **da-sheng**-le Dufu
Libai hit/do-win-Perf Dufu
"Libai defeated Dufu."

(ii) Libai **ku-shi**-le shoupa
Libai cry-wet-Pref handkerchief
"(lit.) Libai cried the handkerchief wet."

It is possible that VVC examples like (i) are formed in the Lexicon, as proposed by Li (1990). The cases like (ii) might be related to the analysis of Sybesma (1992) who follows Hoekstra's (1988) Ergativity Shift Analysis that the Unergative verb *ku* "cry" shifts to ergativitity since (ii) can also have an inchoative counterpart like (iii):

(iii) Shoupa **ku-shi**-le
handkerchief cry-wet-Pref
"The handkerchief got wet from crying."

Moreover, Cheng, Huang, Li & Tang (1997) among others (they argue that VVCs in Mandarin are formed in Lexicon (see note 1)) propose that the based-generated position of object NPs is related to the definiteness of the object NPs in which definite objects are generated in the SPEC of VP and indefinite objects are generated as sister to V. In this article, I will focus on the structure which is so-called "object-sharing" (cf. Baker (1989)) like the sentence (3) and the general structure of Resultative Constructions is like (8) proposed above.

(9) V2s in Mandarin Resultative Constructions contain [+telic] and the feature is required to be checked with the Inner Aspect α.

2.2 Constraints in Resultative Constructions

We have seen that V1s and V2s in Mandarin Resultative Constructions are rigidly formed as VVCs. Unlike the surface Subject-V1-Object-V2 word order in Edo example (2), the objects in Mandarin Resultative Constructions are not allowed to intervene between V1 and V2, as shown in (10b). Moreover, perfective aspect markers[3], such as *-le* in (10c), must be attached to the whole VVCs rather than to V1s on the surface:

(10) a. Libai **tang-ping-*le*** chenshan
Libai iron-flat-Perf shirt
"Libai ironed the shirt flat."
b.* Libai **tang *chenshan* ping**-le
Libai iron shirt flat-Perf
c.* Libai **tang-*le*** **ping** chenshan
Libai iron-Perf flat shirt

Moreover, manner adverbs or Negations can never appear between V1s and V2s, as shown in (11) and (12). Sentences like (11c) and (12c) suggest that further verb movement to higher inflectional projections can never happen:

(11) a. Libai ***hen-kuai-de*** **tang-ping-**le chenshan — Adverb
Libai quickly iron-flat-Perf shirt
"Libai quickly ironed the shirt flat."
b.* Libai **tang *hen-kuai-de*** **ping** chenshan
Libai iron quickly flat shirt
c.* Libai **tang-ping**-le ***hen-kuai-de*** chenshan
Libai iron-flat-Perf quickly shirt

(12) a. Libai ***mei(you)/bu*** **tang-ping** chenshan — Negation
Libai not (Perf.)/not (Gen.) iron-flat shirt
"Libai didn't/doesn't want iron the shirt flat"

[3] Gu (1992) postulates that Mandarin aspect markers are based-generated verbal suffixes and Ernst (1992) makes a similar proposal under a different view. Gu (1992) proposes that AspP in Mandarin does not project its head and Spec morphologically, but Asp^0 node contains aspectual features [+perfective], [+durative], etc., which must be licensed at LF as required by Full Interpretation (FI). The semantic aspectual content in Asp^0 requires that in the feature checking process an aspectual verbal suffix moves with its host verb because the latter is the main predicate of an action or an event for which the aspectuality is relevant. I would further suggest that the whole event consisting of ACTION and RESULT is the relevant event in the case of Resultative Constructions. The aspect marker *-le* contains [+perfective] and is licensed at LF by the requirement of FI. I speculate that *-le* could be related to the analysis of the Inner Aspect α which contains [+telic] feature. However, I leave this as an open question.

b.* Libai **tang** ***mei(you)*** **ping** chenshan
Libai iron not (Perf.) flat shirt
c.* Libai **tang-ping** ***mei(you)*** chenshan
Libai iron-flat not (Perf.) shirt

The example in (13), however, shows that Negation *bu* and its positive counterpart *de* are exceptionally allowed to appear between V1s and V2s. Li & Thompson (1981) note that the *bu* in (13) is different from the *bu* in (12a) since the positive counterpart *de* never appears in structures like (12a). They maintain that *bu* and *de* are adverbs expressing "unachievably" and "achievably" respectively. The phenomenon in (13) can be considered as evidence against the lexical approach that VVCs are formed in Lexicon.

(13) Libai **tang** ***bu/de*** **ping** (zhe-jian) chenshan
Libai iron cannot/can flat this-CL shirt
"(lit.) Libai cannot/can iron the shirt flat."

The following examples in (14) and (15) further show that V1s and V2s can syntactically and semantically function as independent verbs in sentences.

(14) a. Libai **tang-ping**-le chenshan
Libai iron-flat-Perf shirt
"Libai ironed the shirt flat."
b. Libai **tang**-le chenshan
Libai iron-Perf shirt
"Libai ironed the shirt."
c. chenshan **ping**-le
shirt flat-Perf
"The shirt is flat."

(15) a. Libai **jiao-xing**-le Dufu
Libai call-wake-Perf Dufu
"(lit.) Libai called Dufu awake."
b. ta **jiao**-le Libai
he call-Perf Libai
"He called Libai."
c. Libai **xing**-le
Libai awake-Perf
"Libai is awake."

Unlike *ping* "flat" in (14c) and *xing* "awake" in (15c), verbal particles such as *-wan* "finish" in (16c) are difficult to be independent verbs on their own, but can act as V2s in Resultative Constructions, as shown in (16a). It has been observed (Chu (1976), Tai (1984) and Smith (1991), among others) that Mandarin does not have any single verbs expressing the interpretation of Accomplishments. The interpretation of an Accomplishment in Mandarin must be compositionally expressed by "process" V1 and "change of state" V2, that is, Accomplishment interpretation must be fulfilled by V1 and V2 together rather than by any one of them alone. The argument can be evidenced by the defeasible example (17a) where the Activity verb *xie* "write" itself can only express a "process" but not a "change of state". To denote Accomplishments in Mandarin, an Activity verb must combine with a resultative verb, like *ping* "flat" in (14a) or *xing* "awake" in (15a)[4], or a particle like *-wan* "finish" in (16a). The English counterpart (17b) shows that the verb *write* is already an Accomplishment verb itself. There is no need to add any resultative verbs or particles to express the interpretation of an Accomplishment. Thus, unlike the Mandarin's case (17a), defeasible sentences like (17b) in English are contradictory and unacceptable.

(16) a. Libai **he-wan**-le san-ping jou
Libai drink-finish-Perf three-bottle (CL) wine
"Libai drank off three bottles of wine."
b. Libai **he**-le san-ping jou
Libai drink-Perf three-bottle wine
"Libai drank three bottles of wine."
c.? san-ping jou **wan**-le
three-bottle (CL) wine finish/done-Perf
"Three bottles of wine are finished."
(17) a. Libai zuowan **xie**-le yi-fen xin, keshi **mei xie-wan**
Lib last night write-Perf one-CL letter but not write-finish/done
"(lit.) Libai wrote a letter last night, but he didn't finish it."
b.* John **wrote** a letter last night, but he **didn't finish** it.

2.3 Category of V2

In the view of Baker & Stewart (1996), the category of V2s in Resultative Constructions are Statives or Unaccusatives rather than Adjectives. In this section, I will propose that in general V2s in Resultative Constructions are Unaccusatives, more precisely, either Stative Unaccusatives in the case of Edo or Achievement Unaccusatives in the case of Mandarin.

2.3.1 TELIC Feature of V2s in Mandarin Chinese

Since Chinese languages lack of rich inflectional system, syntactic contexts may provide important clues for the identification of syntactic categories. Mandarin Adjectives do not usually take copulas like those in English. Nevertheless, degree markers such as *geng* "more" in (18a) and *hen* "very" in (18b) or *HEN* "very" with the addition of emphasis, as in (18c), are often utilized to identify Mandarin Adjectives (cf. Tang (1979)):

[4] Notice that the perfective marker *-le* in (14c) and (15c) does not indicate "completion" but only "termination" (cf. Smith (1991)). As cited in Tang (1997:219, note 15), however, Sybesma (1997) holds a different opinion that the aspect marker *-le* is a resultative verb.

(18) a. ta **shou**, ni ***geng*** **shou**
he thin you more thin
"He is thin and you are thinner."

b. ta ***hen*** **shou**
he DEG thin
"He is thin."

c. ta **HEN** **shou**
he **VERY** thin
"He is **VERY** thin."

Historical evidence shows that Adjectives or Statives in Classical Chinese functioned as Causatives. In (19) *hou* "thick" and *xiao* "small" were used as Causative verbs meaning " to thicken" and "to make something small".

(19) a. **hou** qu qiang-yuan (*Zuo-zhuan*, 400 B.C.)
thick their walls (Li & Thompson (1977))
"(They) thicken their walls."

b. deng Tai-san er **xiao** tienxia (*Meng-zi*, 300 B.C.)
reach Mount. Tai then small the world
"To reach Mount. Tai, one may make the world small."

In modern Mandarin, Adjectives or Statives can shift the interpretation to be Achievements by taking the perfective aspect marker *-le*, as shown in (20a), or act as Causatives, as illustrated in (20b), or even function as V1s in Resultative Constructions, as given in (20c). The verb *shou* "thin" in these cases has the expression of Achievements or Activities rather than Statives. I postulate that verbs like *shou* "thin" are Achievements containing telicity features which Statives lack. The evidence comes from the facts that *shou* in (20a) and (20b) is compatible with the adverbial *(zai) yi-ge yue/xiaoshi nei* "in one month/hour" functioning as a TELIC verb indicating COMPLETION of an endpoint, whereas it is an ATELIC verb in (20d), expressing PROCESS when occurring with the adverbial *san-ge yue* "for three months":

(20) a. ta ***(zai) yi-ge*** ***yue*** ***nei*** **shou-le**
he in one-CL month in thin-Perf
"He became thin in one month."

b. zhe-ci zhuce ***(zai) yi-ge*** ***xiaoshi nei*** **shou-le** wo-de hebao
this-CL registration in one-CL hour in thin-Perf my purse
"(lit.) The registration thinned my purse in one minute."

c. zhe-ci zhuce ***(zai) yi-ge xiaoshi nei*** **shou-bien**-le wo-de hebao
this-CL registration in one-CL hour in thin-flat-Perf my purse
"(lit.) The registration thinned my purse flat in one minute."

d. ta **shou**-le ***san-ge*** ***yue***, keshi tizhong you huilai le
he thin-Perf three-CL month but weight again come back CRS
"He had thinned for three months, the weight came back again."

Activity verbs such as *pao* "run" in (21a) and *fei* "fly" in (21b), on the other hand, should not involve natural endpoints since they are compatible with the ATELIC adverbial *yi-ge xiaoshi* "for one hour". Interestingly, as shown in (22a) and (22b), *pao* and *fei* are compatible with TELIC adverbial *(zai) yi-ge xiaoshi nei* "in one hour" as well. If we take the compatibility with the adverbials "in one hour" and "for one hour" as a considerable condition of identifying telicity values of verbs, that is, verbs which are compatible with "for one hour" are ATELIC whereas those co-occurring with "in one hour" are TELIC, we may say that *pao* "run" or *fei* "fly" are ATELIC (Activities) in (21a) and (21b) whereas they are TELIC (Achievements) in (22a) and (22b):

(21) a. Libei **pao**-le ***yi-ge xiaoshi***
Libai run-Perf one-CL hour
"Libai ran for one hour."
b. nei-qun nao **fei**-le ***yi-ge xiaoshi***
that-CL birds fly-Perf one-CL hour
"Those birds flew for one hour."

(22) a. (nei-zuo jianyu) ***(zai) yi-ge xiaoshi nei*** **pao**-le wu-ge fanren
that-CL jail in one-CL hour in run-Perf five-CL criminal
"(lit.) The jail made five criminals run away in one hour."
b. (nei-jia naodien) ***(zai) yi-ge xiaoshi nei*** **fei**-le shi-zhi nao
that-CL bird shop in one-CL hour in fly-Perf ten-CL bird
"(lit.) The bird shop made ten birds fly away in one hour."

From an aspectual point of view, there is no mismatch at all between the different uses of the same verbs in (21) and (22). While speakers of English will generally assume that verbs such as *run* and *fly* in (21) are Actives, for Mandarin speakers these verbs pattern as Achievements in (22) because of their compatibility with "in one hour". Furthermore, the fact that Causative sentences in (22) also have inchoative counterparts (23) proves that *pao* and *fei* in (22) and (23) are actually Unaccusatives. It is then not surprising that these verbs are found acting as V2s in Resultative Constructions (24):

(23) a. wu-ge fanren ***(zai) yi-ge xiaoshi nei*** **pao**-le
five-CL criminal in one-CL hour in run-Perf
"Five criminals run away in one hour."
b. shi-zhi nao ***(zai) yi-ge xiaoshi nei*** **fei**-le
ten-CL bird in one-CL hour in fly-Perf
"Ten birds fly away in one hour."

(24) a. jingcha **gan-pao**-le naoshi-de qunzhong
policemen drive-run-Perf cause trouble-R mob
"(lit.) The policemen drove the trouble making mob run away."
b. qiang sheng **xia-fei**-le yi-qun nao
gun sound scare-fly-Perf one-CL birds
"(lit.) The sound of the gun scared the birds fly away."

By examining the data above, categories seem to be "underdetermined" in Mandarin since there is no clear or identifiable morphology to separate different categories. A verb in this language thus can have different situation types. Without clear identification, V2s would not be able to express the "change of state" or "endpoint" in Resultative Constructions. However, categories can be determined as TELIC or ATELIC by their compatibility with certain adverbials, such as "in one hour" or "for one hour", or by other syntactic contexts. The interpretation of "change of state" or "endpoint" in Resultative Constructions thus can be fulfilled only in the case when V2s are Achievements containing [+telic] feature. Hence, V2s in Mandarin are categorized as Achievement Unaccusatives. Since V2s contain [+telic] feature in Resultative Constructions, the feature needs to be checked with the Inner Aspect α which contains [+telic] feature for the interpretation of Accomplishments. V2s thus are triggered to move to α for the purpose of feature checking and the movement results the occurrence of VVCs in Mandarin. The [+telic] feature, as I propose, is the crucial factor that supports the parameter (9) for Resultative Constructions.

2.3.2 V2s in Edo Resultative Constructions

Baker & Stewart (1996) note that Edo distinguishes different categories with identifiable morphology (different tones), as shown in (25a-c). V2s in Edo are restricted to Statives. The Stative verb *mòsé* is marked low-high tone in (26a) instead of Adjective *mòsè* (26b) or Achievement *mó!sé* (26c).

(25) a. èmèrí **mòsé** (Baker & Stewart (1996))
Mary be.beautiful ($V_{Stative}$)
"Mary is beautiful."

b. èmèrí yé **mòsè**
Mary be beautiful (Adj.)
"Mary is beautiful."

c. èmèrí dòó ghá **mó!sé** (p.c. Stewart)
Mary Incep. pre-verb be.beautiful ($V_{Achievement}$)
"Mary became beautiful"

(26) a. Úyi **kòkó** àdésúwà **mòsé** (Stewart (1998))
Uyi raise Adesuwa be.beautiful ($V_{Stative}$)
"Uyi raised Adesuwa to be beautiful."

b.* Úyi **kòkó** àdésúwà **mòsè**
Uyi raise Adesuwa be beautiful (Adj.)

c.* Úyi **kòkó** àdésúwà **mó!sé** (p.c. Stewart)
Uyi raise Adesuwa be.beautiful ($V_{Achievement}$)

Edo, like Mandarin and other languages, is certainly required to denote the interpretation of the eventuality as an Accomplishment in its Resultative Constructions. Accordingly, the entire sentences have to be compatible with TELIC adverbials, such as *vbè ùkpó ìsén* "in five years" in (27a), but not with ATELIC adverbials, such as *là ùkpó ìsén* "for five years" in (27b).

(27) a. Úyi **kòkó** àdésúwà **mòsé** ***vbè ùkpó ìsén*** (Stewart (1998))
Uyi raise Adesuwa be.beautiful in year five
"Uyi raised Adesuwa to be beautiful in five year."
b.* Úyi **kòkó** àdésúwà **mòsé** ***là ùkpó ìsén***
Uyi raise Adesuwa be.beautiful for year five
"Uyi raised Adesuwa to be beautiful for five year."

Like *fei* "fly" in Mandarin (21b), Edo Activity verbs, such as *tín* "fly" in (28a), have Unergative use. However, unlike the *fei* in Mandarin (24b), the verb *tín* can never function as an Unaccusative acting as V2 in Resultative Constructions like (28b). Certainly, Causative use like Mandarin *fei* in (22b) is never allowed in Edo, as illustrated in (28c). To form a Causative sentence, a functional causative marker *yá* is required, as shown in (28d).

(28) a áhiánmwèn **tín** (p.c. Stewart)
birds fly
"Birds fly."
b.* Òzó **sùá** áhiánmwèn **tín**
Ozo push birds fly
"Ozo pushes birds fly."
c.* **tín** áhiánmwèn
fly birds
d. Òzó ***yá*** áhiánmwèn **tín** (Stewart (1998))
Ozo cause/make birds fly
"Ozo causes birds fly."

According to the observation above, V2s in Edo Resultative Constructions are rigidly restricted to Statives. Activities or Achievements can never be allowed acting as V2s in Edo. As indicated in (7), temporal telicity is not applicable to Statives. Nevertheless, in Edo the interpretation of an Accomplishment for Resultative Constructions can still be ensured by the [+telic] feature of α since TELIC adverbials like "in five years" in (27b) are licensed by the [+telic] feature[5]. V2s in Edo Resultative Constructions do not raise since no such [+telic] feature checking with α is required. Verb incorporation does not happen in Edo and SVCs then are presented on the surface. Mandarin V2s, on the other hand, are Achievements containing [+telic] feature. The [+telic] feature renders V2-movement to α for feature checking. VVCs are therefore formed by verb incorporation in Mandarin.

[5] Smith (1991:158) notes that different telicity values of distinctive situation types of verbs and adverbials would cause an aspectual clash. She claims that the telicity values of verb types can be reinterpreted in the context of appropriate adverbials. I suggest that telicity values of adverbials in sentences are actually licensed by the telicity values of the situation types.

Ìgbo, another West African language, also presents VVCs in Resultative Constructions, as exemplified in (29a-b). Déchaine (1993: 242) claims that V2s has to be governed by a past Tense morpheme *-ru* which then attracts V2-movement and results VVCs order. Markers like *-o* in (29c) (glossed as "Á" by Déchaine (1993)) also have the interpretation of past Tense but are not allowed to appear in Resultative Constructions. I speculate that *-ru* in (29a) and (29b) might bear certain temporal property ("completion" or "perfective") due to its past meaning and that Ìgbo V2s might be also underdetermined like Mandarin V2s since no "Á" suffix co-occurs in (29b). If so, VVCs in Ìgbo might resemble VVCs in Mandarin in that V2s are triggered by [+telic] feature of α which indicates the telicity of the event.

(29) a. Ò **gbà-gbu-*ru*** Ézè (Déchaine (1993:243))
3s shook-kill-rV Eze
"She/he shot Eze dead."
b. Ò **rí-ju-*ru*** afo
3s eat-be.full-rV stomach
"She/he ate her/his stomach full."
c.* Ò **rí-*ri*** afo **ju-*o*** (Déchaine (1993:202))
3s eat-rV stomach be.full-**Á**
"She/he ate her/his stomach full."

3. Consecutive/Consequential Constructions

Both Mandarin Chinese (30) and Edo (31) show the same SVC order in their Consecutive Constructions (termed as Consequential Constructions in Edo by Stewart (1998)) on the surface. In addition, V1s and V2s in both languages exhibit temporal order in which V1s temporally precede V2s.

(30) Libai **mai** LGB **kan**
Libai buy LGB read
"Libai bought LGB to read."
(31) Òzó **lé** èmiówó **khién** (Stewart (1998))
Ozo cook meat sell
"Ozo cooked the meat and sold it."

As analyzed in Stewart (1998), Edo Consequential Constructions contain a juxtaposition of two separate VP events since there are no rigid aspectual constraint as that in Resultative Constructions (27), as shown in (32):

(32) a.* Òzó **lé** èmiówo **khién** ***vbè ùkpó ìsén*** (Stewart (1998))
Ozo cook meat sell in year five
"Ozo cooked the meat and sold it in five years."
b. Òzó **lé** èmiówo **khién** ***là ùkpó ìsén***
Ozo cook meat sell in year five
"Ozo cooked the meat and sold it for five years."

In traditional literature and in Li (1985), Mandarin sentences like (30) have been analyzed as constructions containing a postverbal VP in the structure of [NP VP1 VP2]. This approach, as pointed by Tang (1990), does not seem to be correct. Following Tang (1990), Consecutive Constructions like (30) should be treated to resemble Purposive Constructions. Directional aspect markers *lai* "come" or *qu* "go" in (33) indicate that the action of V2 *kan* "read" is actually a "purpose" of the V1 phrase *mai LGB* "buy LGB".

(33) Libai **mai** LGB **(lai/qu)** **kan**
Libai buy LGB come/go read
"Libai bought LGB to read."

In the following sections, I will argue that Mandarin and Edo in fact contain different structures in their Consecutive Constructions though they display the same SVC order on the surface. I will provide some evidence to illustrate that Mandarin contains an adjunct CP clause attached to V1'.

3.1 V2 Is in a CP Clauses (IRREALIS Descriptive Clause)

Consequential Constructions in Edo are REALIS constructions since negation markers *má* (past) or *í* (non-past) can never precede V2s, as shown in (34):

(34) a.* Òzó **dé** ìyán ***má*** **lé** (Stewart (1998))
Ozo buy(past) yam not(past) cook
"Ozo bought yam not to cook."
b.* Òzó **dè** ìyán ***í*** **lé**
Ozo buy(fut) yam not(non-past) cook
"Ozo will buy yam not to cook."

Following Li & Thompson (1981), I argue that Mandarin Consecutive Constructions contain an IRREALIS descriptive clause which is actually an adjunct CP in that V2s are involved, as illustrated in (35):

(35)

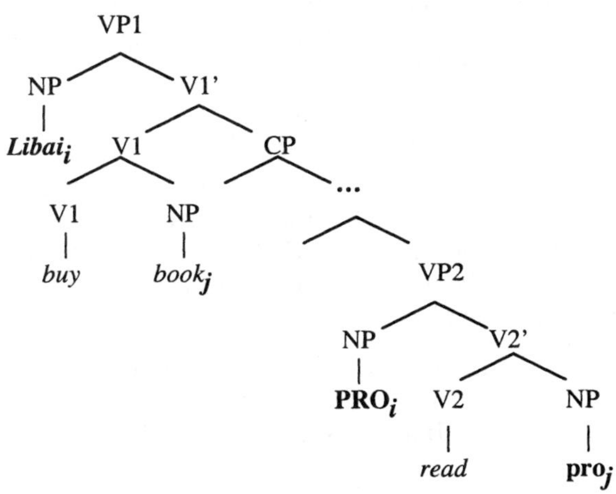

The interpretation of IRREALIS is that the event or the process of V2s might or might not happen. Therefore, Mandarin Negations *mei(you)* and *bu* may precede V2s, as shown in (36a) and (37a). As the Negations *mei(you)* and *bu* precede V1s, the scope that they covers is the entire sentence, as shown in (36b) and (37b). This suggests that V2s are in the domain of V1s.

(36) a. Libai **mai-le** LGB ***mei(you)*** **kan** — Perfective Negation
Libai buy-Perf LGB not (Perf.) read
"Libai bought LGB but he didn't read it."
b. Libai ***mei(you)*** **mai** LGB **kan**
Libai not (Perf.) buy LGB read
"Libai didn't buy LGB to read."
"*Libai didn't buy LGB but he read it."

(37) a. Libai **mai-le** LGB ***bu*** **kan** — General Negation
Libai buy-Perf LGB not read
"Libai bought LGB not to read it."
b. Libai ***bu*** **mai** LGB **kan**
Libai not buy LGB read
"Libai does not buy LGB to read."

In Mandarin, V2s of Consecutive Constructions can co-occur with temporal or locative adverbs such as *mingtien/zai jia* "tomorrow/at home", as shown in (38), or modal adverbs such as *yiding/keneng* "certainly/probably", as shown in (39). As noted in Tang (1990), these kinds of adverbs (or the projections of the adverbs) are not licensed by a verbal projection, rather, they are licensed under IP (or under some other inflectional projection in Tang (1990)). Therefore, it is reasonable to claim that V2s are in the domain of an IP projection.

(38) Libai **mai** LGB ***mingtien/zai jia*** **kan**
Libai buy LGB tomorrow/at home read
"Libai bought LGB and he is going to read it tomorrow/at home."

(39) Libai **mai-le** LGB ***yiding/keneng*** **hui kan**
Libai buy-Perf LGB certainly/probably will read
"Libai bought LGB and he certainly will read it."

Mandarin V2s may occur in cleft constructions like (40), which is headed by a Focus marker *shi* "to be". If cleft constructions can be analyzed as projections within a complementizer layer headed by operator-like focalized elements (cf. Rizzi (1997)), V2s in cleft constructions then are in the scope of a projection where a CP is involved.

(40) Libai **mai-le** LGB [$_{CP}$ ***shi*** yao **kan**]
Libai buy-Perf LGB is (Foc) want(Modal) read
"(lit.) Libai bought LGB and he wants to read it."

The examples in (41) show that adjunct *wh*-questions like (41a) and (41b)[6] and *A-not-A* questions like (41c) may be constructed with V2s. Unlike the cases in (36a) and (37a) where the scope of the Negations *mei(you)* and *bu* covers only V2s, the *wh*-phrases in (41) actually take wide scope. If the assumption that CP2 is an adjunct clause attached to V1' in Consecutive Constructions is correct, the adjunct *wh*-movement in (41) would then move the entire description that contains the adjunct *wh*-expression to the operator position of the matrix clause CP1 as well as the *wh*-expression itself, which moves within the lower CP. The wide-scope expression of the examples in (41) evidences that moving an adjunct *wh*-phrase out of an adjunct clause essentially constructs a Pied-Piping Effect where the [+*wh*] feature of the adjunct has been percolated to the matrix CP without being blocked.

(41) a. Libai mai-le LGB [(yao) **zemeyang** kan]
Libai buy-Perf LGB want how read
"(lit.) Libai bought LGB how to read it?"
b.? Libai mai-le LGB [**weisheme** (yao) kan]
Libai buy-Perf LGB why want read
"(lit.) Libai bought LGB why to read?"
c. Libai mai-le LGB [**kan-bu-kan**]
Libai buy-Perf LGB read-not-read
"(lit.) Libai bought LGB to read it or not?"

Given the observation and analyses above, Consecutive Constructions in Mandarin do not structure as [NP VP1 VP2] but actually [NP VP1 CP] with an adjunct CP containing V2. However, some other possibilities also have to be considered that the CP might be something else other than an adjunct clause, such as a coordinated clause or a relative clause.

3.2 CP2 Is an Adjunct Clause of V1'

It is manifest that CP2 is not a complement clause of V1 since CP2 is not strictly subcategorized by V1 and it is optional. In this section, I will show two other possible alternatives, CP coordination constructions and relative clause constructions, for Mandarin Consecutive Constructions and provide some empirical evidence to prove that CP2 in Mandarin Consecutive Constructions is actually an adjunct clause attached to V1'.

3.2.1 CP2 Is NOT in a CP Coordination Construction

First, by considering the scope of the perfective Negation *mei(you)*, I would like to compare a CP Coordination Construction like (42) with the previous Consecutive Construction sentence (36b) which is illustrated as (43):

---

[6] The reason that the example (41b) is not perfectly acceptable may be attributed to different semantic representation since the answer of this sentence can be "He may give LGB away instead of reading it."

(42) [$_{CP1}$ Libai ***mei(you)*** [$_{VP1}$ **mai** rou]] [$_{CP2}$ Dufu [$_{VP1}$ **he**-le jou]]
Libai not (Perf.) buy meat Dufu drink-Perf wine
"Libai didn't buy meat and Dufu drank wine."

(43) [$_{CP1}$ Libai [***mei(you)*** [$_{VP1}$ [$_{V1'}$ **mai** LGB] [$_{V1'}$ [$_{CP2}$ [$_{VP2}$ *e*1 **kan** *e*2]]]]]]
Libai not (Perf.) buy LGB read
"Libai didn't buy LGB to read."
"*Libai didn't buy LGB but he read it."

In the CP Coordination Construction (42), the scope of the perfective Negation of *mei(you)* covers only V1 *mai* "buy" but not V2 *kan* "read". As noted previously, the scope of the Nagation *mei(you)* in the Consecutive Construction (43) covers not only just V1 *mai* "buy" but also V2 *kan* "read". Since V2 is in an adjunct clause CP2 which is attached to V1', the entire sentence is in the scope of the perfective Negation *mei(you)*.

Secondly, unlike (41a), the *wh*-phrase *weisheme* "why" in (44) does not take wide scope expression since the [+*wh*] feature of *weisheme* can only be percolated to the operator position of CP2 rather than CP1. Moving the *wh*-expression to CP1 will violate Coordinate Structure Constraint (CSC).

(44) Libai shou [[$_{CP1}$ Dufu **zou**-le] erqie [$_{CP2}$ Baijuyi ***weisheme*** **lai**-le]]
Libai said Dufu leave-Perf and Baijuyi why come-Perf
"Libai said Dufu left and why Baijuyi came."

Thirdly, if CP2 is in a Coordination Construction, which is a coordinate clause containing irrelevant information of V1, like the ones in (42) and (44), the sentence (45) should then be accepted. However, this is not the case. As exemplified in (45), V1 *mai* "buy" and V2 *he* "drink" do not involve any "consecutive" relation in the sentence. CP2 in Mandarin Coordination Constructions therefore is not a CP coordination clause.

(45) * Libai **mai**-le shu **he**-le
Libai buy-Perf book drink-Perf

3.2.2 CP2 Is NOT a Relative Clause

Compare the relative clauses in (46) with the adjunct CP clauses in (41), the argument *wh*-extraction from the relative clause in (46a) is grammatical whereas the adjunct *wh*-extraction in (46b) and (46c) is illegitimate.

(46) a. Libai **mai**-le [$_{CP}$[**shei** xie] de] shu
Libai buy-Perf who write D book
"(lit) Libai bought the book who wrote it?"

b.* Libai **mai**-le [$_{CP}$[**weisheme** xie] de] shu
Libai buy-Perf why write D book

c.* Libai **mai**-le [$_{CP}$[**xie-bu-xie**] de] shu
Libai buy-Perf write-not-write D book

As suggested by Nishigauchi (1990), what is relevant to the facts here is the distinction in terms of syntactic categories. A *wh*-phrase, according to Nishigauchi's Pied-Piping Mechanism, must be "identical" in syntactic category, such as [±N], to the dominating node in order for its [+*wh*] feature to be percolated. There are several possibilities with respect to how the procedure works. As illustrated in (47a), if the operator X is identical in [−N] feature to the dominating CP, the [+*wh*] feature percolation can then be licensed. Accordingly, the grammatical extraction of the adjunct *wh*-phrases from the adjunct CP2s in (41a-c) is attributed to the fact that the adjunct *wh*-question and *A-not-A* clause contain the identical [−N] feature. Hence, the [+*wh*] feature in (41a-c) can be percolated to the matrix clauses. The grammatical (46a) also is explained by the reason that the *wh*-phrase *shei* "who", which contains [+N] feature identified by the dominating CP, is identical to the [+N] feature of the relative clause. Therefore, the [+*wh*] feature in (46a) can be legitimately percolated. However, as indicated in (47b), the percolation of a [+*wh*] feature will never be licensed if the operator X and its dominating CP contain different values. This explains why the adjunct *wh*-phrases in (46b) and (46c) fail to extract from the relative clauses. The [−N] feature of the adjunct *wh*-phrases is not identical to the [+N] feature of its dominating CP, the relative clauses, therefore the [+*wh*] feature in (46b) and (46c) cannot be percolated to the matrix clauses.

(47)

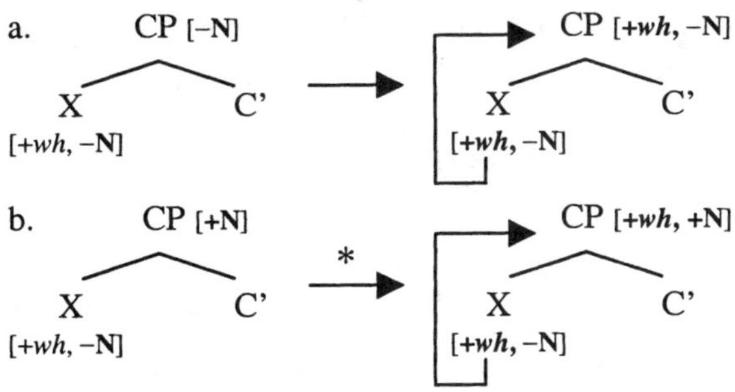

Given the analysis above, the distinction between the extraction of adjunct *wh*-phrases from a relative clause and that from an adjunct clause may then be captured by a theoretical way that the occurrence of Pied Piping Effect is due to proper feature percolation. It is thus evidenced that CP2 is an adjunct clause rather than a relative clause.

3.2.3 CP2 Is an Adjunct Clause

It has been presented previously that the claim that CP2 is an adjunct clause attached to V1' can be captured by Pied-Piping Effect. Given this analysis, we may explain why the pied-piping answer in (48a), rather than the short answer in (48b), is appropriate as one of the possible answers of (41a).

(48) a. Libai mai-le LGB [[**han xuecheng**] (yiqi) **kan**]
Libai buy-Perf LGB with student together read
"(lit.) Libai bought LGB to read it with students."
b.* **han xuecheng**
with student

The interpretation of (48) can be essentially captured if we assume that the LF representation for (41a) is something like (49), where the entire description *y* that contains the *wh*-adjunct *x* is moved to the operator position of the matrix sentence CP1 by Pied-Piping Effect. Notice that the entire expression that corresponds to *zemeyang kan* "how to read" occupies the operator position of CP1 as well as it matches the pied-piping answer (48a) rather than the short answer (48b) since, according to Pied-Piping Effect, [+*wh*] feature percolation of the adjunct *wh*-phrase is not blocked.

(49) [$_{CP1}$ ***y*** [Libai [$_{V'}$ **mai**-le LGB] [$_{V'}$ [$_{CP2}$ [*e*1 [**WH*x***]$_x$ **kan** *e*2]$_y$]]]]
Libai buy-Perf LGB read

The facts that adjunct *wh*-phrases have undergone Pied-Piping movement within an adjunct CP clause and that the [+*wh*] feature has been percolated to the matrix clause can give a proper account for the illegitimate sentences in (50) and (51). The failure of the extraction of *wh*-adjuncts in (50a) and (50b) is attributed to the interference of another *wh*-adjunct *weisheme* "why" which occurs in the matrix clauses and causes *Wh*-island Constraint.

(50) a.* Libai ***weisheme*** mai LGB [(yao) **zemeyang** kan]
Libai why buy LGB want how read
b.* Libai ***weisheme*** mai LGB [**kan-bu-kan**]
Libai why buy LGB read-not-read

The Negation *mei(you)* in (51a) and (51b) also throws impediments in the way of the adjunct *wh*-extraction and thus causes the problematic sentences.

(51) a.* Libai ***mei(you)*** mai LGB [(yao) **zemeyang** kan]
Libai not (Perf.) buy LGB want how read
b.* Libai ***mei(you)*** mai LGB [**kan-bu-kan**]
Libai not (Perf.) buy LGB read-not-read

The Pied-Piping Effect of adjunct *wh*-phrases properly provides a support for the claim that although Mandarin and Edo share the same SVC order on the surface, differing from Edo, Mandarin Consecutive Constructions contain an adjunct CP clause attached to V1' in the structure. However, the fact that Mandarin and Edo share the same SVC order brings out some questions: Is the fact a mere coincidence or it has psychological reality? What kind of parameters that children of Mandarin and Edo set up would end up exhibiting the same surface structure? These are the questions that need to be explored in the future work.

4. Conclusion

In this article, I have argued that V2s in Mandarin Resultative Constructions are Achievement whereas those in Edo are Stative. An inner aspectual head α is proposed as a projection selected by CAUSE verb and functionally it contains [+telic] feature which requires the ACTION-RESULT event in Resultative Constructions to achieve the property of "completion" in the Accomplishment interpretation. V2s in Mandarin, unlike those in Edo, contain a temporal aspect feature [+telic]. This aspectual property is the crucial parametric factor that triggers Mandarin V2s to raise to and check the [+telic] feature with the Inner Aspect α. Eventually VVCs are formed by verb incorporation in Mandarin and the V2-movement causes the different distribution of Mandarin Resultative Constructions. Consecutive Constructions in Mandarin, I propose, contain an adjunct CP clause attached to V1'. Pied-Piping Effect provides empirical evidence to show that this CP is not in a coordination construction, or a relative clause modifying the object of V1. Although Mandarin and Edo have the same SVC order in their Consecutive Constructions, the evidence provided in this paper proves that these two languages are in fact structurally distinctive.

References

Baker, M. (1989) "Object sharing and projection in serial verb constructions", *Linguistic Inquiry* 20, 513-553.

Baker, M & O. T. Stewart (1996) "Unaccusativity and the adjective-verb distinction: Edo evidence" *NELS 27.*

Baker, M. (1997) "Thematic roles and syntactic structure", *Elements of Grammar*, 73-137, ed. by Liliane Haegeman, Kluwer Academic Press, Dordrecht, the Netherlands.

Cheng, L. L.-S. & C.-T. J. Huang (1994) "On the argument structure of Resultative Compounds", In *Honor of William S.-Y. Wang: Interdisciplinary Studies on Language and Language Change*, eds. M. Y. Chen and O. J.-L. Tzeng, 187-221, Pyramid Press, Taipei.

Cheng, L. L.-S., C.-T. J. Huang, Y.-H. A. Li & C.-C. J. Tang (1997) "Causative compounds across Chinese dialects: A study of Cantonese, Mandarin and Taiwanese", *Chinese Languages and Linguistics* 4, 199-224, Academia Sinica, Taipei.

Chu, C.-C. (1976) "Some semantic aspects of action verbs", *Lingua* 40, 43-54.

Déchaine, R.-M. (1993) *Predicates Across Categories*, Doctoral dissertation, University of Massachusetts, Amherst.

Ernst, T. (1992) "On the negation in Mandarin Chinese", paper presented at *NACCL 4*, University of Michigan, Ann Arbor.

Gu, Y. (1992) *The Syntax of Resultative and Causative Compounds in Chinese*, Doctoral dissertation, Cornell University.

Hale, K. & S. J. Keyser (1993) "On argument structure and the lexical expression of syntactic relations", in K. Hale & S. J. Keyser (eds.), *The View from Building 20*, 53-110, MIT Press, Cambridge, Mass.

Hoekstra, T. (1988) "Small clause results", *Lingua* 74, 101-139.

Levin, B. M. Rappaport Hovav (1995) *Unaccusativity: At the Syntax-Lexical Semantics Interface*, MIT Press, Cambridge, Mass.

Li, C. & S. Thompson (1977) "Development of the causative in Mandarin Chinese: Interaction of diachronic processes in syntax", *Syntax and Semantics* 6, 477-492, ed. Masayoshi Shibatani, Academic Press, New York.

Li, C. & S. Thompson (1981) *Mandarin Chinese: A Functional Reference Grammar*, University of California, Berkeley and Los Angles, California.

Li, Y.-F. (1990) "On V-V Compounds in Chinese", *Natural Language and Linguistic Theory* 8, 177-207.

Li, Y.-H. A (1985) *Abstract Case in Chinese*, Doctoral dissertation, University of Southern California.

Nichigauchi, T. (1990) *Quantification in the Theory of Grammar*, Kluwer Academic Press, Dordrecht.

Rizzi, L. (1997) "The fine structure of the left periphery", *Elements of Grammar*, 281-337, ed. by Liliane Haegeman, Kluwer Academic Press, Dordrecht, the Netherlands.

Smith, C. (1991) *The Parameter of Aspect*, Kluwer Academic Press, Dordrecht, the Netherlands.

Stewart, O. T. (1998) *The Serial Verb Construction Parameter*, Doctoral dissertation, McGill University.

Sybesma, R. (1992) *Causatives and Accomplishments: The Case of Chinese Ba*, Dordrecht: Holland Institute of Generative Linguistics.

Sybesma, R. (1997) "Why Chinese verb-*le* is a resultative predicate", *Journal of East Asian Linguistics* 6.

Tai, J. H.-Y. (1984) "Verbs and times in Chinese: Vendler's four categories", *Papers From the Parasession on Lexical Semantics*, eds. D. Testen, V. Mishra and J. Drogo, 289-296, Chicago Linguistic Society.

Tang, C.-C. J. (1990) *Mandarin Chinese Phrase Structure and The Extended X'-Theory*, Doctoral dissertation, Cornell University.

Tang, S.-W. (1997) "The parametric approach to the Resultative Construction in Chinese and English", *UCI Working Papers in Linguistics* 3, eds. L. C.-S. Liu and K Takeda, 203-226, Irvine.

Tang, T.-C. C. (1979) *Studies in Mandarin Chinese Syntax*, Student Book Co., Taipei.

Travis, L. (1997) "The Syntax of Achievements", *Proceedings of AFLA III*.

Travis, L. (forthcoming) *Inner Aspect*, Kluwer Academic Press, Dordrecht, the Netherlands.

Wo pao-le ge feikuai and Reanalysis of the Classifier *ge*

ZOE WU
University of Southern California

1. Introduction

This paper is an examination of the status of the classifier *ge* in nominal and verbal environments. There are two types of related elements pronounced as *ge* in Mandarin Chinese. One is a general classifier which is commonly used to "type" or individuate a noun which follows it for purposes of counting. The other *ge* will be shown to be used to count the event denoted by the predicate in which *ge* itself occurs as a single event. While the first use of *ge* has long been known as the most general classifier in Mandarin, the second type of *ge* has not been investigated thoroughly in the literature. The discussion in this paper will be focused on the second type of *ge*, and is organized as follows. Section 2 briefly notes the use of ge as the most general classifier for count nouns. Section 3 then discusses the distribution and semantic contribution of the event classifier *ge*. Section 4 outlines the syntactic properties of the event classifier *ge* and section 5 makes a proposal to structurally encode *ge* within the DP in a way which mirrors

On the Formal Way to Chinese Languages.
Sze-Wing Tang and Chen-Sheng Luther Liu (eds.).

these central syntactic properties. Section 6 then finally argues for the grammaticalization and reanalysis of event *ge* from the status of a classifier to that of a new indefinite determiner.

2. *Ge* as a General Classifier for Nouns

The most frequent use of *ge* is to serve as a classifier for its following noun, preceded by a numeral and directly followed by a noun, as in (1):

(1) wo you liang ge pingguo.
I have two GE apple
'I have two apples.'

When the numeral preceding a classifier is "one," it is well-noted that this numeral can in fact be deleted, as shown in example (2):

(2) wo chi-le (yi) ge juzi.
I eat-LE (one) GE tangerine
'I ate a tangerine.'

Ge as a general noun classifier is defined as "individual classifier" by Chao (1968). The noun following *ge* is a count noun denoting an object which usually does not have great volume and has to be a separable entity in the physical world. That is, the entity is physically "bounded" in Allen's (1966) sense. The verbs that can occur with the noun classifier *ge* are diverse, and stative verbs, action verbs and achievement verbs are all possible.

3. *Ge* as a Classifier for Events Denoted by the Predicates

The second use of *ge*, which constitutes the main focus of this paper, is where it occurs preceded by a verb and followed by a bare noun, a classifier-measure string, an adjective, or a clause-like idiom. In what follows, this second *ge* will be shown to contribute to the aspectuality of the predicate and makes the denoted activity counted as a single event.

3.1 Occurrence Between a Verb and Its Cognate Object

Although in its most common use *ge* follows a numeral and introduces regular concrete count nouns, it may also occur between certain V-O compounds. In (3a), the object part of the compound is only licensed to occur when together with the verbal part of the compound, and in (3b), the verbal part *tiao* 'jump' can only mean 'dance' when it occurs with the object part *wu* 'dance'. When *ge* occurs separating the verb and its object, the sequence *ge*-O functions like an individuated cognate object of the verb:

(3) a. women qu you ge yong ba!
we go swim GE swim Prt
'Let's go for a swim (do a swimming)!'
b. women zuotian qu na-jia wuting tiao-le ge wu.
we yesterday go that-CL club jump-LE GE dance
'We went to that club and did an activity of dancing.'

Some speakers even accept examples such as (4), in which *ge* intervenes between the verbal members of a V-V compound:

(4) xue ge xi
study GE study
'do an activity of studying'

In these cases, it can be argued that *ge* is used to help count out a single event and cause the action to be interpreted as being telically bounded. For example, if *ge* is omitted in (3a), the interpretation of the verb *youyong* is as a simple unbounded action of 'swimming'. However, when *ge* occurs between the two syllables of 'swim', (3a) in fact means to 'do a swimming' (and there is a single swimming event). Similarly in (3b), *ge* allows in the interpretation of one dancing event. This event may consist of one dance or more than one dance; the main point is that *ge* helps count out the event as a whole.

Above in example (2) with nominal classifier *ge* it has been observed that the classifier is optionally able to appear without a preceding numeral, and that when this happens, the numeral 'one' is implied. Consequently here where these V-O and V-V sequences occur with a 'bare' *ge* intervening, it can similarly be suggested that the numeral one is implied and that the occurrence of *ge* makes the action verb countable as one event. Indeed, it is possible to insert the element *yi* 'one' in (3) and (4):

(5) a. you yi ge yong
swim one GE swim
'do a swimming'

b. xue yi ge xi
study one GE study
'do an activity of studying'

3.2 Occurrence Between a Verb and an Indefinite Object

Ge can also directly occur between a verb and a regular non-cognate object nominal. This post-verbal nominal is usually indefinite and is often a bare noun, as in (6). Note that the appropriate specific/non-general classifier for *yu* 'fish' is *tiao* as in (7). As in the examples in (3), it can be suggested that when *ge* comes in between the V-N sequence it functions to quantify over the predicate/event and results in a single buying event. Note that in (6) the interpretation when *ge* is used is that there is a single delivery event which could involve several fish, whereas in (7) with the regular/specific classifier *tiao*, the interpretation is that only a single fish is delivered. Consequently the use of *ge* might seem to relate more to counting the event/predicate than the nominal object:

(6) wo qu song ge yu.
I go deliver GE fish
'Let me go do a fish-delivering.'

(7) wo qu song tiao yu.
I go deliver CL fish
'Let me go deliver a fish.'

(8) shows the occurrence of a locative object introduced by *ge*:

(8) a. women lai tiao ge sheng. (see also Liu 1993)
we come jump GE rope
'Let's do a rope-jumping.'
b. women qu zou ge lu.
we go walk GE road
'Let's go take a walk (do a walking on the road).'

Here (8) is in contrast with (6) and (7) where it is possible to have either the specific classifier or the 'event' classifier *ge*. Examples with locative objects such as (8a/b) however do not allow for similar substitution of a noun's specific classifier, as shown in (9):

(9) a. *women lai tiao gen sheng
we come jump CL rope
b. *women qu zou tiao lu.
we go walk CL road

From this it can be concluded that *ge* is not a simple replacement for more specific nominal classifiers and does not simply function to introduce a regular NP object. Whereas *tiao-sheng* 'jump-rope' in (8a) does allow *ge* to introduce *sheng* 'rope,' in (9a) this same sequence does not allow for the regular classifier *gen* (which would be an appropriate classifier for *sheng* in other situations). There is consequently an important difference between *ge* and other classifiers whose function is to introduce and individuate simple NP objects.

Next it can be noted that the post-verbal nominal following *ge* is often a numeral-measure phrase. This numeral-measure phrase can be an object of an action verb (10a) or occur as a duration/frequency phrase (10b):

(10) a. chi ge san wan fan
eat GE 3 bowl rice
'do an eating of 3 bowls of rice'

b. qu Bali wan-le ge liang tian
go Paris play-ASP GE 2 day
'did a 2-day trip to Paris'

Comparing (10a/b) with (11a/b) it is found that when *ge* is used, the whole verb phrase has to be interpreted as a single event or a single group of events. For example, in (10a), the inclusion of *ge* has the interpretative effect that the eating of the three bowls of rice has to be understood to take place at one specific time, while in (11a), the three bowls of rice could be eaten at different meals.

(11) a. chi san wan fan
eat three bowl rice
'eat three bowls of rice'

b. wan-le liang tian
play-ASP 2 day
'had fun for 2 days'

This single-event interpretation associated with the predicate can be highlighted by the interaction of quantified or plural NP subjects and *ge*-marked objects. Sentence (12) means Zhangsan ate three bowls of rice at one time and Lisi ate three bowls of rice at one time. Strictly speaking, although there may be two events involved, *ge* functions to set the boundary of the activity denoted by the predicate: for each person the three bowls of rice is necessarily consumed during one eating event.

(12) Zhangsan he Lisi ge chi-le ge san wan fan.
Zhangsan and Lisi each eat-LE ge three bowl rice
'Zhangsan and Lisi each at one time ate three bowls of rice.'

3.3 *Ge* introducing a Simple Resultative/Descriptive Adjective

Ge can also be used to follow an action verb and precede certain adjectives in an adverbial usage. As shown in (13), *ge* can be used to introduce a descriptive adjective, which otherwise cannot follow the verb. This intervention of *ge* again results in the interpretation that a single event (of 'fast-running') occurred:

(13) Pingchang kan-bu-chu-lai, zuotian de yundonghui ta dao pao-le ge kuai
usually can-not-see yesterday 's sports event he but run-ASP GE fast
'I can't see that in him in daily life, but he demonstrated a fast running in yesterday's sports meet.'

With many adjectives the interpretation is that the activity depicted by the verb is carried out until the point described by the adjective is reached:

(14) a. wo yao chi ge bao.
I want eat GE stuffed
'I want to do a satisfying eating (keep eating until I am stuffed)'

b. ta ma-le ge gou.
he curse-ASP GE enough
'He kept cursing until it was enough.'

Concerning the use of *ge* with adjectives/stative verbs here, it can be suggested that *ge* in fact has an aspect-related function. Following ideas in Tenny (1987) and Borer (1994), it can be assumed that the occurrence of certain nominal objects may be necessary to convert atelic activity predicates into telic bounded events, and that *ge* here critically functions to convert a non-nominal category into a nominal type which will result in such an interpretation (nominal elements 'measuring-out' an event and resulting in an event being bounded when the object is fully 'consumed'-- see Tenny (1987)/Borer (1994). The use of *ge* as a simple nominal classifier can therefore be suggested to have widened significantly and may now be used to convert elements of adjectival/stative verb type into nominal type elements.

A further peculiarity of the *ge*-construction is that when the adjective/stative verb following *ge* can be made more complex by being combined with some kind of degree-type modifier, such an expression generally sounds better than an unmodified *ge*-O sequence, as seen in (15a) and (15b). The modified adjective preceded by *ge* in these examples denotes an activity carried out to some extreme point/degree.

(15) a. he-le ge ?(da-)zui
drink-ASP GE big-drunk
'did a completely-drunk drinking'

b. pao-le ge ?(fei-)kuai
run-ASP GE fly-fast
'did a fast-as-flying running'

Concerning this effect of adding a 'modifier' to an adjective in (15) vs. (14), it can be suggested that if the object is modified and in a certain way made more specific/identifiable then this enables it to function as a delimiter more easily, either providing an end-point or otherwise measuring out the event to make it telic. If the end-point is some kind of extreme (a 'big drunk') then the telic reading appears to be more easy to license.

3.4 *Ge* introducing an Idiom or Fixed Expression

Above in section 3.3 it was shown that the element introduced by *ge* can be an adjective/stative verb, and the suggestion was made that *ge* may be functioning to provide an essentially nominal complement to the verb which precedes it. Here it can be noted that the element which is introduced into the VP via *ge* can actually also be a *clause-like idiom*, expressing the extreme result of some action.[1] Again in such instances the preceding verb is an action verb and the *ge*-XP has the function of converting the predicate into an accomplishment:

(16) a. ping ge ni-si-wo-huo
fight GE you-die-I-live
'make a terrible fight

b. nao-le ge ji-quan-bu-ning
fuss-ASP GE chicken-dog-not-peace
'caused a big turmoil'

3.5 *Ge* with Perfective but not Imperfective Aspect

There are also certain aspectual restrictions on *ge*-forms, and when the predicate has an overt aspect marker, as in (17) and (18), it is found that event classifier *ge* can co-occur with the perfective marker *-le*, but not with the imperfective markers *zai* and *-zhe.* This may perhaps be because imperfective aspect markers focus on the internal stages of an event (as in Smith 1997) and event classifier *ge*-marked objects are interpreted as the objects of an unanalyzable single event with no visible internal stages, in this sense being more like instantaneous achievement-type predicates. Such an unanalyzable single event property will also account for the fact that in *ge*-marked objects which have numerals, such as (10) and (12) above, there can only be a single event interpretation and no possibility of a multiple event reading - the internal parts of a *ge* object are simply unavailable for individual interpretation/imperfective aspectual modification:

(17) *Wo zheng zai die ge tou-po-xie-liu.
I right at fall GE head-break-blood-flow
Intended: ‘I am falling so hard that I got a broken bleeding head.'

(18) Wo die-le/*zhe ge tou-po-xie-liu.
I fall-PERF/IMP GE head-break-blood-flow
'I fell/*am-falling so hard that I got a broken bleeding head.'

[1] These sequences are 'clause-like' in the sense that a full, overt argument structure is present.

3.6 Apparent Constraints on Verb Selection

While it was noted in section 2 that noun classifier *ge* can occur with a stative verb, an action verb, or an achievement verb, most of the occurrences of event classifier *ge* actually follow an action verb, and often *ge* may not occur with a stative verb:

(19) *Ta xiang you ge san zhi bi.
he want have GE three CL pen

This constraint on verb selection can be shown to be aspectual in nature. If the *ge*-XP is able to express an end point, even stative verbs are in fact permissible. For example, in (20), the subject wants to experience love to a certain exciting endpoint/degree. Once again it seems therefore that the *ge*-XP functions to change an atelic predicate into a telic predicate.

(20) Ta xiangyao ai ge si-qu-huo-lai.
ta want love ge die-go-live-come
'He wants to experience an extreme romance.'

4. Syntactic Properties

4.1 Event *ge* introducing a Non-predicational Adjective

Here I would like to note a further restriction on the event *ge* which can be observed when *ge* combines with adjectives. Basically it is found that the adjective in such cases cannot be in predicational form but rather must be "bare."[2] When adjectives occur as predicates in declarative sentences they are accompanied by a modifier such as *hen* 'very' or *tai* 'too' as in (21), whereas when they occur attributively they appear bare, as in (22):

(21) a. Ta hen piaoliang.
ta very pretty
'She is very pretty.'

b. Zhe-ge fangzi tai jiu.
this-CL house too old
'This house is too old.'

[2] Note that earlier it was observed that sometimes an adjective is more natural with *ge* if it is combined with an element indicating high/extreme degree of the adjective, as in example (15). This kind of modification does not result in predicational forms, unlike the use of *hen* and *tai* attempted in (23) and so still leaves the adjectives 'bare' in a certain sense.

(22) xin shu
new book
'new books'[3]

Turning to *ge*-forms it is found that adjectives which occur following *ge* cannot be modified by *hen* 'very' or *tai* 'too', as shown in (23).

(23) a. *shuo-le ge hen qingchu
say-ASP GE very clear
b. *chi-le ge tai bao
eat-ASP GE too full

Secondly, there is a further restriction found in adjectival reduplication forms. Chinese allows for bisyllabic adjectival reduplication in two basic forms commonly referred to as the AABB Form and the ABAB form. The AABB reduplication form is referred to as the 'vivid' adjectival form, while an ABAB reduplication is said to be predicational reduplication and occurs in standard predicate type positions as in (24) (see here Chao 1968):

(24) a. Mingtian women chuqu tongkuaitongkuai.
tomorrow we go out enjoy
'Let's go out and enjoy ourselves tomorrow.'
b. Jintian ni hua-yixia-zhuang, rang ziji piaoliangpiaoliang.
today you put one makeup let self beautify
'Why don't you put on makeup and make yourself look beautiful today.'

In the *ge*-construction it is found that adjectives may be reduplicated according to the AABB pattern but not the ABAB predicational pattern:

(25) a. chi ge tong-tong-kuai-kuai
eat GE over-enjoyed
'do a very satisfying eating'
b. daban ge piao-piao-liang-liang
dress-up GE beautiful
'dressed to be very beautiful'

(26) a. *chi ge tongkuai-tongkuai
eat GE over-enjoy
'eat until satisfied'
b. *daban ge piaoliang-piaoliang
dress-up GE beautiful
'dressed up beautifully'

A third restriction on the combination of *ge* with adjectives is that the adjective following *ge* cannot be syntactically negated. As shown in (27), *ge* cannot introduce an adjective syntactically negated by *bu* 'not'.

---

[3] If *hen* 'very' is added to the adjective, the element *de* must also occur, suggesting that this is a relative clause structure and a predication, e.g.:
(i) hen xin *(de) shu
very new DE book
'books that are very new'

(27) *shuo-le ge bu qingchu
say-ASP GE not clearly
'say (it) not clearly.'

However, if the negation is part of a fixed negative adjective, as in (28), it is a legitimate item to follow *ge*. Being able to be *syntactically* negated is another characteristic of a syntactic predicate, so again there is evidence that a predicational adjective cannot follow *ge*.

(28) shuo-le ge bu-qing-bu-chu
say-ASP GE not-clearly
'make a vague statement'

Lastly, an adjective following *ge* cannot be A-not-A questioned. As shown in (29), *ge*-sentences cannot be made into an A-not-A question by questioning the adjective. This is another predicational characteristic that the adjective selected by *ge* is lacking.

(29) *Ta shuo ge qing-bu-qing-chu?
he say GE clear-not-clear
'Did he make it clear?'

I would like to suggest that these restrictions may be essentially similar in kind to other restrictions noted to constrain *nominalization* forms in certain languages, and may be explained if it is assumed that (a) *ge* is functioning as a nominalizer (a categorization in fact suggested in S. Lü 1984), and (b) *ge* selects for a complement which is syntactically less than a full clausal predicate.

Specifically concerning point (b), it has been noted that in languages such as Korean there is variation in the type of predicate constituent selected by different nominalizers. Following initial work in Yoon (1990), Lapointe & Nielsen (1996) show that Korean Type II and Type III nomimalizations have certain critically different clusters of properties. The nominalizer in the former selects for a full clausal complement which has an overt tense morpheme, a nominative subject and allows for sentential negation, sentential adverbs and clause-internal scrambling. The nominalizer in the latter however seems to select for a more restricted constituent which does not allow scrambling, negation, sentential adverbs, nominative subjects or tense/aux elements (subjects instead occur in genitive case). Such a contrastive patterning can be captured quite simply if it is assumed that the Type II nominalization involves selection by the nominalizer of a TP-level constituent, whereas in Type III nominalizations the nominalizer selects a VP-type level constituent.

Returning to Chinese, with *ge* one finds that although a predicate may be selected and even project its arguments (as in the idiom cases in 16), there are certain syntactic properties associated with full regular clauses which may not occur in the predicate sequence following *ge*, e.g. clausal/sentential negation and A-not-A question forms. Such syntactic properties, and possibly also the type of reduplication found with predicational adjectives noted may all be assumed to require a certain minimal amount of clausal structure in order to be licensed. For example, clausal/sentential negation would occur located in the functional part of a clause and not low down within VP/AdjP, and A-not-A forms arguably require the presence of a Q-morpheme in I^0, hence the functional projection IP, etc. This absence of clausal negation, A-not-A questions and predicational adjectival reduplication can consequently be suggested to indicate that the functional structure necessary to support such properties is also absent, in a way which is rather similar to Korean Type III nominalizations. Similar to Korean Type III nominalizations, I would therefore now like to suggest that *ge* is in fact a nominalizer which takes as a potential complement simply a bare predicate (maybe an AdjP) without allowing any of the higher clausal functional projections which would be necessary to support negation, A-not-A and predicational reduplication, etc.[4]

4.2 *Ge* Licensing the Expletive 'It'

Here I would like to note a last interesting aspect of the *ge* paradigm: its occurrence with *ta* 'it' in object expletive contexts. Lin (1993) shows that expletive *ta* can often co-occur with object DPs and suggests that an expletive-associate chain is formed between *ta* and the real argument DP, the argument raising to replace *ta* in SpecAgrOP at LF. (30) illustrates this use of *ta* with an object associate:

(30) wo kan-le ta san-ben-xiaoshuo
I read-ASP it 3-CL-novel
'I read three novels.'

Here it can be shown that *ge*-XPs may also often co-occur with the expletive *ta* 'it' (called by Lin 1993 an expletive object). The element

[4] Given the well-formedness of (28) it may need to be assumed that some instances of negation are combined with other elements *in the lexicon*. This is a position which has actually frequently been adopted in the past, for example by certain authors working on contracted negative auxiliary elements such as English 'can't', 'won't', etc (in Zwicky 1977), or Cantonese *mo* = *mei* + *yau* in (Matthews & Yip 1994).

introduced by *ge* when following *ta* can be either an adjective or an indefinite nominal which is a measure phrase (or more marginally a bare noun), as shown in (31):

(31) a. chi ta ge tongkuai
eat it GE satisfied
'have a satisfying eating'

b. pao ta ge san quan
run it GE 3 rounds
'do a three-lap running'

c. ??tiao ta ge wu
dance it GE dance
'do an activity of dancing'

What is important to note is that *ta* in these object expletive structures always requires a DP associate. This therefore implies that *ge* is crucially functioning to provide a nominal DP expression in the event *ge* construction, sometimes converting non-nominal categories (such as adjectives) into DP elements. Secondly, *ta* has been noted by Lin to tolerate only DP associates which are headed by *weak determiners* such as *ji*-CL-N 'several N' and *yi-xie* 'some NP', and not DPs headed by strong determiners such as *nei*-CL-N 'that NP' or *mei*-CL-N 'every NP':

(32) wo yao kan ta ji-ben/yi-xie lishi-xiaoshuo
I want look it few-CL/some history novel
'I want to read a few/some history novels.'

(33) *wo yao kan ta nei-ben/mei-ben lishi-xiaoshuo
I want look it that-CL/every-CL history novel

This would seem to indicate that the *ge*-headed nominals must also be DPs with some weak determiner element in the D-head position.[5] [6]

---

[5] Lin (1993) and Borer (1994) essentially both assume that the DP-object-associate raises to SpecAgrO/AspP at LF. For Borer this has the effect of inducing a telic reading, activating the Asp-head which is associated with telicity.

[6] Note that when *ge* is not present, only the (b) example in (31) survives, as shown in (i).

(i) a. *chi ta tongkuai
eat it satisfied

b. pao ta san quan
run it three CL-rounds
'run three rounds'

c. *tiao ta wu
dance it dance

This is because the expletive *ta* requires a weakly-quantified DP associate, as noted. Where *ge* is present, this provides the necessary type of DP object associate for *ta*, but when it is removed only (b) has a weakly-quantified DP following *ta*; (a) and (c) can be suggested to unacceptable because *tongkuai* and *wu* are interpreted as verbal/non-nominal and hence of the wrong categorial type to constitute associates for *ta*.

5. The Proposal: *ge* as a Weak Unselective Determiner in D^0

Having provided a characterization of a number of restrictions and patterns found with what has been referred to loosely as 'event *ge*', I would now like to argue that the evidence presented would all seem to indicate a single solution: the element *ge* is currently used not only as a regular numeral classifier, but also now as a weak unselective determiner with a non-specific indefinite specification. It will be pointed out that this element is similar in certain respects to the unselective determiners reported to exist in Salish languages by Davis and Matthewson (1997).

5.1 *Ge* as a Nominalizer

In order to reach the conclusion above, a brief review of the patterns observed earlier will be helpful. In section 3 it was observed that the element *ge* may occur preceding nouns which are already quantified by numeral-classifier expressions, as for example in (34):

(34) he ge san-ping jiu (see also 10a/b)
drink GE three-CL wine
'drink three bottles of beer at one time'

It was also significantly shown that *ge* may occur introducing not only elements which are clearly nominal (as in 34), but also other XP-types which may not be nominal at all, a common case being adjectives as in (35a), but also clause-like idiom expressions as in (35b) and sub-parts of V-V compounds as in (35c):

(35) a. chi ge bao
eat GE full
'do a satisfying eating'

b. wen ge shui-luo-shi-chu
ask GE water-fall-rock-out
'do a thorough interrogation'

c. xue ge xi
study GE study
'do an activity of studying'

In this sense it seems that *ge* is rather unselective in terms of the syntactic category type it selects and introduces into the object position.[7]

---

[7] The *output* of applying *ge* to any of its possible complement XP types is however assumed to be consistent, and *ge* as a nominalizer applied to any of these XP will result in a constituent YP $[_{YP}$ *ge* XP$]$ which is outwardly specified as being a nominal-type projection.

A comparison was also made between *ge* and other regular classifier types and it was argued that *ge* is not simply replacing a more specialized regular classifier when it occurs in certain objects, as the attempt to replace *ge* with a regular classifier is often found to be unacceptable:

(36) tiao ge/*gen sheng
jump GE/CL-strip rope
'do a rope jumping/*jump one rope'

This would seem to indicate that *ge* is not simply occurring in the standard classifier position and that "event *ge*" forms do not result from simple deletion of the numeral *yi* 'one'. Rather, *ge* would appear to have a rather different status from standard classifiers and is arguably occurring in a different syntactic position.

It was also shown that the *ge*-XP has an important aspectual function, often serving to provide either an end point for an activity predicate or an object which can be measured-out in the course of the event (and so also naturally bounding the predicate in this function too). Data reviewed indicated that *ge*-XPs could only occur with perfective and not imperfective aspect-markers, this being fully consistent with the assumption that *ge*-XPs function to convert a non-telic predicate into one which is aspectually bounded. Noting that work carried out by Tenny (1987) and Borer (1994) has argued that underlying nominal objects (or unaccusative subjects) may be necessary for the interpretation of a predicate as telic, it was suggested that *ge* might seem to be functioning as a nominalizer in part, converting certain non-nominal categories into object DPs which could then serve as the necessary input for the interpretation of a predicate as telic.

Following this it was noted that there are various further restrictions on *ge*-XPs - it was shown that adjectives introduced by *ge* may not undergo predicate-type ABAB reduplication, that regular syntactic negation may not occur between *ge* and its complement, and that adjectives in *ge*-XPs may not undergo A-not-A question formation. It was suggested that restrictions of this type might be explained by likening such patterns to other similar restrictions found with nominalization phenomena in languages such as Korean. Nominalizers in Korean would seem to differ crucially with regard to the size of the syntactic constituent they may embed, Type II nominalizations embedding a full clausal constituent and allowing for all regular clausal elements and syntax to occur internal to the nominalization, while Type III nominalizations only embed VPs or smaller clausal/lexical projections and disallow elements and syntactic phenomena which are dependent on higher functional heads in the clause. Such differences have also been noted to occur in English (e.g., in Abney 1987), with the *-ing* nominalizer arguably being associated with either an IP-like constituent as in (37), this licensing nominative case and accusative case, or selecting a VP-size complement and forcing genitive case and *of*-insertion for objects (due to the lack of T and AgrO heads) as in (38):

(37) [John reading his book] was encouraging.

(38) [John's reading of his book] was encouraging.[8]

Consequently there might seem to be good evidence for a nominalization hypothesis, the absence of ABAB reduplication, A-not-A question forms and regular negation being attributed to the possibility that *ge* as a nominalizer might be selecting a bare Adj(P) which would not be able to support such syntactic processes.

A final set of evidence relating to patterns found with object expletive *ta* was then argued to confirm this suggestion. Observing that object expletive *ta* always seems to require a weakly-quantified DP associate, a natural conclusion to make is that *ge*-XPs also have such a status, and that the element *ge* is critical in performing a nominalization category-conversion function.

Putting all this information together, it seems that *ge* can be convincingly argued to function as some kind of nominalizer. A natural question to ask now is what the descriptive term "nominalizer" actually corresponds to in formal syntactic terms, and what position in the Chinese DP/NP/CLP (event) *ge* actually occurs in?

5.2 *Ge* as a D^0

Here I would like to suggest that the most natural interpretation of the evidence and patterning found may be to conclude that the element *ge* is actually a determiner in the D^0 position selecting for a variety of complement types and converting them into a 'nominal' output which can then function to provide an aspectual bounding for an activity predicate. The clues which lead to such a conclusion also come from various parts of the evidence presented. First the nominalization function of *ge* has been seen to be suggested by a number of phenomena. The patterns with object expletive *ta* then indicate that the overall category of the *ge*-XP can reasonably be argued to be that of DP, headed by some overt weak determiner (noting that object expletive *ta* will not combine with an NP which does not have any overt weak determiner, cf: **kan ta shu* 'read it

[8] Note also that negation can occur in the (37)-type form and not in (38), supporting the suggestion that (37) contains an IP clausal projection whereas (38) is a simple nominalized VP:
(i) [John not reading his book] upset us.
(ii) *[John's not reading of his book] upset us.

book(s)'). This consequently might seem to indicate that *ge* itself must be interpreted as the weak determiner head of the DP.

As *ge* is elsewhere assumed to have the category of classifier however, one might perhaps question whether this suggested (re-)assessment of (event) *ge* as a determiner type is actually correct. Other evidence indicates that such a conclusion is in fact rather well-supported. First of all it was seen that (event) *ge* may often not be simply replaced by a more specialized classifier (example 36), which may be taken to indicate that *ge* is not just instantiating the regular classifier position but is inserted as some other syntactic category type. Secondly we saw that (event) *ge* may also precede a full numeral-classifier expression as in (34), which indicates rather clearly that *ge* cannot in fact be occurring in the regular classifier position but must be located in some higher functional head.[9] A natural conclusion then is that this higher functional head is in fact D^0, and that the occurrence of *ge* in D^0 results in the nominalization of whatever complement it is that *ge* introduces.

5.3 Further Evidence

Event *ge* is therefore now suggested to be a weak determiner instantiating D^0 and occurring higher in the nominal functional structure than simple numeral-classifier units. There are two further consequences of such an analysis which can be argued to support it further. First of all if *ge* is in D^0 and not the regular Classifier position CL^0, we can explain why *ge* may not be preceded by numerals such as *san* 'three' and *si* 'four' etc - numerals will occur lower in the functional structure and not raised in D^0 or SpecDP:

[9] It might perhaps be suggested that *ge* in these cases corresponds to something like a "group classifier" and therefore does still occur in a higher classifier position. However, event *ge* can also embed adjectives with no group meaning. If one intends to aim for a uniform analysis of event *ge* it would therefore seem that *ge* is best analyzed as something other than a straightforward classifier in CL. It can also be noted that *ge* can precede a singular-marked object accompanied by the numeral 'one' and a classifier in certain cases where this has the interpretation that the action is unusual/excessive as in (i). This again suggests that a "group classifier" description of *ge* is not appropriate:

(i) Ta pingchang bu he jiu. Jintian tai gaoxing le. Jingran zai wu-fenzhong nei
he regularly NEG drink alcohol today too happy LE surprisingly in 5-minute within
he-le ge yi da-ping jiu.
drink-ASP GE one big-bottle wine
'He does not drink normally. Today he was too happy and surprisingly drank a big bottle of wine in 5 minutes.'

(39) a. Wo xiang chi ge/yi-ge bao.
I want eat GE/one-GE full
'I want to keep eating until I am stuffed.'
b. *Wo xiang chi san/si ge bao.
I want eat three/four GE full

Elsewhere (e.g. in S. Lü 1984) it has been suggested that event *ge* is actually the abbreviated form of *yi-ge* 'one-*ge*' and hence that *ge* should in fact be in the regular CL position, simply with a deleted number one. Here I would like to suggest that there may in fact be a deleted or covert *yi* occurring with *ge*, but that this element is not in fact the regular number one but rather an equivalent to the indefinite article 'a/an' in English. While certain languages do have indefinite articles which are phonologically distinct from the number one (as e.g., English), there are many languages which make use of the number one also as an indefinite article (e.g., German *ein*, French *un* etc.). Chinese can therefore be suggested to belong to this latter (far larger) group and allow for *yi* to be syntactically employed either as the number one or as an indefinite article.[10] The distributional facts reported here would also seem to support the treatment of *yi* as an indefinite article syntactically distinct from the number one *yi* too - only the article *yi* can occur (with *ge*) preceding a numeral-classifier-N sequence:

(40) a. ta e-jile, henhende chi-le (yi) ge san-wan-fan.
he hungry-very fiercely eat-ASP one GE three-CL-rice
'He was very hungry, so he fiercely ate three bowls of rice.'
b. *ta e-jile, henhende chi-le si ge san-wan-fan.
he hungry-very fiercely eat-ASP four GE three-CL-rice

The second set of evidence supporting a treatment of *ge* as a weak determiner giving rise to an interpretation of the DP it heads as a non-specific indefinite comes from the unacceptability of *ge*-XPs in environments other than object position. The examples in (41) and (42) show that *ge*-XPs cannot occur in subject position and cannot be topicalized. This can be simply ascribed to the suggestion that *ge*, as a weak determiner with a non-specific indefinite interpretation, is barred from occurring in positions which only allow for either definite or specific indefinite DPs, hence neither subject nor topic position. Note that bare NPs/DPs may in fact occur in subject/topic position (with definite/generic

[10] Concretely I would actually like to assume that *yi-ge* is a single "collapsed" grammaticized X^0 head and does not consist in two discrete parts/heads (noting that neither *yi* nor *ge* can be substituted for by any other numbers or classifiers when this unit occurs in the D^0 position preceding other numerals and classifiers or adjectives). It is therefore *yi-ge* as an X^0 which is the D^0 indefinite determiner equivalent to English 'a/an'. I furthermore suggest that simple bare *ge* is fully equivalent to *yi-ge* and results from simple reduction of *yi-ge* to *ge*.

interpretations); the fact that *ge*-XPs are fully unacceptable in subject/topic position can therefore only be related to the presence of *ge* and the proposal that *ge* as a weak determiner forces a particular non-specific indefinite interpretation.

(41) a. *ge wu tiao-wan-le.
GE dance dance-finish-LE

b. *ge san quan pao-wan-le.
GE 3 lap run-finish-LE

(42) a. *ge wu, ta tiao-le.
GE dance he dance-LE

b. *ge san quan, ta pao-le.
GE 3 lap he run-LE

Similar considerations account for the non-occurrence of *ge*-XPs in *ba*- and *bei*- constructions - in both such environments the *ba-/bei*-raised DP must be specific, but *ge*-XPs are necessarily non-specific.

(43) a. *ta ba ge wu tiao-le.
he BA GE dance dance-LE

b. *ta ba ge san quan pao-le.
he BA GE 3 lap run-LE

(44) a. *ge wu bei ta tiao-le.
GE dance BEI he dance-LE

b. *ge san quan bei ta pao-le.
GE 3 lap BEI he run-LE

Finally, the weak determiner analysis of *ge* can be suggested to account for the non-occurrence of *ge* with demonstratives as in (45):

(45) *ta chi-le ge na san wan fan.
he eat-ASP GE that three CL rice
'He ate those three bowls of rice at one time.'

Examples such as (45) can be ruled out in either of two possible ways. Possibly it could be suggested that the demonstrative must be located in D^0 and therefore if *ge* is also an instantiation of D^0 they simply cannot occur. A second way to account for the unacceptability of (45) is to suggest that demonstratives are base-generated lower in the DP and not in D (as per Simpson, this volume), but that there must be necessary definiteness concord/agreement obtaining between a lower demonstrative/quantifier and any instantiation of D^0, and as *ge* is specified as being indefinite, this will conflict with the [+definite] specification of the demonstrative, resulting in the unacceptability of (45).

Finally, concluding this section, one might ask whether there is any supporting *precedent* for the analysis of *ge* as an element of the type proposed. Essentially it has been argued that (event) *ge* is an unselective determiner which is able to embed a complement which may be of a variety of syntactic types, from clearly nominal types through to adjectives and apparent clausal idioms. Whereas determiners (and functional elements in general) cross-linguistically are commonly assumed to be lexically specified for a single complement type, the proposal that *ge* as a nominalizing determiner should tolerate a variety of complement types might seem to be somewhat unusual. However, looking further across other languages it can be noted that a range of rather different evidence has in fact led to a highly similar proposal being made for a patterning found in the Salish languages of North America. Davis and Matthewson (1997) argue at length and present convincing evidence that there are determiners in Salish which are unselective in terms of their complement category, optionally selecting for either a nominal NP or a verbal VP complement: "In Lilloet Salish the lexical projections of N and V are morphologically and syntactically distinct. However, this distinction is neutralized at the DP/IP level. In (46) [numbering changed here] the determiner */kwu/* indiscriminately takes either an NP or an (infinitival small clause) VP as its complement:' (Davis & Mathewson 1997, handout p.3):

(46) wa ka ama-s-as [kwu calis]/[kwu qwul-xal]
PROG appear good-CAUS-3ERG [DET cherry]/[DET cook-INTR]
'He likes cherries/likes to cook.'

Likewise the determiner [*ti...a*] introduces either an NP or a (finite small clause) VP:

(47) ama [ti citx sw a] / [ti s xiq sw a]
good [DET house 2SG.POSS DET]/[DET FIN arrive 2SG.POSS DET]
'Your house is good/Your arriving is good.'

It can therefore be suggested that the existence of unselective determiners of different types might actually be a phenomenon which exists across a number of languages and may not be linguistically odd in any way.

6. Grammaticalization, Re-analysis and *ge*

In this last main section of the paper, I would finally like to approach the question of how it is that *ge* might come to be an element in the D^0-position. I would like to suggest that a plausible explanation can be offered in terms of an approach to grammaticalization proposed in Simpson (1998) and Roberts and Roussou (1999) and developed further in Simpson and Wu (1999) and Wu (2000). In these works it is argued that grammaticalization frequently results from a combination of movement and re-analysis within the functional structure projected above a lexical element. It is proposed that various instances of syntactic category change (i.e., re-analysis of an element of one category-type as instantiating a second category-type) may occur when a lexical element first raises up to some functional head dominating a lexical head and then later on becomes re-interpreted as actually being base-generated in the higher functional head position. For example, if a functional structure consisting of three functional heads F1-F3 is projected dominating a lexical head L as in (48), it is possible that F1-F3 may be filled by discrete overt functional elements which are actually base-generated in F1-F3, or it is possible that the lexical head L raises to these heads. In the latter case the lexical element may be taken to be base-generated with morphological features which are checked against the higher F-heads either overtly (as in overt N-to-D raising in DPs in Romance languages, see e.g., Longobardi 1994, Grosu 1988) or later on at LF.

(48)

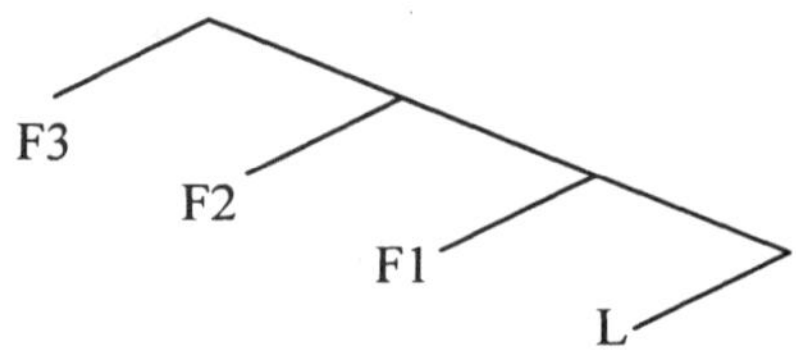

Considering the case where L raises up to one or more of the functional heads, supposing the morphological features corresponding to these heads are covert/phonologically zero, it is possible that the lexical element itself may become interpreted as actually instantiating the features of the higher functional head(s). If the lexical element also undergoes a loss of descriptive content (i.e. semantic "bleaching") while simultaneously becoming more associated with the functional properties of the F-head/s it raises to, it is argued that the lexical element may then ultimately undergo categorial reanalysis and be re-interpreted as base-generated in the functional super-structure dominating L rather than originating in L. This will consequently result in a syntactic category change and grammaticalization of the lexical element L as a functional element of type F_1 (or $F_{2/3}$).

A commonly attested instantiation of this "upward" process of grammaticalization is the frequent reanalysis of lexical verbs as auxiliary-verb elements, a development in which a lexical V^0 first raises up to a higher Infl-type head from V^0 and then is later simply base-generated in the higher functional head.[11] In support of the movement-based approach to grammaticalization, it is noted that changes going in a "downward" direction do not seem to take place. For example, whereas root modals which are canonically situated low down in the functional structure dominating VP commonly turn into structurally higher epistemic modals

[11] Such a change and reanalysis is assumed to have occurred in the creation of the modal verb series in English and other languages (see e.g. Lightfoot 1979).

with sentential scope, the opposite type of change of epistemic modal into root modal is critically not found (see e.g., Bybee, Perkins & Pagliuca 1994). Significantly it would seem to be the case that change and re-analysis consistently occurs in an upwards direction, mirroring the direction of syntactic movement.

Turning back to Chinese and *ge*, I would like to suggest that a rather simple natural hypothesis can now be made about *ge*'s occurrence in the D^0 position. It is fairly clear that *ge* must have originated as a classifier and would therefore have been originally base-generated in the classifier head position CL^0. Synchronically it has been suggested that *ge* has however a rather different function now and occurs as an unselective determiner in D^0 embedding a variety of complement types as a nominalizer, functionally allowing these elements to occur as the nominal/DP objects of a verb. Historically I would like to suggest that the current status of *ge* is a direct result of *ge* undergoing a sequence of movement and reanalysis in the functional super-structure of the DP essentially very similar to that schematized in (48). It can be suggested that *ge* was indeed originally base-generated in CL^0 but then later underwent raising to the higher D^0 position and then ultimately became re-analyzed as an element of type D^0 directly base-generated in the D^0 head. Concerning the motivation for the hypothetical movement to D^0, here a useful clear parallel can be drawn with the development of English 'a/an'. The English indefinite determiner 'a/an' is well-documented as having developed historically from the numeral one (see e.g., Osawa 1998); if one assumes that numerals are base-generated in a distinct functional head Num^0 (as e.g., in Ritter 1991) and that indefinite determiners occur in D^0, then 'a/an' can be taken to have developed from 'one' via raising from Num^0 to D^0 and eventual full re-analysis in D^0. It can be assumed that 'a/an/one' underwent a change in its interpretation and functional role and that from a time when it was licensed as a numeral signaling the number one in contrast to other numbers it later came to be interpreted primarily as a simple indefinite element which embeds an NP as its argument. As an indefinite counterpart to 'the' it can therefore be assumed to have raised to D^0 and then have undergone full reanalysis as a D^0 element. Turning back to Chinese now, the element *ge* is in ways quite similar to English 'a/an', functioning as an embedding element with a clear indefinite value like English 'a/an'. Recall here also the fact noted earlier that when no numeral occurs with the simple classifier *ge* it has a natural default interpretation of 'one'; in such cases there is critically no feeling of contrast between the numerical value one and other possible numbers and *ge* is much more naturally translated as English 'a/an'. Consequently it can be suggested that when *ge* was not accompanied by a numeral in the past, it came to be potentially licensed not just as a classifier associated with a covert numeral 'one' but also as an indefinite embedding element higher in

D^0. Essentially then in both English and Chinese an element such as *ge*/a/an/one would be base-generated and remain in CL^0/Num^0 if its role was primarily numerical and contrastive with other possible number values, but raise to D^0 or be directly base-generated in D^0 if its primary function were to serve as an indefinite embedding element. The hypothetical raising of *ge* to the D^0 position can therefore be given a reasonable explanation which furthermore has cross-linguistic support.[12]

Diachronically, I would therefore like to suggest the following sequence of developments underlie the present reanalysis of *ge* as a D^0:

(49) Stage 1: *ge* was base-generated and remained in CL^0 as a classifier.
Stage 2: *ge* was base-generated in CL^0 and also raised to D^0
Stage 3: *ge* was fully re-analyzed as a D^0 and consequently base-generated directly in the D^0 position

Supposing one assumes a DP structure in which D^0 selects for a NumP, and Num^0 in turn selects for a CLP, (50-52) below would represent the hypothetical sequence of change:

(50) Stage 1

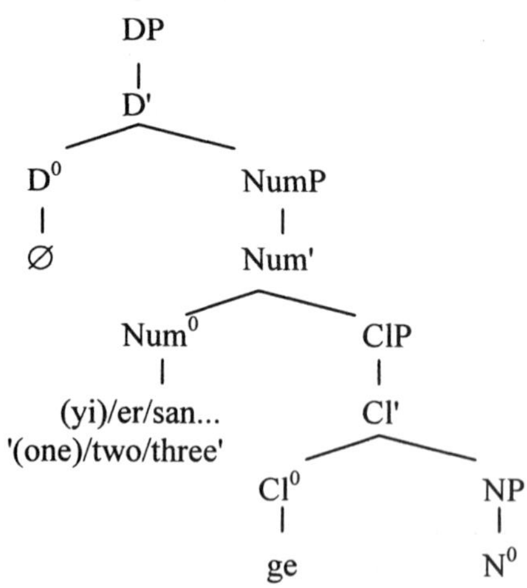

[12] See here Szabolcsi (1994) and Simpson (this volume) on the suggestion that elements in D^0 may be licensed in virtue of being embedding elements similar to complementizers in the clausal domain.

(51) Stage 2

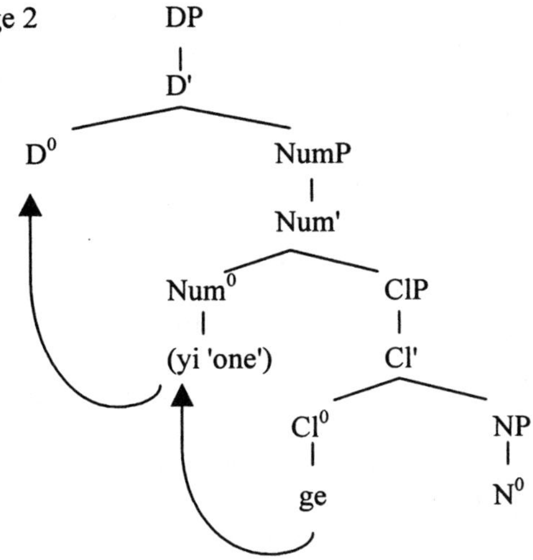

(52) Stage 3

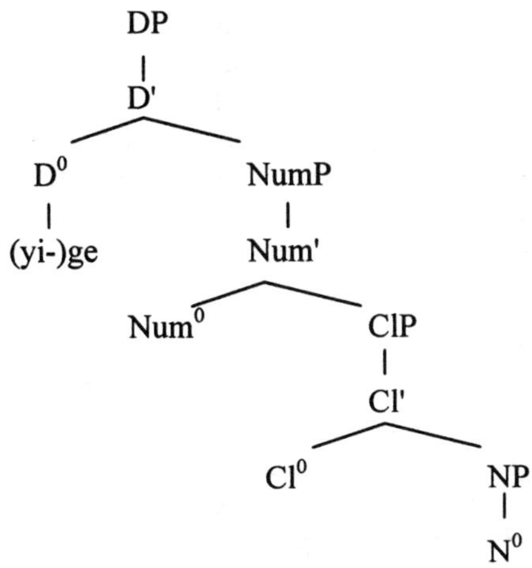

In (51) where no numeral (other than 'one') occurs in Num^0 *ge* raises to this position and is essentially interpreted as 'one', and then moves higher to D^0 where it is licensed as an embedding indefinite determiner-type element.[13] In stage 3, *ge* is re-analyzed as being base-generated in D^0 and functions

[13] Earlier it was noted that *ge* alternates with *yi-ge* as an indefinite determiner in D^0 and that *ge* and *yi-ge* are essentially equivalent (see footnote 10). There are two possible ways in which *ge* could have come to combine with *yi* in D^0. One possibility is that *yi* was located in Num^0 in Stage 2 and allowed for *ge* first to raise up to it and then *yi* and *ge* together raised higher to D^0 as *yi-ge*. A second possibility is that *yi* was actually located in D^0 as an indefinite determiner in Stage 2 and *ge* raised up to adjoin to it in D^0.

just as an embedding indefinite determiner. Significantly at this point when *ge* is not interpreted as having undergone raising from CL^0 and Num^0 it then becomes possible for these positions to become filled with other overt elements and sequences such as (53) become possible:

(53) ta he-le ge san-ping-jiu
he drink-LE GE 3-CL-wine
'He did a drinking of three bottles of wine.'

Ultimately then it is indeed possible to arrive at a principled and also plausible explanation of how the element *ge* has grammaticalized and developed from a classifier into a functional element of some higher type within the DP. This can consequently be suggested to add further good support and justification for the synchronic treatment of event *ge* as an element of type D^0 as indeed proposed here. Finally it can be noted that when *ge* reaches stage 3 of the grammaticalization process outlined above and can hypothetically be base-generated directly in the D^0 position, at this point it can be suggested that it becomes possible for the complement to *ge* in D^0 to be instantiated by constituents other than NumPs (hence AdjPs or VPs as in (15) and (16)), and *ge* develops the distinctive property of being an *unselective* determiner similar to determiners in the Salish languages. No longer being raised to D^0 from a lower CL^0 and Num^0 when the hypothetical stage 3 is reached, it is no longer necessary for a NumP and a CLP to occur in the structure embedded by *ge* and this potentially allows for constituents of other types to be realized as the complement to *ge* in D^0.

7. Concluding Remarks

Briefly summarizing the main conclusions of the paper now, sections 2 and 3 began by showing that the Mandarin element *ge* functions not only as a general classifier but also occurs in a secondary use employed to count out an event. Semantically this use of *ge* was suggested to have the function of making an atelic predicate telic by bringing out or reinforcing the end point of the event depicted by the predicate. In section 4 a variety of the syntactic properties of event *ge* were highlighted and in section 5 these properties were all suggested to indicate that event *ge* is actually now a weak determiner base-generated in the D^0 position. As a D^0, *ge* was argued to be essentially equivalent to a non-specific indefinite article, but one which is also significantly unselective and allows for a variety of complement types, converting them into "nominal" outputs which can then provide aspectual boundings for activity predicates. Finally, section 6 attempted to show how this event *ge* may have diachronically undergone change from being an instantiation of CL^0 to become a D^0, following a path of change upwards in the DP essentially equivalent to the development of the English indefinite article 'a/an' from the numeral 'one'.

References

Abney, Steven. 1987. The English noun phrase in its sentential aspect. PhD Dissertation, MIT.

Allen, R. L. 1966. *The verb system of present-day American English.* The Hague: Mouton.

Borer, Hagit. 1993. The projection of arguments. Ms, University of Massachusetts, Amherst.

Bybee, Joan, Perkins Revere and William Pagliuca. 1994. *The evolution of grammar.* Chicago: University of Chicago Press.

Chao, Y.-R. 1968. *A grammar of spoken Chinese.* Berkeley: University of California Press.

Davis, Henry & Lisa Matthewson. 1997. Determiners, finiteness, and the entity/event distinction. Paper presented at the 1997 conference of the North Eastern Linguistics Society (NELS), Toronto.

Grosu, Alex. 1988. On the distribution of genitive phrases in Roumanian. *Linguistics* 26: 931-949.

Lapointe, Steven and Sarah Nielsen. 1996. A reconsideration of type III gerunds in Korean. In *Japanese/Korean Linguistics* 5, eds. Noriko Akatsuka, Shoichi Iwasaki and Susan Strauss, 305-320. Stanford: Center for the Study of Language and Information.

Li, Charles & Sandra Thompson. 1981. *Mandarin Chinese: A functional reference grammar.* Berkeley: University of California Press.

Li, Fang. 1993. "Shu+*ge*+bu" jiegou de tantao [On the "verb-*ge*-complement" construction]. Ms, Beijing University.

Lightfoot, David 1979. *Principles of diachronic syntax.* Cambridge: Cambridge University Press.

Lin, Jo-wang. 1993. Object expletives in Chinese. Paper presented at the 5th North American Conference on Chinese Linguistics. University of Delaware.

Liu, Hsiao-Mei. 1993. Fanchou moxing lilun yu Hanyu shuliangci tixi [Categorial model theory and Chinese numeral-measure system]. Ms, Fuda Linguistics Institute, Taipei.

Longobardi, Giuseppe. 1994. Reference and proper names: a theory of N-movement in syntax and logical form. *Linguistic Inquiry* 25: 609-65.

Lü, Shu-Xiang. 1984. *Hanyu yufa lunwenji* [Papers on Chinese syntax]. Beijing: Shangwu.

Matthews, Stephen and Virginia Yip. 1994. *Cantonese: a comprehensive grammar.* London: Routledge.

Osawa, Fuyu. 1998. The emergence of the D-system and the demise of morphological case in English. *University College London (UCL) Working Papers in Linguistics* 10, eds. John Harris and Corinne Iten, 467-98.

Ritter, Elizabeth. 1991. Two functional categories in noun phrases: evidence from modern Hebrew. In *Syntax and Semantics* 26, ed. S. Rothstein, 37-62. New York: Academic Press.

Roberts, Ian & Anna Roussou. 1999. A Formal approach to "grammaticalization." Ms., University of Stuttgart and University of Cyprus.

Simpson, Andrew. 1998. Empty determiners and nominalization in Chinese, Japanese and Korean. Paper presented at the Symposium on the Syntax of East Asian Languages, University of Southern California, Los Angeles.

Simpson, Andrew. (this volume). On the status of 'modifying' DE and the structure of the Chinese DP.

Simpson, Andrew & Zoe Wu. 1999. The grammaticalization of formal nouns and nominalizers in Chinese, Japanese and Korean. Paper presented at the Sheffield Conference on Language Change in Japan and East Asia. To appear in *Language Change in East Asia,* ed. N. Tranter. Curzon: London.

Smith, Carlota. 1997. *The parameter of aspect.* Dordrecht: Kluwer.

Szabolcsi, Anna. 1994. The noun phrase. In *Syntax and Semantics 27: The structure of Hungarian*, ed. K. Kiss, 179-274. New York: Academic Press.

Tenny, Carol Lee. 1987. Grammaticalizing aspect and affectedness. PhD dissertation, MIT.

Wu, Zoe. 2000. Grammaticalization and the development of functional categories in Chinese. PhD Dissertation, University of Southern California.

Yoon, James. 1990. Korean nominalizations, lexicalism, and morphosyntactic interfaces. Ms., University of Illinois, Urbana-Champaign.

Zwicky, Arnold. 1977. *On clitics.* Bloomington: Indiana University Linguistics Club.

Focus Adverbs CAI and JIU in L1 Acquisition of Mandarin Chinese: A Preliminary Study*

XIAOLU YANG
Tsinghua University

1. Introduction

There has been a growing interest in one aspect of natural language, the focus phenomenon (Kratzer 1991, von Stechow 1991, Krifka 1992, Rooth 1992, 1996). Focus adverbs such as *even*, *only* and *still* in English and their counterparts in other languages, particularly in German, have been

* The materials presented here were first presented at the "On the Formal Way to Chinese Languages' held at University of California, Irvine in December, 1997 and have been incorporated into my Ph.D. dissertation. I am much indebted to Dr. Thomas Lee, my supervisor, for his valuable counsel at every point in this research. I also thank Beijing Ke Xing Nursery School and the Elementary School Affiliated with Beijing University of Aeronautics and Astronautics for their help with my data collection. I would also thank two anonymous reviewers for their insightful comments on an earlier version of the paper. This research was supported by a Postgraduate Studentship from the Chinese University of Hong Kong.

On the Formal Way to Chinese Languages.
Sze-Wing Tang and Chen-Sheng Luther Liu (eds.).

substantively studied (Horn 1969, Jackendoff 1972, Kattunen and Peters 1979, Kay 1990, Konig 1991, Michaelis 1996). In the study of focus adverbs in Mandarin Chinese, CAI and JIU have attracted researchers' attention due to their subtle meaning properties. As focus adverbs, they both contribute to the sentence meaning by focusing a specific element of the sentence and at the same time relating the focused element to a range of alternatives. As shown by the example sentences, CAI and JIU can focus on time as in (1), on quantity as in (2), and on an antecedent conditional clause as in (3).[1,2]

(1) a. Lisi *san dian* cai lai.
Lisi three o'clock CAI come
'It was only at three that Lisi came.'
b. Lisi *san dian* jiu lai le.
Lisi three o'clock JIU come LE
'Lisi has already been here at three.'

(2) a. Ta chi le *san ge* pingguo cai bao.
he eat LE three CL apples CAI full
'He became full only after eating (as many as) three apples.'
b. Ta chi le *san ge* pingguo jiu bao le.
he eat LE three CL apples JIU full LE
'He became full after only eating (as few as) three apples.'

(3) a. *Lisi qu* wo cai qu.
Lisi go I CAI go
'I will go only if Lisi goes.'
b. *Lisi qu* wo jiu qu.
Lisi go I JIU go
'I will go if Lisi goes.'

It has long been observed that although they are similar in many respects, especially syntactically, CAI and JIU contrast semantically and pragmatically. JIU indicates earlier-than-expected or smaller-than-expected values and sufficient conditions while CAI denotes later-than-expected or larger-than-expected values and necessary conditions. The English translation of each sentence from (1) to (3) has shown such contrast. The relative ordering of values associated with CAI and JIU is argued to be related to an underlying pragmatic scale (Paris 1985, Biq 1987, Lai 1995). Given the subtleties and intricacies of the meaning of CAI and JIU, including their meaning contrast, one may wonder how they get acquired by

[1] The following abbreviations are used in the examples: LE for the aspect marker *le*, CL for classifier, DE for nominal modifier *de* and post-verbal *de*, SFP for sentence final particles.
[2] The focused constituent in each sentence is in italics.

Mandarin-learning children. An answer to this question will surely offer insight into our understanding of the acquisition of focus adverbs in general.

The present paper presents an experimental study of Mandarin-speaking children's understanding of the CAI and JIU meaning contrast. The second section is a discussion of Lai's (1995) analysis of CAI and JIU which serves as the theoretical framework for the present study. Section 3 is devoted to the relevant acquisition issues concerning CAI and JIU. In Section 4, we describe the experiment, followed by a presentation of the results in Section 5. A speculative account of the findings is offered in Section 6. The concluding remarks are given in the final section.

2. Rejected expectation (Lai 1995)

Drawing on comparative studies of similar focus adverbs in German and English (Löbner 1989, van der Auwera 1993, Garrido 1992, Michaelis 1993), Lai characterizes the meaning properties of CAI and JIU in terms of rejected expectation. Her idea is that the various uses of CAI and JIU are related by virtue of their common link to one uniform semantic structure. It is argued that CAI and JIU presuppose a change of state in the truth value of a proposition and they presuppose that this change happens at a different point from where it is expected to happen. Such properties of CAI and JIU can be represented in terms of scales. Specifically, the semantic representations of CAI and JIU contain two kinds of scales: the expected alternative scales (e-scales) indicating possible expected points of change and the asserted scale (a-scale) expressing the real point of change. The meaning contrast between CAI and JIU is in that for CAI, the asserted value or the focused value is located 'farther up' on the scale than the expected value whereas for JIU, the asserted value is located 'farther down' on the scale than the expected value.

In what follows, we will illustrate Lai's analysis with the examples given in (1), (2) and (3), which reflect the use of CAI and JIU in three different domains, namely, the time, quantity and conditional domains.[3]

2.1 CAI and JIU in the time domain

Following Lai's analysis, the meaning representations of sentences (1a) and (1b) are (4) and (5) respectively, together with the scalar diagrams.

What (4) says is that, the change from *Lisi's not coming* to *Lisi's coming* didn't happen until three o'clock although it was expected that it could have happened alternatively at some earlier time. (5) says that, due to the meaning contribution of JIU, the change from *Lisi's not coming* to *Lisi's*

[3] It should noted, however, that Lai's treatment of CAI and JIU is not restricted to these three domains.

coming already happened at three o'clock although it was expected that it could have happened at some later time. Hence CAI in (4) indicates lateness and JIU in (5) denotes earliness.

(4) cai (Lisi x lai) (sandian)

e(xpected): $\exists t\ [t < 3 \wedge$ Lisi came at t]
a(sserted): Lisi came at 3 $\wedge \neg\exists t\ [t < 3 \wedge$ Lisi came at t]

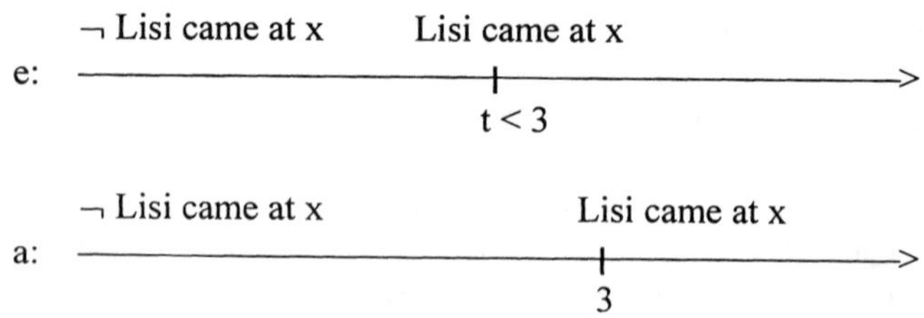

(5) jiu…le (Lisi x lai) (sandian)
e(xpected): $\neg$Lisi came at 3 $\wedge\ \exists t\ [3 < t \wedge$ Lisi came at t]
a(sserted): Lisi came at 3

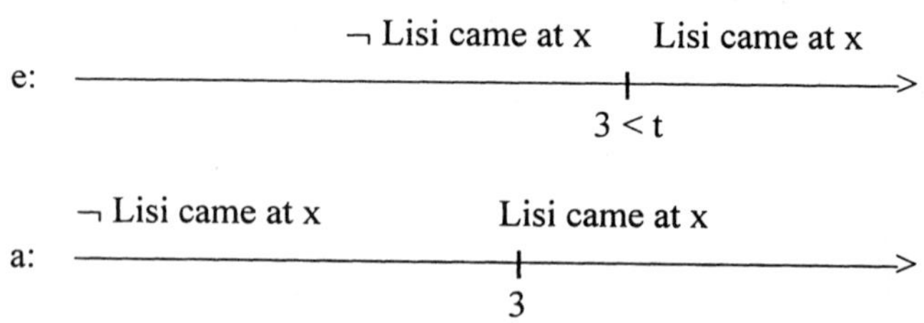

2.2 CAI and JIU in the quantity domain

The semantic structures of CAI and JIU for (2a) and (2b) are given in (6) and (7). Now CAI and JIU focus on a value on a quantity scale. The scale indicates the number of apples that has changed Lisi's state from not feeling full to feeling full. The structure in (6) for CAI suggests that the asserted amount is more than the expected amount and JIU in (7) expresses that the asserted amount is less than the expected amount.

(6) cai (ta bao x pingguo) (sange)
e(xpected): $\exists b\ [b < 3 \wedge$ He became full after eating b apples]
a(sserted): He became full after eating 3 apples $\wedge \neg\exists b\ [b < 3 \wedge$ He became full after eating b apples]

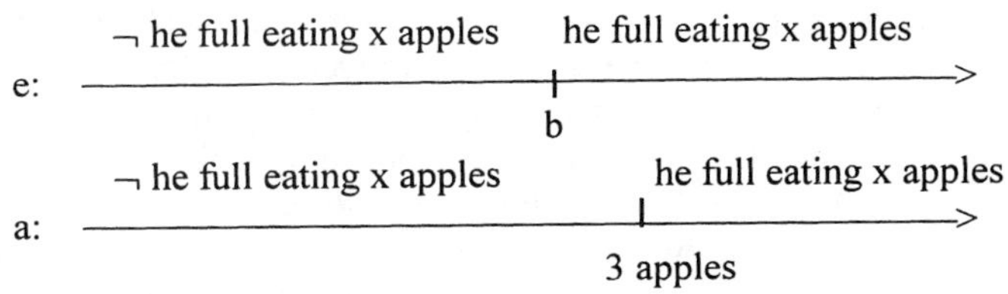

(7) <u>jiu….le (ta bao x pingguo) (sange)</u>
e(xpected): $\neg$He became full after eating 3 apples $\wedge\ \exists$b [3 < b $\wedge$ He became full after eating b apples]
a(sserted): He became full after eating 3 apples

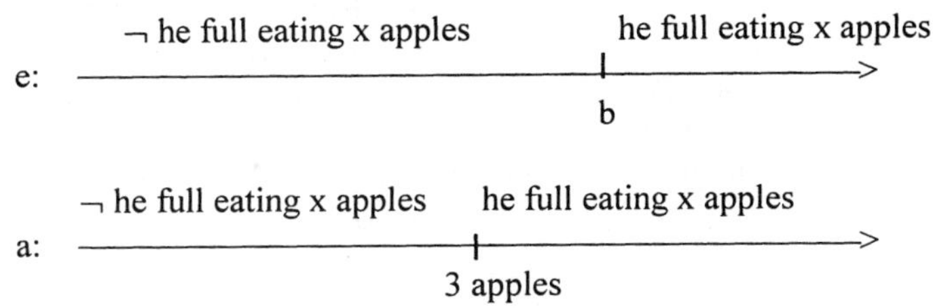

2.3 CAI and JIU in the conditional domain

According to Lai, the same semantic structures for CAI and JIU can be constructed in the conditional domain as in the time and quantity domain. But what is constructed is a hierarchical scale with different propositions, rather than a linear scale with different values of time or quantity.

The use of CAI and JIU in the conditionals relates the focused antecedent to the alternative propositions that can potentially make the consequent clause true. For instance, the possible alternative antecedent sets for the example sentences in (3) are given in (8).

(8) The possible alternative set for *Lisi qu wo CAI/JIU qu*
{Lisi goes, Zhangsan goes, … , Lisi and Zhangsan go, …
The weather is nice, …
I am in a good mood, …
I won a lottery, ….}

(9) <u>path</u>

if p_1 then q $\Rightarrow$ if p_2 then q, as p_2 is more specific than p_1.

These alternative propositions form a hierarchical scale which is determined in terms of informativeness. In other words, all the alternative antecedents are partially ordered according to their informativeness. An antecedent that provides less specific information is ranked lower in that order and is considered as weaker. The lower an antecedent is, the weaker it is and hence the stronger the whole conditional statement is. And a lower antecedent that satisfies the consequent entails that every other antecedent that is higher on the scale would also satisfy the consequent. The two propositions on the scale can be captured in terms of the notion of 'path' which is illustrated in (9). (9) demonstrates the relation between p1 and p2 in the same path.

Following (9), one may argue that *Lisi goes* and *Zhangsan goes* in the alternative sets in (8) are less specific or informative than *Lisi and Zhangsan go*, hence that they rank lower in the hierarchical scale. One may also argue that the propositions like *The weather is nice* or *I am in a good mood* are not in the same path as *Lisi goes*.

Now let's look at the scalar representations for CAI in (3a) and JIU in (3b). They are given in (10) and (11) respectively.

(10) <u>cai (wo qu)(Lisi qu)</u>

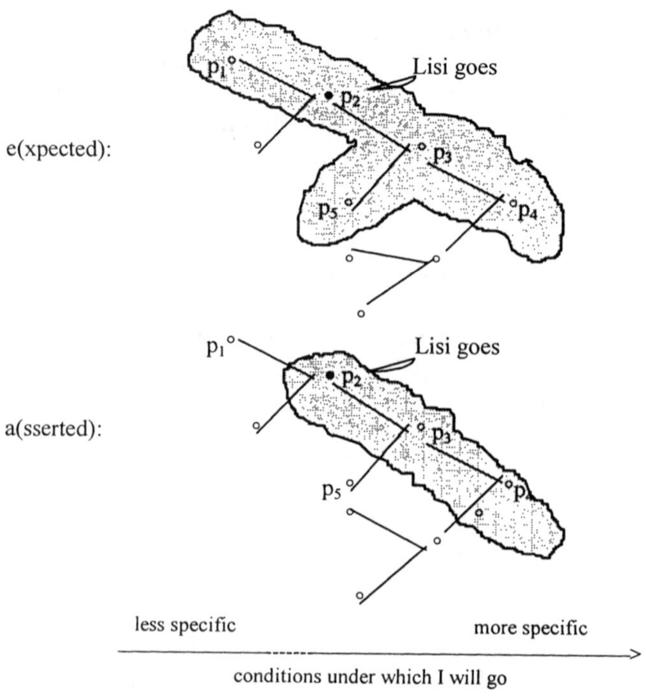

What (10) says is that the speaker will not go unless Lisi goes. With CAI, it is asserted that only the propositions in the shaded area of the diagram, including the focused proposition p_2 *Lisi goes* and the propositions on the same path higher than *Lisi goes* (i.e., p_3, p_4) will make *I go* true. But it is expected that the possible conditions that will make *I go* true properly include the alternatives ranking lower than the focused assertion as indicated by p_1 or alternatives that are simply not on the same path as the focused assertion as indicated by p_5.

(11) jiu (wo qu)(Lisi qu)

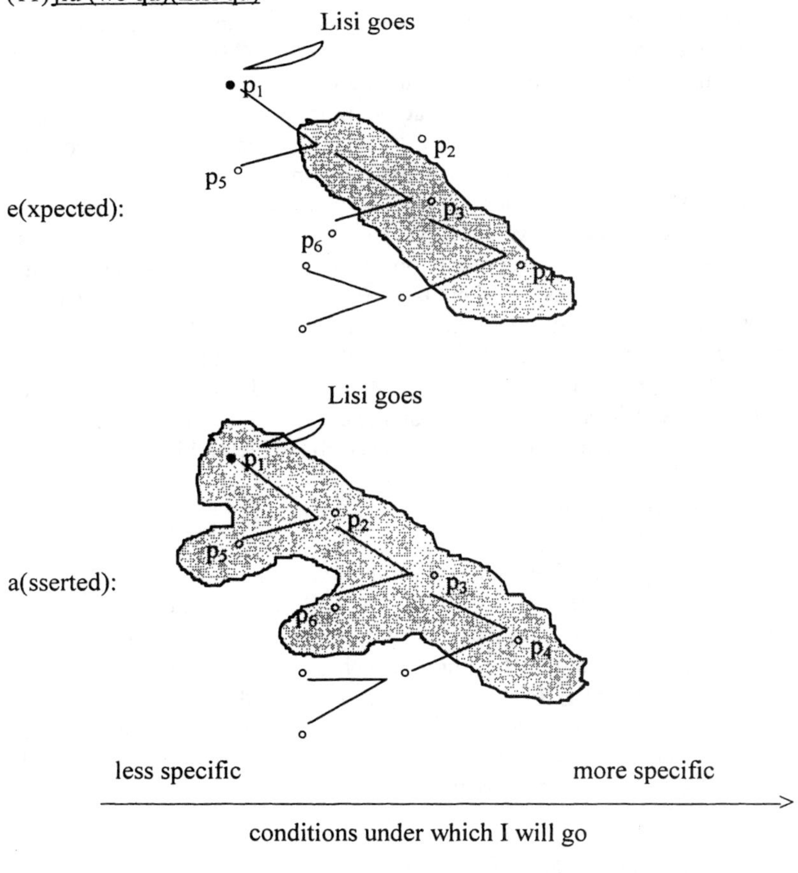

(11) shows is that it is asserted that the information provided by p_1, *Lisi goes,* is sufficient to make *I go* true and as soon as the focused proposition contains enough information to satisfy *I go,* so does every condition that contains more specific information, as indicated by p_2, p_3, and p_4 in the

shaded area of the diagram. The diagram also shows that some other alternative propositions indicated by p_5, or higher information states on other paths as indicated by p_6 might satisfy the consequent as well. However, the expectation is that *I go* would be true with some more specific information-providing antecedent as indicated by p_2, p_3, and p_4 in the shaded area of the e-structure.

It is clear from the structures in (10) and (11) that CAI marks a stronger condition than JIU on the scale. In addition, it is worth noting that to determine what alternative antecedent propositions are relevant for the consequent clause is a dynamic process, i.e., it relies on the speaker-hearer shared knowledge in the on-going communication. So, in different contexts, the possible alternative antecedent sets for *Lisi qu wo CAI/JIU qu* may vary.

To summarize, Lai attempts to relate the various uses of CAI and JIU to one underlying superstructure.[4] What is important about the underlying semantic structure is that, in using CAI and JIU, the asserted or focused value (proposition) on the a-scale is different from those expected values (propositions) on the e-scales, that is, the asserted value is always a 'rejection' of the expected values. The meaning contrast of CAI and JIU is reflected in their semantic representations: the focused value (proposition) picked up by CAI lies 'farther up' on the a-scale than the values (propositions) on the e-scales, i.e., later on the time scale, larger on the quantity scale and higher on the hierarchical scale. On the other hand, the focused value (proposition) selected by JIU is located 'farther down' on the a-scale than the values (propositions) on the e-scales, i.e., earlier on the time scale, smaller on the quantity scale and lower on the hierarchical scale.

3. Acquisition issues

So far we have outlined Lai's analysis of the meaning properties of CAI and JIU. An interesting question arises as to how children acquire such subtle properties of CAI and JIU, in particular their meaning contrast. A survey of Mandarin-speaking children's natural speech shows that they learn to use CAI and JIU quite early (Tse et al 1991). They produce CAI and JIU as early as 3 years of age, although their use of CAI and JIU becomes more productive after 4 years of age. (12) to (16) are examples of the use of CAI and JIU in the speech of three- year-olds.[5]

[4] Lai (1995) is consistent with Paris (1985) and Biq (1987) in this respect.

[5] The child data in Tse et al (1991) has one defect: it fails to provide the contexts for children's utterances, e.g. linguistic contexts such as utterances preceding and following the child's utterances, and non-linguistic contexts. This makes the analysis of CAI/JIU in their utterances difficult since the use of CAI/JIU is closely associated with semantics and pragmatics. But we can still get a glimpse into the use of CAI and JIU in their speech.

(12) Baba bao bao jiu hao. (3;0)
Dad hold hold JIU good
'It will be good if Dad holds (me).'

(13) Toufa bao bao cai bu hui leng. (3;2)
hair wrap wrap CAI not will cold
'(You) won't feel cold only if (you) wrap up your hair.'

(14) Deng yi xia jiu hui jia a? (3;4)
wait a while JIU return home SFP
'Shall (we) go home after a while?'

(15) Women zhe kou chi wan jiu lai. (3;6)
we this CL eat finish JIU come
'We will come soon after we have eaten this mouthful (of food).'

(16) Yao gei liang kuai cai xing. (3;8)
want give two piece CAI do
'It will do only if (you) give (me) two pieces.'

Given the fact that three-year-old children have already used CAI and JIU in their speech, one wonders whether they really understand the subtle meanings of CAI and JIU. If they have mastered the meaning properties of CAI and JIU, the CAI and JIU meaning contrast should constitute part of their knowledge of the meaning of CAI and JIU. In addition, if CAI and JIU are each associated with one underlying semantic structure, as Lai claims, a prediction would be that, once the children have acquired the CAI/JIU contrast in one domain, they should be able to identify the contrast in other domains as well. In other words, it is expected that children acquire the CAI/JIU contrast in all domains simultaneously. Specifically, two research questions are formulated in (17) and (18), which were investigated in the experiment that is to be reported in the following sections.

(17) Do children understand the CAI/JIU contrast, that is CAI marks greater-than-expected values and necessity whereas JIU marks smaller-than-expected values and sufficiency?

(18) Do they show sensitivity to the CAI/JIU contrast in the three domains investigated (namely, the time, quantity and conditional domains) at the same time?

4. The Experiment

4.1 Subjects

60 Mandarin-speaking children participated in the study, who were divided into three age groups: 4;0 - 4;11, 5;0 - 5;11, 6;00 - 6;11. The distribution of the subjects is given in (19). The children were drawn from a day-care and

an elementary school in Beijing. Apart from children subjects, 13 Mandarin-speaking adults from Beijing also participated in the experiment as controls. Each subject was individually interviewed by the experimenter. The interview lasted about half an hour for each child subject.

(19) The distribution of the subjects
Age 4 (4;0-4;11), n=20
Age 5 (5;0-5;11), n=20
Age 6 (6;0-6;11), n=20
Adults (23-32), n=13

4.2 Design

The development of a task to test Mandarin-speaking children's understanding of the CAI and JIU meaning differences turned out to be extremely difficult. As made clear in our discussions, the interpretation of CAI or JIU relies on a set of expectations about events. Such expectations are usually determined by the context in which CAI and JIU sentences occur. Due to this nature of CAI and JIU sentences, we were unable to utilize more standardized tasks in our study, such as truth value judgment tasks, act-out tasks, and picture identification tasks (McDaniel et al. 1996). Since a rich context must be set up, comprehension tasks like a truth value judgment task are difficult to apply for our purpose. Picture identification tasks do not work either because it is difficult to convey a rich set of expectations in a picture. An act-out task would also be difficult to use because of the complexity of the interpretation. To circumvent the problems raised by CAI and JIU, and to serve the specific purposes of the present study, we developed a new method. It involved a request for the child to select the 'right' sentence out of two based on a preceding discourse context. The task developed in this way is similar in nature to a truth-value judgment task since it elicits the child's judgment of a sentence. But our task is different from the standardized truth value judgment tasks in that it requires the child to judge between two sentences and that a discourse context is set up to provide clues for the judgment.

The experiment looked at the CAI/JIU contrast in three domains, i.e. the time domain, the quantity domain, and the conditional domain, as exemplified in sentences (1), (2), and (3). For each domain, two contexts were designed: one context was biased toward the use of CAI and one biased toward the use of JIU. This can be illustrated with an example from the quantity domain. The short passage in (20a) provides a context which is biased toward the use of the CAI sentence. In other words, the CAI test sentence in (20c) is appropriate in this context whereas the JIU test sentence in (20b) is not. The short passage in (21a), on the contrary, provides a context which is biased toward the use of the JIU sentence. Here, the test sentence with JIU in (21b) is appropriate according to the context while the sentence with CAI is (21c) is not.

(20) the context biased toward CAI (*cai*-biased context)

a. Dongdong ti wan qiu hui lai, mama de fan ye shao
Dongdong kick finish ball return come, mother DE meal also burn

hao le. Dongdong chi de ke duo la, mama gei ta cheng
well LE. Dongdong eat DE very many SFP, mother give him ladle

le liang da wan fan, ta hai jue de bu gou. Ta rang
LE two big bowl rice, he still feel DE not enough. he let

mama zai gei ta cheng yi wan fan. Ta shuo:
mother again give him ladle one bowl rice. he say

'When Dongdong came back after playing football, his mother had already got the meal ready. Dongdong ate a lot; his mother ladled him two big bowls of rice, but he still didn't feel full enough. He asked his mother to ladle him another bowl of rice. He said …

b. wo chi san wan fan jiu bao.
I eat three bowl rice JIU full
'I become full after only eating (as few as) three bowls of rice.'

c. wo chi san wan fan cai bao.
I eat three bowl rice CAI full
'I become full only after eating (as many as) three bowls of rice.'

(21) the context biased toward JIU (*jiu*-biased context)

a. Chi wufan le, Dongdong hui lai le. Ta hao kou ke, he
eat lunch LE, Dongdong return come LE. he good mouth thirsty, drink

le yi da ping kele. Mama zuo le feichang hao he de tang.
LE one big bottle cola mother did LE very good drink DE soup

Dongdong he le yi wan tang, mama you gei ta cheng le
Dongdong drink LE one bowl soup, mother again give him ladle LE

yi wan. Dongdong yaoyao tou. Ta shuo:
one bowl. Dongdong shake-shake head. he say

'Dongdong came back when it was lunch time. He was so thirsty that he drank a big bottle of cola. His mother had made very delicious soup. Dongdong drank a bowl of soup and his mother ladled him another. Dongdong shook his head. He said …'

b. wo he yi wan jiu bao le.
I drink one bowl JIU full LE
'I became full after only drinking (as few as) one bowl.'

c. wo he yi wan cai bao
I drink one bowl CAI full
'I became full only after drinking (as many as) one bowl.'

A three-by-two factorial design with repeated measures yielded a total of 18 pairs of test sentences, each with a corresponding discourse context.[6] They were deliberately built into three coherent stories, each story containing 6 contexts biased toward the use of CAI and JIU in the three domains. For instance, the contexts and the test sentences in (20) and (21) which pointed to the use of CAI and JIU in the quantity domain constituted two contexts of a story about a young boy named Dongdong. The contexts described Dongdong's various interactions with his sister or mother and all the test sentences were spoken by Dongdong. The second story was about a rabbit and a tortoise. The third story was about a spaceman and a little girl. The order of the contexts of each story and that of the two test sentences for each context was randomized except for the story about Dongdong, in which the order of the contexts followed automatically from the narrative order of the story. All the contexts and the test sentences were tape-recorded. Note that the contexts and the test sentences were differentiated by two voices in the recording.

4.3 Procedure

Before the test was given, all children were given four sentences for pre-test training. The purpose of the pre-test training was to familiarize the child

[6] An anonymous reviewer pointed out that one should also include control sentences (ones without CAI or JIU) too in order to avoid a bias in children's response, e.g. they might tend to select the second of the two sentences they hear. Although there didn't seem to be such a bias in our child subjects' actual responses, we would include control sentences in our future studies.

with the type of questions that he was going to handle in the real task.[7] He was told that of the two sentences he heard, only one was 'right' in describing a picture which was shown to him. He was expected to choose the 'right' one and repeat it. As two 'right' sentences were the first sentences and two the second sentences, the practice also made the child know that it was possible to choose either the first or the second sentence. The child who was not able to handle the pre-test training sentences was considered to be unsuitable for the experiment and therefore not included in the experiment.

In the experiment, the experimenter first introduced the main characters of the story by showing them a picture. Then the experimenter told the child that of the two sentences he heard at the end of each context, one was 'right' and one was 'wrong'. He was expected to select the 'right' sentence and repeat it. After the introduction, the recording of the first context and the two test sentences was played. Once the child completed the repetition, the experimenter played the recording of the second context and the test sentences. The same procedure was followed for the second and the third story. In order to cut down the child's memory load, there was visual support for each context, that is, a picture was also shown to the child when he was listening to the recording.[8] If the child failed to respond, the recording would be played again. An experiment helper would write down the child's repeated sentences verbatim on the experiment record. In addition, the interview was tape-recorded and later transcribed in order to check the written record. For adult subjects, the procedure was the same except that they were not given the warm-up as well as the picture support.

In the next section, we will display the results of the experiment.

5. Results

[7] In designing the pre-test, we tried to focus the child's attention on preverbal items since CAI and JIU always occur preverbally. Here are two examples of the pre-test training stimuli. Note that in (i), the two sentences differ in that in the first one there is a preverbal negator. In (ii), there is a difference in that one has a preverbal quantifier 'all' and one has a preverbal negator.

(i) a. zhe ge xiao gege mei dai maozi.
this CL little brothe r not wear hat
'This little brother does not wear a hat.'

b. zhe ge xiao gege dai le maozi
this CL small brother wear LE hat
'This little brother is wearing a hat'.

(ii) a. zhe san ge xiao pengyou quan zai tiaowu.
this three CL little friends all PROG dance
'These three little children are all dancing.'

b. zhe san ge xiao pengyou meiyou tiaowu.
this three CL little friends not dance
'These three little children are not dancing.'

[8] Of course it is impossible to depict everything in one single picture. It's also impossible to depict expectations in the pictures. We only included events that were closely related to the test sentences in the picture. What's more important, the time and quantity expressed in the test sentences were made clear in the picture.

5.1 Overall performance in using JIU and CAI

We will first take a look at the overall performance of the subjects' use of JIU and CAI in the JIU-biased and CAI-biased contexts. Table (1) is a frequency table indicating the use of JIU and CAI by different groups of subjects. Here the categories of 'use of CAI' and 'use of JIU' refer to children's selection of CAI and JIU sentences respectively.[9] The category of 'deletions of CAI/JIU for children' are children's repetitions without CAI or JIU.[10] The category of 'acceptance of both CAI and JIU for adults' means that the adult subjects either made a choice but responded by explaining that both were possible or responded directly by saying that both were possible.

Table 1 Use of JIU and CAI in *jiu*-biased and *cai*-biased contexts (Raw number of responses followed by % of total responses)

Use of JIU						
	Time domain		Quantity domain		Conditional domain	
Age group	*jiu*-biased	*cai*-biased	*jiu*-biased	*cai*-biased	*jiu*-biased	*cai*-biased
age 4 (n=20)	35(58%)	19(32%)	23(38%)	22(37%)	22(37%)	18(30%)
age 5 (n=20)	39(65%)	20(33%)	26(43%)	15(25%)	19(32%)	20(33%)
age 6 (n=20)	47(78%)	20(33%)	48(80%)	31(52%)	36(60%)	27(45%)
adults (n=13)	38(97%)	4 (10%)	39(100%)	1 (3%)	37(94%)	10(26%)
Use of CAI						
	Time domain		Quantity domain		Conditional domain	
Age group	*jiu*-biased	*cai*-biased	*jiu*-biased	*cai*-biased	*jiu*-biased	*cai*-biased
age 4	8 (14%)	28(47%)	18(30%)	29(48%)	18(30%)	25(42%)
age 5	15(25%)	34(57%)	30(50%)	38(63%)	32(53%)	34(57%)
age 6	10(17%)	32(53%)	11(18%)	26(43%)	20(33%)	32(53%)
Adults	1 (3%)	28(72%)	0 (0%)	38(97%)	1 (3%)	23(59%)
Others: deletion of CAI/JIU for children /acceptance of both CAI and JIU for adults						
	Time domain		Quantity domain		Conditional domain	
Age group	*jiu*-biased	*cai*-biased	*jiu*-biased	*cai*-biased	*jiu*-biased	*cai*-biased
age 4	17(28%)	13(21%)	19(32%)	9 (15%)	20(33%)	17(28%)
age 5	6 (10%)	6 (10%)	4 (7%)	7 (12%)	9 (15%)	6 (10%)
age 6	3 (5%)	8 (14%)	1 (2%)	3 (5%)	4 (7%)	1 (2%)
Adults	0 (0%)	7 (18%)	0 (0%)	0 (0%)	1 (3%)	6 (15%)

[9] Sometimes the sentence repeated by the child didn't copy the test sentence exactly, but as long as its meaning and CAI/JIU was retained, we still put it under the category of 'use of CAI' or 'use of JIU'.

[10] In fact, one type of deletion should not be considered as pure deletion of CAI or JIU: these were cases where other particles were used other than CAI or JIU. For instance, some children used HAI ('still') or ZAI ('again'). At the present stage, we are not clear why HAI or ZAI were used instead of CAI or JIU. It's possible that both these particles are phonetically similar to CAI (all have the same diphthong [ai]) and therefore HAI or ZAI were phonetical variants of CAI in children's language at this level. However this explanation is not satisfactory at all, particularly when the data shows some children consistently used HAI or ZAI whereas some children never did so.

The table demonstrates that, for children of all age groups, there were occurrences of JIU and CAI in both JIU-biased and CAI-biased contexts, but it is clear that adult speakers tended to use JIU mostly in the JIU-biased contexts and use CAI only in CAI-biased contexts. This indicates that children have problems in differentiating between CAI and JIU even when they are 4- or 5- years old. In addition, the table also indicates the unsurprising fact that children's differentiation between CAI and JIU was better as they grew older: children at age 6 generally performed better in using JIU and CAI than younger children. Another interesting finding was that some adults used JIU or accepted both CAI and JIU in the CAI-biased contexts but not vice versa.

5.2 JIU in *jiu*-biased contexts and *cai*-biased contexts

To determine whether children understand the CAI/JIU meaning contrast, we first compare children's use of JIU and then their use of CAI in the *jiu*-biased and *cai*-biased contexts. Table (2) displays the mean results of the use of JIU in the two contexts.

Table 2 Use of JIU in *jiu*-biased contexts and *cai*-biased contexts (Mean number of responses with a range of 0-3)

	Time domain		Quantity domain		Conditional domain	
Age group	*jiu*-biased	*cai*-biased	*jiu*-biased	*cai*-biased	*jiu*-biased	*cai*-biased
age 4 (n=20)	1.75	0.95	1.15	1.10	1.10	0.90
age 5 (n=20)	1.95	1.00	1.30	0.75	0.95	1.00
age 6 (n=20)	2.35	1.00	2.40	1.55	1.80	1.35
Adults(n=39)	2.92	0.31	3.00	0.08	2.85	0.77

The results in the time domain suggest that children across all age groups (4, 5, 6) used JIU significantly more in the *jiu*-biased contexts than in the *cai*-biased contexts (age 4: t=4.29, p=.000; age 5: t=4.50, p =.000; age 6: t=6.47, p=.000). This indicates that Mandarin-speaking children are sensitive to the CAI/JIU contrast in the time domain at 4, and such sensitivity emerges at 4 or even earlier.

In the quantity domain, children in the two older age groups (age 5, 6) selected JIU in the *jiu*-biased contexts significantly more than in the *cai*-biased contexts (age 5: t=2.60, p=.017; age 6: t=3.34, p=.003), but no significant difference was found for the group of children at age 4 (age 4: t=.29, p=.772). It suggests that children are not sensitive to the CAI/JIU contrast in the quantity domain at age 4 but they begin to detect the CAI/JIU contrast when they enter their fifth year of life.

Children at age 4 and 5 do not differentiate between CAI and JIU in the conditional domain: no significant difference was detected when comparing their use of JIU in the two contexts (age 4: t=.94, p=.359; age 5: t=.22, p=.825). But there was a significant difference for the group of children at age 6 (age 6: t=2.27, p=.035). A possible interpretation for this is that children have not acquired the CAI/JIU meaning contrast until 6.

5.3 CAI in *jiu*-biased contexts and *cai*-biased contexts

Table (3) displays the mean results of the use of CAI in the two contexts. Here a similar developmental pattern is observed, particularly in the time and conditional domain.

Table 3 Use of CAI in *jiu*-biased contexts and *cai*-biased contexts (Mean number of responses with a range of 0-3)

	Time domain		Quantity domain		Conditional domain	
Age group	*jiu*-biased	*cai*-biased	*jiu*-biased	*cai*-biased	*jiu*-biased	*cai*-biased
age 4 (n=20)	0.40	1.40	0.90	1.45	0.90	1.25
age 5 (n=20)	0.75	1.70	1.50	1.90	1.60	1.70
age 6 (n=20)	0.50	1.60	0.55	1.30	1.00	1.60
Adults(n=39)	0.07	2.15	0.00	2.92	0.08	1.77

In the time domain, children across all age groups chose the CAI sentences in the *CAI*-biased contexts significantly more than in the *JIU*-biased contexts (age 4: t=4.36, p=.000; age 5: t=4.79, p=.000; age 6: t=6.24, p=.000), indicating their early sensitivity to the CAI/JIU meaning contrast in this domain.

In the quantity domain, the overall trend is that children chose CAI sentences more in the *CAI*-biased contexts than in the *JIU*-biased contexts although the difference was not significant at age 5 (age 4: t=2.98, p=.008; age 5: t=1.71, p=.104; age 6: t=2.78, p=.012). For children at age 5, there was also a clear tendency that more CAI sentences were chosen in the CAI-biased contexts than in the JIU-biased contexts.

In the conditional domain, children at age 6 significantly selected CAI sentences in the CAI-biased contexts more than in the JIU-biased contexts (age 6: t=3.04, p=.007), but no significant difference was found for those at age 4 and age 5. In other words, only children of age 6 showed propensity to correctly choose the CAI sentences in the *cai*-biased contexts and refute CAI sentences in the *jiu*-biased contexts.

A comparison of our child subjects' use of CAI and JIU in both *cai*-biased and *jiu*-biased contexts provides evidence that the CAI/JIU contrast in the time domain and quantity domain develops earlier while the CAI/JIU contrast in the conditional domain is acquired late.

6. Discussion

It has been shown in the previous section that the three groups of children in my study, namely, 4-, 5- and 6- year-olds, could not fully differentiate between CAI and JIU. This does not match with the findings evidencing children's early use of CAI and JIU (Tse et al 1991). Furthermore, our subjects did not show sensitivity to the CAI/JIU contrast in the three domains at the same time. Specifically, children in my study exhibited sensitivity to the CAI/JIU contrast in the time and quantity domain relatively earlier, namely before 6, but their sensitivity to the CAI/JIU contrast in the conditional domain didn't develop until 6. Our prediction that children should acquire the CAI/JIU meaning contrast in all domains simultaneously isn't borne out. One may interpret it as evidence against Lai's claim that there is a single semantic representation underlying the use of CAI and JIU in all domains. But this interpretation is too rash. Jackendoff (1983) has argued for the advantage of relating various uses of a polysemous lexical item to one underlying structure from the acquisitional perspective: the existence of 'formal relations among apparently distinct readings of a polysemous word ... would make it easier for the language learner to acquire one reading, given another.' (p13). The similar pattern observed in the acquisition of CAI/JIU in the time and quantity domains in the present study provides further support for a close relation between temporal CAI/JIU and quantity CAI/JIU. On such grounds, we argue that Lai's treatment of CAI and JIU is correct. A possible explanation of the data presented is that there exists asymmetry in the acquisition of the CAI/JIU contrast in different domains. In what follows, we will discuss this possibility as well as the question as to why there is a gap between findings from the present study and those production data.

6.1 Focus adverbs CAI and JIU in child language acquisition

As mentioned earlier, it is found that Mandarin-speaking children produce CAI and JIU in their speech as early as 3 years of age. But what we have shown is that children's knowledge of focus adverbs CAI/JIU is far from complete. At age 6, they have not yet completely mastered the CAI/JIU contrast. Such findings are consistent with what has long been observed in child language acquisition: there is a gap between children's production of certain forms or structures and their development of the semantic properties of such forms. They may produce the forms quite early, but it will take them some time to map the meanings onto the forms. An example is the development of subordinating conjunctions. Although many subordinate conjunctions are used in speech before six, studies of comprehension show that children rarely learn the full logical implications of these conjunctions until much later (cf. studies cited in Wing and Scholnick 1981, Relly 1986) It is argued that the source of difficulty of these structures lie not only in the logical relations they express but also in the pragmatic concepts they convey (Wing and Scholnick 1981). In addition, the acquisition of the word pair with subtle meaning distinctions proves to be difficult and there is a stage at which children mix up the words before they finally reach the state of differentiation which characterizes the adult's knowledge (cf. the study of the acquisition of the meaning of the word pair *before* and *after* in Clark 1971). This seems to be the case with the acquisition of focus adverbs CAI and JIU in Mandarin Chinese.

A complete understanding of the meanings expressed by CAI and JIU may develop fairly late due to their complex and subtle meaning properties. One of the complexities is related to the fact that CAI and JIU are used in various domains. The use of CAI and JIU in some structures in particular, such as conditionals, pose difficulties for children at first. The issue concerning conditional CAI and JIU is taken up in the next section.

6.2 The delayed acquisition of the CAI/JIU contrast in the conditional domain

The data suggests that there exists asymmetry in the acquisition of the CAI/JIU contrast in different domains: children do not acquire the CAI/JIU contrast in all domains simultaneously. We would argue that the delayed development of the CAI/JIU contrast in the conditional domain may be due to the complexities involved in the conditional use of CAI and JIU.

Remember that in our discussion of Lai's analysis, CAI and JIU in the conditional domain are associated with a hierarchical scale while they are associated with a linear scale in the time and quantity domain. If this characterization is correct, then intuitively, the hierarchical scale in the conditional domain may be more difficult for children to acquire than the linear scale in the time and quantity domain. In the time and quantity domain, the focused values and alternative values are linearly ordered on the scale. There is presumably less difficulty for young kids to establish the relationship between the focused values and the expected alternative values. Consequently, the different implications carried by CAI and JIU are easier to detect.

In the conditional domain, on the other hand, the acquisition of the hierarchical scale is more complicated. The hierarchical scale involves partial ordering of relevant antecedent conditions. To determine what alternative antecedents are relevant for the consequent is not an easy process. In addition, the ordering of the alternatives is determined in terms of informativeness. The more informative an antecedent is, the stronger it is, hence the weaker the whole conditional statement. JIU marks a weaker condition on the scale, hence related to sufficiency and CAI marks a stronger condition on the scale, hence related to necessity. Again, the ordering of possible conditions to satisfy the consequent is not an easy task. The young child is incapable of differentiating between JIU and CAI, that is to say, he does not tell from necessity from sufficiency. This is possibly a reflection of the delay in the construction of the scale of informativeness. Before a complete mastery of the scale of informativeness, the child may treat CAI and JIU as carrying the same implication in the conditional domain: CAI and JIU are the same in that both mark a unique condition that satisfies the consequent clause. In other words, the child tends to mark a stronger condition with both CAI and JIU. An interesting observation from the data is that in the conditional domain, the subjects used CAI a lot in the JIU-biased contexts, where adults rarely use CAI. This account of the delayed development of the CAI/JIU contrast in the conditional domain, however, needs to be further justified.

6.3 Why do adults use JIU or accept both JIU and CAI in *cai*-biased contexts?

For adults, the situation is reversed: they would use JIU or accept both JIU and CAI in the CAI-biased contexts in the conditional domain as shown in Table 1. One may argue that this is a consequence of the invited inferences of conditionals. Geis and Zwicky (1971) points out that, given the sentence in (22), the speaker never asserts (23). Yet listeners will invariably infer the latter, is also true. This conclusion by the listener is not a deduction that follows from logical rules, but rather it is an inference that was invited by uttering (22) in normal circumstances.

(22) If you mow the lawn I'll pay you $5.
(23) If you don't mow the lawn, I won't pay you $5.

CAI and JIU conditionals in Mandarin Chinese are interesting in that CAI is directly related to the invited inferences, in other words, this is what CAI contributes to the sentence meaning. Hence, in uttering (24a), the speaker implies (24b).

(24) a. *Lisi qu* wo cai qu.
Lisi go I CAI go
'I will go only if Lisi goes'
b. Lisi bu qu wo bu qu.
Lisi not go I not go
'I won't go if Lisi doesn't go'

JIU's meaning contribution to the conditional statement is to mark a sufficient condition; however, one may still get the invited inferences. When one utters (25a), he may imply (25b) or (25c), but the listener may still infer

(25d) from (25a). In other words, (25a) can have any of the three interpretations from (25b) to (25d).

(25) a. *Lisi qu* wo jiu qu.
Lisi go I JIU go
'I will go if Lisi goes'

b. Lisi bu qu wo ye qu.
Lisi not go I too go
'I will go if Lisi doesn't go.'

c. Lisi bu qu wo keneng qu keneng bu qu.
Lisi not go I may go may not go
'I may or may not go if Lisi doesn't go.'

d. Lisi bu qu wo bu qu.
Lisi not go I not go
'I won't go if Lisi doesn't go'

The above discussion shows that in some cases JIU overlaps with CAI. But how JIU overlaps with CAI and what role this overlapping plays in comprehension remains unclear. This, nevertheless, may account for the fact that the adult subjects in the experiment used CAI or accepted both CAI and JIU even when the context was biased toward CAI.[11]

7. Conclusion

What has been reported in the present paper is a preliminary investigation into Mandarin-speaking children's acquisition of focus adverbs CAI and JIU. The findings suggest that Mandarin-speaking children cannot fully appreciate the semantic distinctions between CAI and JIU before 6 and that they acquire the CAI/JIU meaning difference in the time and quantity domains earlier than in the conditional domain. We have offered a tentative account of the findings, arguing that a) it takes time for children to fully understand the complex meaning properties of CAI and JIU although they have used both in their production and b) the lag in the acquisition of the CAI/JIU meaning contrast in the conditional domain is related to the hierarchical structure underlying CAI and JIU in their conditional use. More revealing information concerning children's knowledge of the meaning of CAI and JIU is still waited to be disclosed by systematic attempts.

[11] The anonymous reviewer pointed out that even judgments concerning truth conditions for conditionals without focus adverbs are often complex for adult subjects. (See, for instance, Talpin (1971)

References

Auwera, J. van der. 1993. 'Already' and 'still': beyond duality. *Linguistics and Philosophy* 16:613-653.

Biq, Y.O. 1987. *The Semantics and Pragmatics of Cai and Jiu in Mandarin Chinese.* Bloomington, Indiana: Indiana University Linguistic Club.

Clark, E.V. 1971. On the acquisition of the meaning of *before* and *after.J ournal of Verbal Learning and Verbal Behavior* 10:266-275.

Geis, M. and Zwicky, A.M. 1971. On invited inferences. *Linguistic Inquiry* 2:561-566.

Garrido, J. 1992. Expectations in Spanish and German adverbs of change. *Folia Linguistica* XXVI:357-402.

Horn, L. 1969. A presuppositional approach to 'only' and 'even'. *Papers from the 5th Regional Meeting*, Chicago Linguistics Society, 98-107.

Jackendoff, R. 1972. Focus and presupposition, in *Semantic Interpretation in Generative Grammar*. MIT Press.

---1983. Semantics and Cognition. Cambridge: MIT Press.

Karttunen, L and Peters, S. 1979. Conventional implicature, in C.-K. Oh and D.A. Dinneen, eds., Syntax and Semantics 11: Presupposition, 1-56. New York: Academic Press.

Kay, P. 1990. Even. *Linguistics and Philosophy* 13: 59-111.

Konig, E. 1991. *The Meaning of Focus Particles*. London: Routledge.

Kratzer, A. 1991. The representation of focus, in A. von Stechow and D. Wunderlich, eds., *Semantik/Semantics*. Berlin: Walter de Gruyter.

Krifka, M. 1992. A framework for focus-sensitive quantification, in C. Barker and D. Dowty, eds., *Proceedings of the Second Conference on Semantics and Lingusitic Theory*. Dept. of Linguistics, Ohio State University.

Lai, H.-L. 1995. *Rejected Expectations: the Scalar Particles CAI and JIU in Mandarin Chinese*. Ph.D. dissertation. The University of Texas at Austin.

Löbner, S. 1989. German 'schon-erst-noch': an integrated analysis. *Linguistic and Philosophy* 12:167-212.

McDaniel, D., McKee, C., and Cairns, H. S. eds. 1996. *Methods for Assessing Children's Syntax*. Cambridge: MIT Press.

Michaelis, L. A. 1996. Cross-world continuity and the polysemy of adverbial *still*, in G. Fauconnier and E. Sweetser, eds., *Spaces Worlds and Grammar*. Chicago: The University of Chicago Press.

Paris, M.- C. 1985. The semantics of JIU and CAI in Mandarin Chinese. *Computational Analysis of Asian and African Languages* No. 24:181-196.

Reilly, J. 1986. The acquisition of temporals and conditionals, in E. Traugott, A. ter Meulen, J. Relly and C.Ferguson, eds., *On Conditionals*. Academic press.

Rooth, M. 1985. *Association with Focus*. Doctoral Dissertation. University of Massachusetts at Amherst.

---1992. A theory of focus interpretation. *Natural Language Semantics* 1: 75-116.

--- 1996. Focus, in S. Lappin, ed., *The Handbook of Contemporary Semantic Theory*. London: Blackwell.

Taplin, J.E. 1971. Reasoning with conditional sentences. *Journal of Verbal Learning and Verbal Behavior* 10:219-225.

Tse, K.- P., Tang, T.- C., Shi, Y. and Li, E. 1991. *Chinese Children's Language Acquisition and Development*, National Science Council Research Report. Dept. of English, National Taiwan Normal University.

von Stechow, A. 1991. Current issues in the theory of focus, in A. von Stechow and D. Wunderlich, eds., *Semantik/Semantics*. Berlin: Walter de Gruyter.

Wing, C. and Scholnick, E. 1981. Children's comprehension of pragmatic concepts expressed in 'because', 'although', 'if' and 'unless'. *Journal of Child Language* 8: 347-365.

Part II

Phonology

The Role of Markedness in Onset Change

MOIRA YIP
University of California, Irvine and
University College London

Many Min dialects exhibit a type of reduplication in which one onset changes to a fixed segment, usually [l] (or [n] in nasal contexts). In some cases there are also special changes in tones and/or rhyme segments too. I will show that this onset change can be fully understood as an attempt to minimize the markedness of the output, and is not the result of some sort of affixation. This phenomenon thus falls under the first type of "fixed segmentism" identified in Alderete et al (1997), an instance of The Emergence of the Unmarked (TETU). A similar phenomenon is found in secret languages, but in one such language, Kunshan's Mo-pa secret language, the "fixed onsets" vary so widely that a markedness account appears implausible. I shall show that a straightforward markedness-based explanation is available here also. However, I will argue that the change here is not *caused* by markedness, but rather by the need for obfuscation, and markedness selects from various obscure outputs. A secondary line of argument will show that reduplication without onset change results when markedness considerations are over-ridden by positional faithfulness of several kinds. The analysis supersedes Yip (1993,5), in which onset change was the result of *ECHO constraints, and the role of markedness, though crucial, was not itself the cause of the change.

The paper is organized as follows. Section 1 looks at Chaoyang verbal reduplication, and uses these data as the basis for the central analysis. Section

On the Formal Way to Chinese Languages.
Sze-Wing Tang and Chen-Sheng Luther Liu (eds.).

two looks at Fuzhou, and extends the analysis to a sketch of tonal and rhymal markedness. Section three looks at secret languages, and focuses particularly on the Kunshan case. Section four shows that not all secret language facts can be explained by markedness, and that in some types affixation *is* involved. The final section sums up the findings.

1. Chaoyang verbal reduplication:

The following data (Zhang 1979a,b, 1980, 1982) contrasts two types of verbal reduplication. For space reasons I will not discuss polysyllabic inputs, or onomatopoeia. The first set of data shows onset-changing reduplication, and the second set shows non-onset-changing reduplication:

(1) *Onset change*:

a. *resultatives:* kuaʔ kuaʔ luaʔ tŋ 'cut off'
b. *directional complements* kiã kiã niã lai 'walk-come'
c. *durational complements* paʔ paʔ laʔ e 'pat once'

(2) *No onset change:*

a. *non-reduplicative compounding/affixation:*
teŋ tioʔ 'heavy weight'
b. *all other types of reduplication, including verbal, nominal, adjectival/adverbial, measure word*
hou bui bui 'rain slight' kuaŋ kuaŋ aŋ 'blush red'
haŋ toi toi 'alley's end' zik zik tsiõ paŋ 'everyday go to work'

These data raise two puzzles: (I) Why do onsets change at all, and why to [l] or [n]? (ii) Why can only some onsets change? I will propose the following answers: (I) Onsets change to reduce markedness. There is no affix. (ii) Marked onsets resist change if *either* a. they are the only surface correspondent of the input onset *or* b. they are initial in the morphological word *or* c. they are final in X".

1.1 Why do onsets change at all, and why to [l] or [n]?

The basic facts are given below:

(3) *Onsets become [l] if original onset and vowel are oral:*
kuaʔ luaʔ tŋ 'cut off' paʔ laʔ e 'pat once'
tsuŋ luŋ ta 'twist dry' tui lui tik 'pull straight'

b. Onsets become [n] if original onset or nucleus are nasal:

kiã niã lai 'walk-come' k'ŋ nŋ muã 'hide things'

kuẽ nuẽ k'u 'close-go' mueʔ nueʔ tiau 'finish up'

ŋaŋ naŋ tiau 'dig out with nails'

c. Only onset of second syllable changes.

ts'u lu tik *lu ts'u tik * lu lu tik

d. Second syllable must have onset; first syllable may be onsetless

uãi nuãi tiau 'dig out w. knives' *uãi uãi tiau,*nuãi nuãi tiau

e. Nucleus and coda never change/ delete:

tsuŋ luŋ ta 'twist dry' *tsuŋ lun ta, * tsuŋ lu ta, *tsuŋ liŋ ta

siap liap (siap liap) 'puckery' *siap liat, *siap lia[1]

I start with the assumption that this type of (near) total reduplication is self-compounding, with both halves of the output having equal status. No base-affix relationship exists, so FAITH-BR constraints can play no role. Instead, FAITH -IO constraints relate each half to the input. Reduplication is forced by constraints that require repetition, but I differ from my own previous work in subdividing these constraints into two that I will call ALLITERATE, and RHYME. ALLITERATE governs the initial consonant, RHYME governs the rest of the syllable, including any pre-nuclear glide. The combination of the two thus does the work done by ECHO or REPEAT in Yip (1993,5). RHYME and ALLITERATE must dominate IO-INTEGRITY, since in reduplicated outputs each input segment has *two* output correspondents.

(4)

$/b_1u_2i_3/$	MAX-IO	RHYME	ALLITERATE	IO-INTEGRITY
☞ a. $b_1u_2i_3\ b_1u_2i_3$				***
b. $b_1u_2i_3\ u_2$		*!	*!	*

I shall now show that onset change, resulting in less than full reduplication, is caused by markedness pressures. The central idea is that in reduplication each input segment has two output correspondents, each of which incurs a markedness violation. Replacing one correspondent with a less marked segment is thus a way to improve matters with respect to markedness, without violating FAITH-IO. The fixed segment is an introduced segment, in violation of DEP-IO, not a correspondent of an input segment.

---

[1] No examples of monosyllabic bases given with final labials

One fact, however, makes this approach look unpromising: unlike marked segments in the onset, marked segments in the rhyme survive in both correspondents, in double violation of markedness: /ŋaŋ/ reduplicates as [ŋaŋ naŋ], not [ŋaŋ nan] or [ŋaŋ na]. Final coronals are not allowed in Chaoyang, but complete loss of the final coda would remove a marked segment, and a NOCODA violation, without a FAITH-IO violation, and yet this does not happen. This puzzle is resolved by the division of ECHO into two parts, RHYME and ALLITERATE, with RHYME dominating markedness constraints, which in turn dominate ALLITERATE. The constraints are assessed gradiently; for each segment by which input and output differ in the absence or presence of some segment, or in the features of that segment, incur one asterisk (but see below for fine-tuning, and also for evidence of the active role played by ALLITERATE in Kunshan).

(5) RHYME>> MARKEDNESS >> ALLITERATE

/ŋaŋ/	RHYME	*DORSAL	ALLITERATE
☞ a. ŋaŋ naŋ		***	*
b. ŋaŋ na	*!	**	*
c. ŋaŋ ŋaŋ		****!	
d. ŋaŋ ŋa	*!	***	

In previous accounts (Yip 1993,5) *ECHO or *REPEAT forced non-identity, and markedness chose the best candidate from those that satisfied *ECHO. In this paper, there is no need for *ECHO. Markedness both causes the loss and picks the best candidate, an issue to which I now turn.

The choice of the voiced coronal [l] results from the familiar markedness hierarchy: *LABIAL, *DORSAL >> *CORONAL. The preference for a coronal over no onset at all shows that ONSET >> *CORONAL (cf Gafos (to appear) on Temiar). The choice of [l] over other coronals shows that *[-voice] is high-ranked, selecting the only voiced oral Coronal, /l/ in Chaoyang.[2] On the

[2] /l/ is often taken to be an obstruent in Min dialects: it fills the inventory slot where one would expect to find /d/. In that case, ranking *[-voice] >> *[+voice], as here, is rather dubious. In most cases, the choice of voiced /l/ could be attributed to intersonorant voicing (see below on Kunshan), but /l/ may also follow [ʔ, p, k]. Jie Zhang (p.c.) has suggested to me that [t] may be avoided in these contexts for a separate

choice of [n] in the presence of [nasal], see Yip (1994). All markedness constraints must of course dominate IDENT-IO.

(6)

/p'oi/	*LAB,*DORS	ONSET	*CORONAL	*[-VOICE]
☞a. p'oi loi	*		*	*
b. p'oi toi	*		*	**!
c. p'oi oi	*	*!		*
d. p'oi koi	**!			**

This analysis makes one clear prediction that distinguishes it from Yip (1993,5). If markedness, not *ECHO, drives onset change, then inputs with unmarked /l/ or /n/ onsets will not undergo further change. This is correct, as shown by examples like [lioʔ lioʔ e kiã] or [nuã nuã e]. *ECHO would wrongly predict onset change, even at the expense of a markedness *increase*.

(7)

/lioʔ/	ONSET	*[- VOICE]	ALLITERATE
☞ a. lioʔ lioʔ			
b. lioʔ tioʔ		*!	*
c. lioʔ ioʔ	*!		*

This completes the basic analysis, which in its essentials will extend to the data in the following sections also. I have shown that Chaoyang is an instance of Alderete et al's first type of fixed segmentism, but with the twist that onsets and rhymes behave differently here. Below I compare their schema with that argued for here:

(8) *The Emergence of the Unmarked (TETU) :*
MAX-IO >> MARKEDNESS >> MAX-BR
Chaoyang:
MAX-IO, RHYME >>MARKEDNESS >> ALLITERATE

---

reason: it would be hard to detect after an unreleased, glottalized stop.

1.2 Why can only some onsets change: Positional Faithfulness

The analysis so far would lead us to expect onset change in *all* forms of reduplication, but some onsets resist change. There are three sub-cases. First, only the second onset changes, never the first. The resistance of initial onset to change I assume to be caused by the well-known tendency for word-initial position to be especially faithful, a fact undoubtedly related to the role of word initial onsets in lexical access and processing (Beckman 1996, McCarthy and Prince 1995 Steriade 1997). The relevant constraint here is MAX-WORDINITIAL (MAX-WI). Either MAX-IO or MAX-WI must dominate *LABIAL.

(9)

/paʔ/	MAX-WI	MAX-IO	*LABIAL
☞ a. paʔ laʔ			*
b. laʔ paʔ	*!		*
c. laʔ laʔ	*!	*	

There is one other word-initial effect, but in order to discuss this I must set the scene by discussing the role of ONSET in the grammar. Earlier I showed that ONSET >> *CORONAL. The active influence of ONSET is also shown by the addition of an onset to an onsetless second syllable, at the expense of featural markedness, as in [uãi nuãi]. We therefore obtain the ranking ONSET >> DEP-IO. Returning to word-initial position, we see that there is never any onset addition in the first syllable, showing that DEP-WI >> ONSET.

(10)

/uãi/	DEP-WI	ONSET	DEP-IO
☞a. uãi nuãi		*	*
b. uãi uãi		**!	
c. nuãi uãi	*!	*	*
d. nuãi nuãi	*!		**

1.3 Role of MAX-IO

The second failure of onsets to change may seem obvious, but still demands an explicit account: onsets never change outside reduplication, in other types of affixation or compounding. In the account offered here, this follows from the assumption that reduplication is self- compounding. In reduplication, and only in reduplication, each input feature has two output correspondents. One correspondent is therefore free to change in response to markedness pressures without violating MAX-IO. In non-reduplicated forms the single output correspondent is protected from change by MAX-IO, as shown by the comparison of candidates (a) and (b) below.

(11)

/$k_1$ia $k^h{}_2$u/	MAX-IO	*DORSAL
☞ a. $k_1$ia $k^h{}_2$u		**
b. $k_1$ia lu	*k^h!	*
/$k_1$ua?/		
c. $k_1$ua? $k_1$ua?		**!
☞ d. $k_1$ua? lua?		*

1.4 Reduplication without onset change

The most challenging case is the type of reduplication in which onsets fail to change. The most obvious possibility is that the prosodic structure of the two types of reduplication might be different, so to assess this possibility I turn to the tonal facts. Chaoyang, like most Min dialects, has two allotones of each tone, one found at the end of a "tone group", and one non-finally. These are known as the citation tone, denoted T, and the sandhi tone, denoted T'. There is also a reduced, neutral tone, T". The status of the tone group as a prosodic domain is unclear, see Chen (2000) for a recent overview. Some relevant data are given below. The (a) cases show that in tone groups of the structure [T'..T'T], we find both onset-changing (12a) and non-onset-changing (13a) reduplication; the syllable whose onset changes, or fails to change, occupies the penultimate position in the tone group (whose end is marked with a final #). Whether or not the onset changes, then, cannot be conditioned either directly by the tonal context, or by its prosodic position or head/non-head status. The syllable whose onset changes, or fails to change, is underlined.

(12) *Onset-changing cases:*

a. *Changed syllable has sandhi tone: resultatives, duration/frequency with full numerical sense.*

kuaʔ luaʔ tŋ 'cut off'
T' T' T#

b. *Changed syllable has base tone, and is followed by neutral tone:directionals, durational/frequency complements:*

kiã niã lai 'walk-come'
T' T T"#

c. *Changed syllable has base tone, and is final in tone group:*
NONE

(13) *No onset change cases:*

a. *non-changed syllable has sandhi tone:*

kuaŋ kuaŋ aŋ 'blush red'
T' T' T#

zik zik tsiõ paŋ 'everyday go to work'
T' T' T' T #

b. *non-changed syllable has base tone, and is followed by neutral tone:* NONE

c. *non-changed syllable has base tone, and is final in tone group.*

hou bui bui 'rain slight'
T # T' T #

haŋ toi toi 'alley's end'
T' T' T #

What alternative is there? The following observations help us focus in on a solution. Observation I: Changing onsets are found in cases of either post-verbal complements (duration/frequency) within the VP, or plausible compounds (resultatives). Directionals could be either. Schematically, with the affected syllable underlined: $[[\text{V-}\underline{\text{V}}]_{\text{v}}\ \text{AdvP}]_{\text{v"}}$ or $[[\text{V-}\underline{\text{V}}\text{-Adj}]_{\text{v'}}]_{\text{v"}}$ Observation II: Non-changing onsets are found in predicates, NP's, or pre-verbal modifiers arguably outside VP: NP $[\ \text{V-}\underline{\text{V}}]_{\text{v"}}$ or $[\text{Adj-}\underline{\text{Adj}}]_{\text{Adv"}}\ [\text{V..}]_{\text{v"}}$. All and only the non-changing syllables are final in their X". It thus appears that this position is a privileged one, and protects the onset from change. Formulated as a constraint, we have:

(14) MAX-X"F: Onsets of syllables final in an X" cannot change.

This is of course a controversial move, making as it does direct reference to the syntax, but the data appear to warrant it. For relevant literature, see Chen 1990, Hayes 1990, and other papers in Inkelas and Zec 1990. With this in hand, it remains to rank this constraint above the markedness constraints, and we explain the resistance of the onsets to change.[3] In the table below I show only markedness violations for onsets.

(15)

/kuaŋ/	MAX-X"F	*DORSAL
☞ a. kuaŋ kuaŋ]$_{ADJ"}$		**
b. kuaŋ luaŋ]$_{ADJ"}$	*!	*
/kuaʔ/		
a. kuaʔ kuaʔ tŋ]$_{V'}$]$_{V"}$		**!
☞ b. kuaʔ luaʔ tŋ]$_{V'}$]$_{V"}$		*

I have now answered the questions with which I began this section. In the following sections I extend the analysis to other dialects with similar but interestingly different systems.

2. Fuzhou: onset loss, tonal neutralization, and rhyme simplification

Fuzhou (Zheng 1983) has a type of verbal reduplication whose onset data are identical to Chaoyang, but in which there is also rhyme change in the first syllable, and tonal change.

(16) Two types of verbal reduplication, strong parallels to Chaoyang:
1. Onset change, to /l/:

---

[3] In the version of this paper given at the conference, I speculated on why tones are more prone to neutralize than onsets in Chaoyang (and probably universally), and on why the positions in which onsets are preserved and the positions in which tones are preserved are not the same. For reasons of space, this discussion is omitted here.

[4] A different type of onset (and rhyme) change, onomatopoeia, always ends in the fixed suffix -kio, so the other syllables are never final, and free to change.

- Second syllable changes onset to /l/
- Verbs must have complements or lɛʔ
- First syllable reduced to C(G)V, undergoes special tone sandhi to 44, 31 or 11.

2. No onset change:

- Second syllable unchanged, except for lenition
- Verbs may not have complements
- First syllable segmentally unchanged, undergoes normal tone sandhi

Examples of the onset-change are given below; unlike Chaoyang, the onset is always /l/, never /n/, a fact which follows from the overall phonology of Fuzhou.

(17)	/pieu/	pie lieu ʒouʔ li	'squirt-come-out'
	/kuŋ/	ku luŋ......	'roll'
	/tau/	ta lau	'cover'
	/niaʔ/	nia liaʔ tɔ a	'blink once'
	/loʔ/	lo loʔ	'cover, sheath'
	/tʰaiŋ/	tʰa laiŋ lɛ	'stand straight (lit: stick out chest)'

The analysis for onset-change is precisely identical to Chaoyang. I now turn to the changes in the first syllable. There are two. In Fuzhou, non-final syllables normally undergo a set of sandhi changes shown in the second column below. The non-onset-changing reduplication shows these sandhi. In onset-changing reduplication, there is a further neutralization, as shown in the third column, reducing the set of tones to only three, eliminating the high falling and high rising tones, 53 and 35. Cross-linguistically, high tones are generally agreed to be marked with respect to low tones, and contour tones are marked with respect to level tones (Pulleyblank 1986), so it comes as no surprise to find that it is the high contour tones which go. Descriptively, I will assume a markedness constraint *HIGHCONTOUR which forces these tonal changes.

(18) *Tone sandhi in first syllable*

<table>
<tr><th>inventory of underlying tones</th><th>inventory of tones found in non-onset changing sandhi</th><th>inventory of tones found in onset changing sandhi</th></tr>
<tr><td>44</td><td>44</td><td>44</td></tr>
<tr><td>53</td><td rowspan="2">31</td><td rowspan="3">31</td></tr>
<tr><td>5ʔ</td></tr>
<tr><td>31</td><td>35</td></tr>
<tr><td>213</td><td rowspan="2">53</td><td rowspan="3">11</td></tr>
<tr><td>242</td></tr>
<tr><td>23ʔ</td><td>44/53</td></tr>
</table>

The second change is in syllable structure. Fuzhou syllables are maximally CGVGC, where G stands for glide. In onset-changing sandhi, the first syllable is maximally CGV. I will assume, following (Duanmu 1990) that the pre-nuclear glide in Chinese dialects is a secondary articulation on the onset, so that the resulting syllable is better written as $C^{G}V$, an instance of the unmarked CV syllable. These new syllables observe NOCODA, and NODIPHTHONG (Rosenthall 1994), two syllable structure markedness constraints.

The combination of these two changes results in a less marked first syllable, structurally and tonally, but at the expense of satisfying RHYME. The following tableau shows that NOCODA, NODIPHTHONG, and *HIGHCONTOUR >> RHYME. Note that MAX-IO blocks neutralization from happening in both syllables.

(19) *Normal sandhi would give 53. Differences in segments or tone violate RHYME.*

/tʰaiŋ 213/	NOCODA	NO DIPHTHONG	*HIGH CONTOUR	RHYME
a. tʰaiŋ 53 laiŋ 213	**!	**	*	*
b. tʰai 53 laiŋ 213	*	**!	*	**
c. tʰaŋ 53 laiŋ 213	**!	*	*	**
d. tʰa 53 laiŋ 213	*	*	*!	***
☞e. tʰa11 laiŋ 213	*	*		***

The remaining question is why does the first syllable neutralize its rhyme, and not the second? This I take to be an extension of the general pattern of Fuzhou sandhi: it is always the first syllable that changes. This could be because the second syllable is plausibly the head of the tone group; more likely, the same processing facts that privilege word-initial onsets privilege word-final rhymes: storage and retrieval pay attention to beginnings and ends, as does poetry. Final lengthening strengthens cues in the final rhyme (always assuming comparable stress). If this speculation is correct (something I do not have room to fully explore here), then we may treat the persistence of marked structures and tones in the final rhyme as the mirror-image of our treatment of the word-initial onset in Chaoyang, and propose a constraint MAX-FR (Final Rhyme). Either this constraint or MAX-IO must dominate NO-DIPHTHONG, NOCODA (and *HIGH CONTOUR).

(20)

/tau/	MAX-FR	MAX-IO	NODIPHTHONG
☞ a. ta lau			*
b. tau la	*!		*
c. ta la	*!	*	

3. A different source of fixed segmentism: Obfuscation

I now turn to a superficially identical but in fact rather different type of fixed segmentism, this time in secret languages. I shall show that here the role of markedness is limited to determining the solution, but does not cause the loss. The loss is instead caused by an essential property of these speech games: their secrecy, which I will instantiate as a constraint requiring that no output syllable is completely identical to the input syllable, or O ≠ I.

3.1 Changzhou

Changzhou has a secret language labeled by Chao (1931) as [məŋ-la], after the output from the input /ma/. Data can be found in Chao's paper, and analysis in Yip 1982, Bao 1990, among others. The syllable is reduplicated, the second onset is replaced by [l], and the first rhyme by [əŋ]. I only discuss the onset change here. As in Chaoyang and Fuzhou, the change can be seen as a response to markedness pressures, but there is a crucial difference. Recall that in Chaoyang and Fuzhou, unmarked *inputs* undergo no further change. But in the language game that is not the case: even an unmarked input changes, despite the fact that any change is in the direction of *increasing* markedness. /laɣ/ becomes [ləŋ taɣ], not *[ləŋ laɣ]. The reason is clear: if the onset did not change, the second syllable of the output would be entirely identical to the input syllable, sacrificing the very secrecy these games are designed to achieve. The change is minimal: the next least marked onset, /t/, is chosen instead, so the role of markedness is still clear. The following tableau shows two different inputs to the grammar, /ma/ and /laɣ/, and the role of O ≠ I in forcing an *increase* in markedness.

(21)

/ma/	O ≠ I	*LABIAL	*CORONAL	*[-VOICE]
☞ a. məŋ la		*	*	
b. məŋ ta		*	*	*!
c. məŋ ma	*!	**		
/laɣ/				
☞ a. ləŋ taɣ			**	*
b. ləŋ laɣ	*!		**	
c. ləŋ paɣ		*!	*	*

3.2 Kunshan: A case where markedness fails

A particularly interesting secret language is found in the Wu dialect of Kiangsu, Kunshan, and called the Mo-pa language by Chao. Data are given below:

(22) *Kunshan Mo pa secret language:*

təw	to ləw	vã	vo pã
k'ɛ	k'o ɦɛ	sya	so tsya
d'oŋ	d'o loŋ	nəw	no təw
tsa	tso za	ñən	ño tɕən

The generalizations are as follows. In the second syllable, stops become voiced continuants., nasals and continuants become voiceless unaspirated stops, and place features are always unchanged. At first glance, this hardly looks like a markedness effect, since the new onset can have either value of the features [voice, cont]. Indeed, Yip (1982) analyzed it as dissimilation. I shall show that despite appearances this is also the result of markedness pressures, but here they are not just absolute but also contextual (Steriade 1995), a set of paradigmatic and syntagmatic markedness constraints. An outline of the solution is given below; it is the various constraints on voicing and continuancy that select the preferred output.

(23) *The solution:*

Constraints	Effect
O ≠ I	Forces onset change
ONSET	Blocks onset deletion
IDENT-IO PLACE >> *PLACE	Blocks Place change
*MANNER >>IDENT-IO MANNER	Permits Manner change
*[+VCE, -CONT]	Voiced stops are marked (Maddieson 1984)
*[+CONT]	Stops preferred to fricatives (Maddieson 1984)
*V [-VOICE] V	Intervocalic voicing. Onset of second syllable always intervocalic

The resistance of Place features to change is demonstrated by the tableau below.

(24)

/vã/	O ≠ I	IDENT-PLACE	*LABIAL
☞ a. vo pã			*
b. vo vã	*!		*
c. vo lã		*!	

The next two tableaux show how the grammar selects among various candidates in which Place has been held constant:

(25)

/vã/	O ≠ I	*MANNER			IDENT-MANNER
		*+VCE, -CONT	*V[-VCE]V	*[+CONT]	
☞ a. vo pã			*		*
b. vo vã	*!			*	
c. vo bã		*!			*
d. vo fã			*	*!	

(26)

/tsa/	O ≠ I	*MANNER			IDENT-MANNER
		*+VCE -CONT	*V [-VCE] V	*[+CONT]	
☞ a. tso za				*	*
b. tso tsa	*!		*		
c. tso dza		*!			
d. tso sa			*!	*	*

One final detail: nothing yet blocks deletion of the second onset, plus epenthesis of an unmarked /l/: MAX-IO will only ensure one surviving correspondent, and here we need two. ALLITERATE must be highly ranked, and assessed gradiently (one * for each feature that differs), so that it can eliminate even non-correspondent unmarked segments that do not alliterate in Place:

(27)

v_1ã	ALLITERATE	IDENT-PLACE	*LABIAL
☞ a. v_1o p_1ã	**		**
b. v_1o t_1ã	***!	*	*
c. v_1o tã	***!		*

So far I have argued that fixed onsets result from the interaction of markedness constraints with requirements for identity, such as RHYME and ALLITERATE, and requirements for non-identity, such as O ≠ I. These data fit neatly into the overall picture of Alderete et al in which fixed segmentism is a TETU phenomenon. Not all fixed segmentism, as they are at pains to show, is of this type, and I finish this paper with a case of the second type, in which the fixed segment is indeed an affix.

4. Affixal onset change: Mandarin May-ka

Unlike all the cases we have looked at so far, and unlike the majority of Chinese secret languages, Mandarin's May-ka secret language has [k] as its fixed segment, not [l]. Analyzing [k] as the least marked onset is clearly implausible, so this language serves as an example of Alderete et al's Type II fixed segmentism, in which the fixed segment is an affix. Since the rhyme also has fixed segmentism, [ay], I assume the affix is an unordered bi-partite /k, ay/. MAX-IO will force realization of the affix at the expense of markedness, and the placement of the affix is enforced by ALIGN-L (ROOT), forcing the affix to the inside, and O ≠ I, which as usual outlaws any output that includes the input syllable intact. /k/ cannot be a coda in Mandarin, ruling out *[ak may].

(28)

/ma, k, ay/	ALIGNL(ROOT)	O ≠ I	MAX-IO	*DORSAL
☞ a. may ka				*
b. ka may	*!			*
c. ma kay		*!		*
d. kay ma	*!	*		*
e. may la			*!	

Even in this affixal system, markedness plays a role. Inputs with /k/ as their onset do not take the /k/ affix, but instead surface with [l]: /kaw/ becomes [kay law]. The reason is clear: *[kay kaw] would violate O ≠ I, so the grammar chooses the least marked alternative.[5]

(29) *TETU is still seen under pressure from O ≠ I:*

/$k_1$aw, k_2, ay/	ALIGN L (ROOT)	O ≠ I	MAX-IO	*DORSAL
a. $k_1$ay $k_2$aw		*!		**
☞b. $k_1$ay law			k_2*	*
c. law $k_2$aw	*!	*	k_1*	*

5. Two types of fixed segmentism in Chinese

This paper has uncovered two distinct types of fixed segmentism within Chinese, and between them they illustrate all Alderete et al's Markedness predictions (p.59).

First, let us look at the properties of fixed segmentism based on TETU:

- Markedness constraints will be "inventory-defining" in some other language: true of all of ONSET, Coronal unmarkedness, *[+VCE, -CONT],

[5]Mey-ka language (also Mandarin) ranks Max-IO>> O≠I , so kaw > key kau, not *key lau.

*[+CONT], *V[-VOICE]V (intervocalic voicing), NODIPHTHONG, NOCODA.

- Default segments should also obey markedness constraints: In Chaoyang, Mandarin, and many other dialects, related or not, [l] recurs over and over again as the default onset in reduplication, onomatopoeia, and secret languages.
- "Fixed segmentism" may show contextual variance: Mo-pa is an extreme example of this.
- Unmarked segments may emerge only when copying is imperfect: the May-ka emergence of /l/ is a good example.
- Unmarkedness may show up as a failure to copy: Suzhou violates ONSET in order to reduce markedness by deletion: hɐ > ɐ-hən, pɔ > ɔ-pən.

Now let us look at the properties of fixed segmentism based on affixation:

- A language may have more than one affix: Mandarin has m*ay-k*a, m*ey-k*a, and m*ən-t'*a.
- Must align as an affix: here treated as Align L(Root).
- Context sensitive, should undergo phonological processes of host language: Like all Mandarin velars, /k/ affix palatalizes before high front vowels: ɕiaŋ > ɕiay tɕiaŋ, *kiaŋ. ([iay] also coalesces to[Iɛ])

Acknowledgments:
This paper was written in 1997 with the generous support of a grant from the Chiang Ching Guo Foundation. I would like to thank the organizers of the "On the Formal Way to Chinese Languages" conference, Sze-wing Tang and Luther Liu, my research assistants, Li Xiao-guang, Sze-wing Tang, and Di Wu, and all the participants in the conference. This paper has been greatly improved as a result of comments from the audience, especially Raung-fu Chung and Jie Zhang. All errors are of course my own.

References

Alderete, John, Jill Beckman, Laura Benua, Amalia Gnanadesikan, John McCarthy, and Suzanne Urbanczyk. 1997. Reduplication with fixed segmentism. Ms, U.Mass Amherst. ROA#

Bao, Zhi-ming 1990 "Fanqie Languages and Reduplication" Linguistic Inquiry 21.3:317-350

Beckman, Jill. 1996. Positional Faithfulness and the distribution of phonological features. Ms, UMass Amherst.

Casali, Rod. 1996, *Resolving hiatus.* UCLA Ph D Dissertation.

Chao, Y-R 1931 "Fanqie yu ba zhong (Eight Varieties of Languages Based on the Principle of Fanqie)" Bulletin of the Institute of History and Philology Academia Sinica 2:320-354

Chen, Matthew 1990 "What must Phonology Know about Syntax" The Phonology-Syntax Connection Inkelas, S. and D. Zec, eds. University of Chicago Press.pp 19-46

Chen, Matthew (1987). The syntax of Xiamen tone sandhi. Phonology 4: 109_150.

Chen, Matthew 2000 *Tone Sandhi*. Cambridge University Press..

Du, Tsai-chwun 1988 *Tone and stress in Taiwanese*. PhD Dissertation, U. of Illinois at Urbana-Champaign.

Duanmu, S. (1990). *A formal study of syllable, tone, stress and domain in Chinese languages* MIT Ph. D. Dissertation.

Flemming, Edward 1995 Auditory representations in phonology. PhD Dissertation, UCLA.

Gafos, D. (to appear) Eliminating long-distance consonant spreading. *NLLT*. 16.

Hayes, B. 1990 Precompiled phrasal phonology. The Phonology-Syntax Connection Inkelas, S. and D. Zec, eds. University of Chicago Press.pp 85-108.

Hsu, Chai-Shune 1996 Voicing underspecification in Taiwanese word-final consonants. Paper presented at the 1996 LSA, San Diego. To appear in Margaret MacEachern ed., UCLA Working Papers in Phonology.

Hsu, Chai-Shune, and Sun-ah Jun 1997 Prosodic strengthening in Taiwanese: syntagmatic or paradigmatic? Ms., OSU.

Inkelas, Sharon, and Draga Zec (eds.) (1990). The Phonology-Syntax Connection. Chicago: University of Chicago Press.

Jun, Jongho 1995 *Perceptual and articulatory factors in place assimilation: an Optimality Theoretic approach*. PhD Dissertation, UCLA

Lin, Jowang 1994 Lexical government and tone group formation in Xiamen Chinese. *Phonology* 11:237-76.

Maddieson, Ian (1984). Patterns of Sound. Cambridge: CUP.

McCarthy, John and Alan Prince. 1995. Faithfulness and reduplicative identity. *UMass Occasional Papers in Linguistics 18: Papers in Optimality Theory*. ed. by Jill Beckman, Laura Walsh Dickey, and Suzanne Urbanczyk. 249-384.

Pulleyblank, D. 1986 *Tone in Lexical Phonology*. Reidel, Dordrecht.

Rosenthall, S. 1994. Vowel/glide alternation in a theory of constraint interaction. PhD Dissertation, UMass Amherst.

Steriade, D. 1995 Underspecification and markedness. In John Goldsmith, ed. *The Handbook of Phonological Theory*. Blackwell, Oxford. 114-174.

Steriade, Donca 1997 Phonetics in phonology: the case of laryngeal neutralization. Ms, UCLA.

Tsay, J. and J. Myers 1996 Taiwanese tone sandhi as allomorph selection. *BLS* 22: 394-405.

Yip, M. 1982 "Reduplication and CV Skeleta in Chinese Secret Languages" Linguistic Inquiry 13.4:637-662

Yip, M. 1993 The Interaction of Align, Parse-Place, and Echo in Reduplication. Paper given at ROW-1. Handout to appear in Prince 1993.

Yip, M. 1994 Morpheme-level features: Chaoyang syllable structure and nasalization. To appear in *Proceedings of the Sixth NACCL,* USC 1994. Also ROA-81.

Yip, M. 1995. Identity avoidance in phonology and morphology. To appear in the *Proceedings of the Conference on Morphology and its Relation to Syntax and Phonology*, UC Davis.

Zhang, Sheng Yu. 1979a. Chaoyang fangyan de chongdieshi. [Reduplication in the Chaoyang dialect]. Zhongguoyuwen 1979, 2.106-114.

Zhang, Sheng Yu. 1979b. Chaoyang fangyan de liandu biandiao. [Tone sandhi in the Chaoyang dialect]. Fangyan 1979, 2.93-121.

Zhang, Sheng Yu. 1980. Chaoyang fangyan de liandu biandiao. [Tone Sandhi in the Chaoyang dialect (II)]. Fangyan 1980, 2.123-136.

Zhang, Sheng Yu. 1982. Chaoyang fangyan de xiangshengzi chongdie shi. [The reduplicated onomatopoeic particles in the Chaoyang dialect]. Fangyan 1982, 3.181-182.

Zheng Yi De 1983 Reduplication of mono-syllabic verbs in the Fuzhou dialect (In Chinese). Zhongguo Yuwen 1983.2:30-39.

A Phonetically-Based OT Account for the /n/-/ŋ/ Asymmetry upon /ɻ/-Suffixation in Northern Chinese Dialects*

JIE ZHANG
University of California, Los Angeles

1. Introduction

In many northern Chinese dialects, a retroflex approximant /ɻ/ can be suffixed to a noun to indicate the diminutive or endearing meaning of the noun. This paper focuses on the realization of the coda nasal of the stem—/n/ or /ŋ/—in the /ɻ/-suffixed forms. First, a dialectal survey of the realization patterns of the coda nasals in the suffixed forms is discussed. The survey shows that the stems closed by /ŋ/ are more inclined to preserve the nasality than the stems closed by /n/ upon /ɻ/-suffixation. A phonetic study on Beijing Mandarin is then documented. The results show that in the unsuffixed forms, the /ŋ/-coda induces a longer nasal flow duration than the /n/-coda, and I infer that the nasality induced by the /ŋ/-coda is perceptually more salient than the nasality induced by the /n/-coda.. Based on the results of the phonetic study, I propose an Optimality-Theoretic analysis for the

* I would like to thank Donca Steriade, Bruce Hayes, Yen-Hwei Lin, and two anonymous reviewers for their detailed comments on earlier versions of this paper. I also thank the audiences at the 'On the formal way to Chinese linguistics' conference, the 4th Seoul International Conference on Linguistics, NELS-29, and NACCL-10/IACL-7, where various aspects of this work were presented. All remaining errors are my own responsibility. A substantially revised version of this paper was published in *Phonology* 17.3 (2000) under the title 'Non-contrastive features and categorical patterning in Chinese diminutive suffixation—MAX[F] or IDENT[F]?'

On the Formal Way to Chinese Languages.
Sze-Wing Tang and Chen-Sheng Luther Liu (eds.).

/n/-/ŋ/ asymmetry upon /ɻ/-suffixation in the surveyed dialects. Finally, two previous accounts for the Beijing Mandarin data are reviewed, and the advantages of the OT analysis over these accounts are outlined.

2. A Dialectal Survey

2.1 Dialects in which /CVŋ/ Behaves Differently from /CVn/ upon /ɻ/-Suffixation

In Beijing (Dow 1972, 1984, Lin and Wang 1992), Zhengzhou (Lu 1992), and many other northern Chinese dialects, upon /ɻ/-suffixation, the nasal codas in both /CVn/ and /CVŋ/ stems are lost, but the stem vowel in /CVŋ/+/ɻ/ becomes heavily nasalized while the stem vowel in /CVn/+/ɻ/ stays oral, resulting in neutralization between /CVn/+/ɻ/ and /CV/+/ɻ/. Examples from Beijing and Zhengzhou are given in (1) and (2) respectively.[1, 2]

(1) Beijing

/CV/+/ɻ/→[CVɻ]:	/pʰa/+/ɻ/→[pʰaɻ]	"rake"
	/sɨˢ/+/ɻ/→[sɨˢɻ][3]	"silk"
/CVn/+/ɻ/→[CVɻ]:	/pʰan/+/ɻ/→[pʰaɻ]	"plate"
	/ɕin/+/ɻ/→[ɕiɻ]	"heart"
/CVŋ/+/ɻ/→[CṼɻ]:	/pʰɑŋ/+/ɻ/→[pʰɑ̃ɻ]	"side"
	/ɕiŋ/+/ɻ/→[ɕĩɻ]	"star"

(2) Zhengzhou (Lu 1992)

/CV/+/ɻ/→[CVɻ]:	/tʂʰa/+/ɻ/→[tʂʰaɻ]	"twig"
	/kɤ/+/ɻ/→[kɤɻ]	"pigeon"
/CVn/+/ɻ/→[CVɻ]:	/pan/+/ɻ/→[paɻ]	"work"
	/tʂən/+/ɻ/→[tʂəɻ]	"a while"
/CVŋ/+/ɻ/→[CṼɻ]:	/paŋ/+/ɻ/→[pãɻ]	"side"
	/siŋ/+/ɻ/→[siə̃ɻ]	"star"

Other northern Chinese dialects which have the similar behavior include Juxian (Shi 1995), Changhai (Li 1981), Huojia (He 1982), Harbin (Yin

---

1 Notice that in some of the examples given, aside from nasalization, there are also vowel changes that accompany the loss of the nasal coda. These changes, to the best of my knowledge, are not relevant to the current investigation. Readers are advised to ignore these changes for the time being for simplicity reasons. The tones and tone sandhi processes that accompany the /ɻ/-suffixation are not relevant to the issue in question either and are thus not indicated in the examples.

2 The notations in the original literature are modified to standard IPA.

3 The phonetic symbol [ɨˢ] represents the so-called apical vowel or syllabic fricative which occurs after [s] in northern Chinese dialects.

1995), Wulumuqi (Zhou 1994), Xiangcheng (Liu 1993), Muping (Luo 1995), etc.

In a few other dialects, when the stem has a /Vŋ/ rime, the /ɻ/-suffix cannot blend with the stem to form a rhotacized syllable as in Beijing Mandarin. Rather, it is realized as a separate syllable following the stem, leaving the stem unchanged. But when the stem has a /Vn/ rime, the /ɻ/-suffix overlaps with the stem as in Beijing and Zhengzhou, deleting the nasal coda of the stem and leaving the stem vowel nasalized or non-nasalized.

Mancheng, a dialect spoken in Hebei Province, prohibits the /ɻ/-suffix to overlap with a /Vŋ/ rime, but not with a /Vn/ rime. The stem vowel in a /Vn/ rime is left non-nasalized while the nasal coda is deleted upon /ɻ/-suffixation (Chen 1988). Some examples of Mancheng are given in (3).

(3) Mancheng (Chen 1988)

/CV/+/ɻ/→[CVɻ]:	/pa/+/ɻ/→[pɐɻ]	"handle"
	/tɕi/+/ɻ/→[tɕiəɻ]	"chicken"
/CVn/+/ɻ/→[CVɻ]:	/mən/+/ɻ/→[məɻ]	"door"
	/pʰan/+/ɻ/→[pʰɐɻ]	"plate"
/CVŋ/+/ɻ/→[CVŋ]+[ŋəɻ]:	/iaŋ/+/ɻ/→[iaŋ]+[ŋəɻ]	"sheep"
	/ɕiŋ/+/ɻ/→[ɕiŋ]+[ŋəɻ]	"apricot"

Anqing, a dialect spoken in Anhui Province, behaves similarly to Mancheng except that the stem vowel in a /Vn/ rime is nasalized when the nasal coda is deleted upon /ɻ/-suffixation (Hao 1982). Examples from this dialect are given in (4).

(4) Anqing (Hao 1982)

/CV/+/ɻ/→[CVɻ]:	/po/+/ɻ/→[poɻ]	"ball"
	/xa/+/ɻ/→[xaɻ]	"a while"
/CVn/+/ɻ/→[CṼɻ]:	/pan/+/ɻ/→[pãɻ]	"plank"
	/tɕʰien/+/ɻ/→[tɕʰiẽɻ]	"before"
/CVŋ/+/ɻ/→[CVŋ]+[ŋəɻ]:	/noŋ/+/ɻ/→[noŋ]+[ŋəɻ]	"coop"

2.2 Dialects in which /CVŋ/ Behaves Identically to /CVn/ upon /ɻ/-Suffixation

Dialects in which /CVŋ/ and /CVn/ behave identically in the suffixation process are also attested.

A number of dialects do not have nasalization on the stem vowels in either /CVŋ/+/ɻ/ or /CVn/+/ɻ/. Liaocheng (Zhang 1995), Chengdu (Yuan 1989), Nanjing (Liu 1997), Yinchuan (Gao and Zhang 1997) and Miyang (Li 1996) are cases of this sort. Examples of Liaocheng, Chengdu and Miyang are given in (5) through (7). Nanjing and Yinchuan behave identically as Chengdu. Note that in Miyang, the suffix in question is a retroflex lateral approximant /ɭ/ rather than /ɻ/.

(5) Liaocheng (Zhang 1995)[4]

/CV$_1$/+/ɻ/→[CV$_1$ɻ]:	/pa/+/ɻ/→[pɐɻ]	"handle"
	/i/+/ɻ/→[ieɻ]	"one"
/CV$_1$n/+/ɻ/→[CV$_1$ɻ]:	/in/+/ɻ/→[ieɻ]	"sound"
	/uən/+/ɻ/→[ueɻ]	"lines"
/CV$_1$ŋ/+/ɻ/→[CV$_1$ɻ]:	/pɑŋ/+/ɻ/→[pɐɻ]	"side"
	/iŋ/+/ɻ/→[iəɻ]	"shadow"

(6) Chengdu (Yuan 1989)

/C(V$_1$)V$_2$/+/ɻ/→[C(V$_1$)əɻ]:	/ko/+/ɻ/→[kəɻ]	"song"
	/mau/+/ɻ/→[məɻ]	"cat"
/C(V$_1$)V$_2$n/+/ɻ/→[C(V$_1$)əɻ]:	/pan/+/ɻ/→[pəɻ]	"class"
	/tɕian/+/ɻ/→[tɕiəɻ]	"item"
/C(V$_1$)V$_2$ŋ/+/ɻ/→[C(V$_1$)əɻ]:	/kəŋ/+/ɻ/→[kəɻ]	"thick soup"
	/tsɔŋ/+/ɻ/→[tsuəɻ]	"cup"

(7) Miyang (Li 1996)

/CV$_1$/+/ɭ/→[CV$_1$ɭ]:	/pa/+/ɭ/→[pɜɭ]	"handle"
	/pʰi/+/ɭ/→[pʰiəɭ]	"skin"
/CV$_1$n/+/ɭ/→[CV$_1$ɭ]:	/pan/+/ɭ/→[pɜɭ]	"plank"
	/piɛn/+/ɭ/→[piɜɭ]	"edge"
/CV$_1$ŋ/+/ɭ/→[CV$_1$ɭ]:	/pɑŋ/+/ɭ/→[pɜɭ]	"stick"
	/piŋ/+/ɭ/→[piɜɭ]	"soldier"

On very rare occasions, the stem vowels in both /CVn/ and /CVŋ/ are nasalized upon suffixation. Only one marginal case of this sort was found in the typological study—Jiyuan (He 1981, Duanmu 1990, Lin 1993). It is marginal because there are two diminutive suffixes in Jiyuan, but as argued in Duanmu (1990) and Lin (1993), neither of them is /ɻ/. Duanmu (1990) claims that the first diminutive suffix is a segment with the feature [+back, +round], and Lin (1993) suggests the feature bundle [-back, +round] for the second diminutive suffix.[5] The correspondence between the root rime and the two diminutive rimes is given in (8a) and (8b).

---

4 It is also documented in Zhang (1995) that in various towns around Liaocheng city, the rimes /ɑŋ/, /əŋ/, /iɑŋ/, /iŋ/, /uɑŋ/ and /uŋ/ are realized as [ɑ̃ɻ],[ə̃ɻ], [iɑ̃ɻ], [ĩɻ], [uɑ̃ɻ] and [uə̃ɻ] respectively upon /ɻ/-suffixation.

5 He (1981) claims that the first suffix in Jiyuan is a /zi/ suffix, while only the second suffix is the /ɻ/ suffix in traditional Chinese philology. Both suffixes are diminutive. But since neither suffix has a close resemblance to its claimed segmental composition, we take both suffixes into consideration here.

(8) Jiyuan (He 1981, Duanmu 1990, Lin 1993)

a. Diminutive suffix I:

Root Rime	Diminutive Rime
i, iʔ	iu
u, uʔ	u
a, au, aʔ, e	ɔ
ia, iau, iaʔ, ie	iɔ
ua, uaʔ, ue	uɔ
ye, yaʔ	yɔ
an	ã
ian	iã
uan	uã
yan	yã
aŋ	ɔ̃
iaŋ	iɔ̃
uaŋ	uɔ̃
yaŋ	yɔ̃

b. Diminutive suffix II:

Root Rime	Diminutive Rime
i	iɥ
u	uɥ
y	yɥ
a	æ
ə, aw, ay	ø
əw, əy	əɥ
ən, əŋ	ə̃ɥ
in, iŋ	ĩɥ
un, uŋ	ũɥ
yn, yŋ	ỹɥ
an	ø[6]
aŋ	æ̃

2.3 Summary of the Survey

Although how /CVn/ and /CVŋ/ differ in their realization upon /ɻ/-suffixation is not always the same across dialects, the directionality of the difference is always the same. Namely, it is always more important to preserve the nasality in /ŋ/ than that in /n/. The difference is shown either by nasalization of the vowel in /CVŋ/+/ɻ/, but not in the other, or by simply requiring the /CVŋ/ rimes to be intact upon /ɻ/-suffixation. The opposite situation where the nasality of /n/ is more prominently preserved than that of /ŋ/ is not attested to the best of my knowledge.

---

6 The /an/ rime is not nasalized after suffixation because of an independent constraint *ø̃, proposed by Lin (1993).

3. A Phonetic Study of Unsuffixed Words in Beijing Mandarin

3.1 Hypothesis and Method

To better understand the nature of the /n/-/ŋ/ asymmetry upon /ɻ/-suffixation, a phonetic study on Beijing Mandarin was conducted. The basic question that the phonetic study asked was whether the /ŋ/-coda induced a more salient perception of nasality than the /n/-coda in the unsuffixed words. The reason why this question was asked was that if the answer to the question was positive, then the nasality of /ŋ/ being more prominently preserved than that of /n/ in the suffixed forms would have a phonetically natural explanation.

I seeked to answer this question through an aerodynamic experiment. Specifically, I tested whether there was a longer nasal flow duration during the vowel in /CVŋ/ than the vowel in /CVn/.

The reason why the nasal flow duration during the vowel is a good indication of the strength of nasal perception is three-fold. First, the presence of the nasal flow indicates an opening of the velopharyngeal port, which is necessary for the acoustic coupling of the nasal tract with the oral tract. Such acoustic coupling is the main cue for the perception of nasality (Delattre 1954, House and Stevens 1956, House 1957, Takeuchi et al. 1975, Maeda 1982). Second, a longer nasal coupling during the vowel gives the vowel a stronger nasal percept. This is shown by studies by Delattre and Monnot (1968) and Whalen and Beddor (1989), who have demonstrated that with equal nasal coupling, longer vowels receive higher nasalization ratings than shorter vowels. Third, Whalen and Beddor (1989) have also shown that with unambiguous nasality, there is no effect of duration on perception. Under the assumption that nasal consonants are unambiguously nasal, we should not expect the duration of the nasal coda to affect the strength of the nasal perception. Through this chain of reasoning, we are led to infer that the nasal flow duration during the vowel in /CVn/ or /CVŋ/ can accurately indicate the relative strength of the perceived nasality induced by the nasal coda: the longer this duration, the stronger the nasal percept.

One concern for the present study is the degree of nasal coupling on the vowel in /CVn/ and /CVŋ/. In Delattre and Monnot (1968) and Whalen and Beddor (1989)'s studies, the effect of duration is found under matched nasal coupling conditions (by constant formant configuration in Delattre and Monnot, and constant velopharyngeal port opening in Whalen and Beddor). For the present study, to ensure that any durational differences, if found, translate into perceptual differences, we must also show that the nasal coupling during the vowel in /CVŋ/ is at least as strong as the nasal coupling during the vowel in /CVn/. The parameter that I used to monitor this effect was the average nasal airflow (*ml/s*) during the nasalized portion of the vowel. The degree of nasal coupling is primarily determined by the size of the velopharyngeal opening (House and Stevens 1956, Abramson et al. 1981, Bell-Berti and Baer 1983), and nasal airflow is an indicator of the size of this opening (Benguerel 1974, Cohn 1990, 1993, Huffman 1990). But nasal airflow is also influenced by two factors other than the velopharyngeal opening—the overall glottal flow and the impedance in the oral tract. When the overall glottal flow increases, the nasal flow may increase even when the velopharyngeal opening stays the same; and when the oral impedence increases, given that more air will be forced out of the nasal tract, the nasal flow may also increase when the velopharyngeal opening stays the same. Since the overall glottal flow and oral impedence have been reported to have negligible effects in the acoustic coupling between the nasal and oral tracts (House and Stevens 1956, Bell-Berti and Baer 1983, Krakow and Huffman 1993), it is important for us to factor out their influences on the nasal flow in our study. To factor out the influence of the overall glottal flow, I simultaneously collected the oral flow and calculated the proportion of the nasal flow in the overall flow (=nasal flow + oral flow). To control for the effect of oral impedance, I used matched vowels between /CVn/ and /CVŋ/ to ensure matched oral configurations in these two environments. The nasal coda has two slight allophonic effects on the vowel quality in Beijing Mandarin: the vowel in the /_ŋ/ context is slightly lower (Dow 1972, 1984), which will decrease the oral impedance; but the /_ŋ/ context might also draw the tongue further back, which will increase the oral impedance. Therefore, it is reasonable to assume that these slight allophonic effects on oral impedance generally cancel each other out.

In (9), I lay out the specific hypotheses to be tested in the aerodynamic experiment on Beijing Mandarin.

(9) In the unsuffixed form,
  a. the vowel in /CVŋ/ has a longer nasal airflow duration than that in /CVn/;
  b. the proportion of the nasal airflow in the overall glottal airflow is no less during the nasalized portion of the vowel in /CVŋ/ than during the nasalized portion of the vowel in /CVn/.

Two male native speakers of Beijing Mandarin—JZ (the author) and HL—participated in the study. The test words included six pairs of /CVn/ and /CVŋ/ words. In each pair, C was a matching oral obstruent and V was a matching vowel. Nasal onsets were avoided. All words had a high-level tone (1st tone). The complete word list is given in (10). '˥' indicates high-level tone.

(10)	tan˥	"sheet"	taŋ˥	"crotch (of pants)"
	kan˥	"dry"	kaŋ˥	"jar"
	ɕin˥	"heart"	ɕiŋ˥	"star"
	cɕin˥	"today"	cɕiŋ˥	"spirit"
	kən˥	"root"	kəŋ˥	"thick soup"
	ʈʂən˥	"true"	ʈʂəŋ˥	"argument"

The test words were read in the carrier sentence in (11). Each sentence was read with five repetitions, with randomised order.

(11) [wo ʂʷo ___ tʂɤ kɤ tsɨ]
I say ___ this measure-word character
"I say the character ___."

Macquirer (an aerodynamic data acquisition system developed by SCICON and the UCLA Phonetics Laboratory) was used to collect the nasal flow, oral flow and the audio signal of the sentences. One nasal mask and one oral mask were held by the speaker and pressed tightly around the nose and mouth when the sentences were uttered. These masks were connected to pressure transducers, and the pressures were subsequently converted to electrical signals in millivolts (*mv*). A calibration device was then used to determine the correspondence between the voltage values in *mv* and the nasal flow values in *ml/s*. An example token is given in (12).

(12) [wo ʂʷo cɕiŋ tʂɤ kɤ tsɨ]

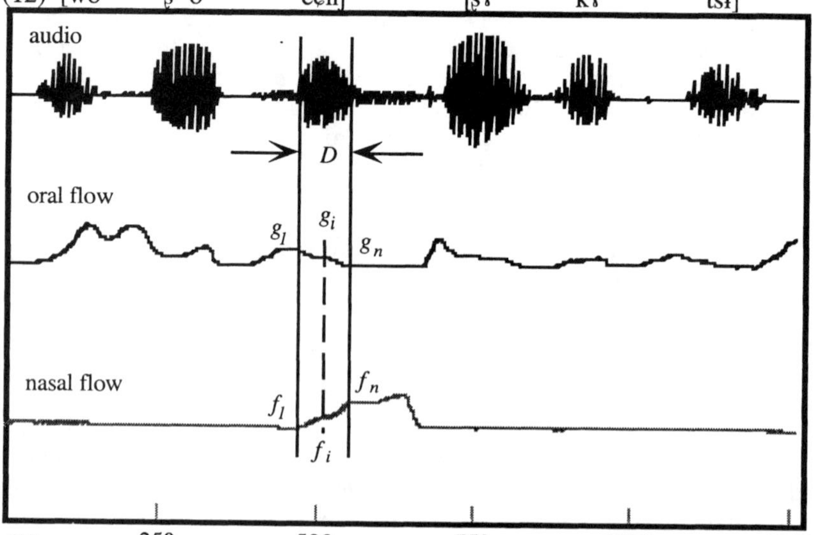

All the recorded tokens were used, as the comparison between the vowel duration in the final and non-final repetitions yielded no significant result. The nasal and oral flow values during the nasalized portion of the vowel of the targeted words were recorded at a sampling rate of 11025Hz (f_1-f_n and g_1-g_n in (12)). The nasalized portion of the vowel was demarcated by the beginning of positive values in the nasal flow signal and the end of the vowel in the acoustic signal. The duration of the entire vowel and its nasalized portion (*D* in (12)) were measured, and the proportion of the nasalized vowel duration to the entire vowel duration was calculated. The duration of the nasal coda in each token was also measured.

The average nasal airflow during the nasalized portion of the vowel was calculated using the formula in (13a). The average proportion of nasal flow in the overall flow in the nasalized portion of the vowel was calculated using the formula in (13b).

(13) a. $\overline{U}_n = \frac{1}{n}\sum_{i=1}^{n} f_i$ b. $\frac{\overline{U_n}}{U_g} = \frac{1}{n}\sum_{i=1}^{n}\frac{f_i}{f_i + g_i}$

The acoustic signals recorded were only used for the purpose of segmentation and duration measurements. No inference on perception was drawn from the acoustic signals, primarily due to the fact that the acoustic consequences of nasal coupling, such as the shift of formant frequencies caused by nasal formants and zeros, are difficult to measure and quantify because of the complexity of the acoustic coupling between the oral and nasal tracts (Cohn 1990, 1993, Krakow and Huffman 1993). Moreover, since an oral mask was used to collect the oral flow during the recording, the acoustic recording was not of high enough quality to do detailed spectrographic analyses.

For each subject, one-way ANOVA's with the nasal place of articulation as the independent factor were carried out for the nasal flow duration, average nasal flow, average overall flow, and average nasal flow proportion, to determine the significance of the effects observed. Obviously, these tests treat subjects as a fixed effect and therefore only allow inference about these two subjects in this study. This is the inevitable limitation of any study that only has a small number of subjects (de Jong and Zawaydeh 1999, Max and Onghena 1999).

3.2 Results and Discussion

The nasal flow duration during the vowel in /CVn/ and /CVŋ/ is shown in (14a). The error bar indicates one standard error. For both speakers, a one-way ANOVA with nasal place as the independent factor indicates a significant effect (JZ: F(1, 58)=18.759, p<0.0001; HL: F(1, 57)=81.226, p<0.0001). Measurements and ANOVA's of the overall vowel duration in /CVn/ and /CVŋ/ indicate that for both speakers, the vowel in the /C_ŋ/ context is significantly longer than the vowel in the /C_n/ context (JZ: V(/_ŋ)=116ms, V(/_n)=92ms, F(1, 58)=16.424, p<0.0005; HL: V(/_ŋ)=133ms, V(/_n)=109ms, F(1, 57)=10.562, p<0.005). To factor out the effect of overall vowel duration, the proportion of the nasalization duration to the overall duration of the vowel was calculated, and the results are shown in (14b). One-way ANOVA's with nasal place as the independent factor still indicate significant effects for both speakers (JZ: F(1, 58)=18.226, p<0.0001; HL: F(1, 57)=34.665, p<0.0001).

(14) a. Nasal flow duration during the vowel (ms) b. Nasalized vowel duration / Overall vowel duration

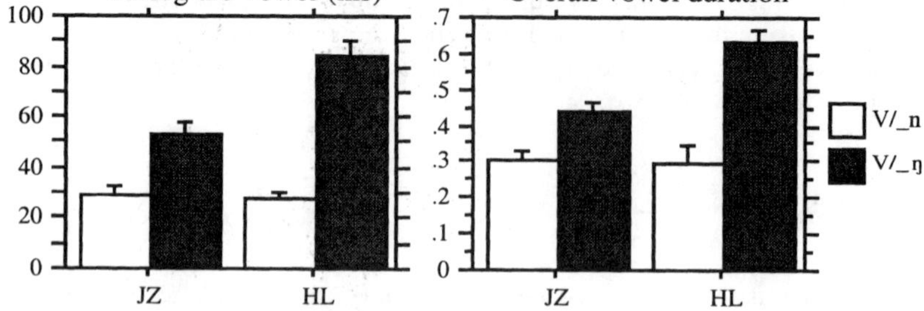

The duration measurements of the nasal codas yielded the following results: for JZ, the average durations for /n/ and /ŋ/ are 168ms and 157ms respectively, with the former significantly longer than the latter, as shown by a one-way ANOVA (F(1, 58)=6.914, p<0.05); for HL, the average durations for /n/ and /ŋ/ are 145ms and 133ms respectively, again with the former significantly longer than the latter, as shown by a one-way ANOVA (F(1, 57)=6.009, p<0.05). But even though the /n/-coda is significantly longer than the /ŋ/-coda, given that the nasality is unambiguous here, this durational difference does not translate into a perceptual difference according to Whalen and Beddor (1989), as I have discussed in §3.1. And if we consider the duration of the nasalized portion of the vowel plus the nasal coda, it is still significantly longer for /Vŋ/ than for /Vn/, for both speakers: for JZ, 211ms for /Vŋ/ and 197ms for /Vn/, F(1, 58)=8.752, p<0.005; for HL, 218ms for /Vŋ/ and 173ms for /Vn/, F(1, 57)=42.218, p<0.0001.

The mean nasal flow values for the nasalized duration of the vowel in /CVn/ and /CVŋ/ are shown in (15a), and the proportion of the nasal flow to the overall glottal flow is shown in (15b). The error bar again represents one standard error. For the mean nasal flow, for both speakers, a one-way ANOVA with nasal place as the independent factor indicates a significant effect (JZ: F(1, 58)=11.428, p<0.005; HL: F(1, 57)=4.636, p<0.05). But for the mean proportion of the nasal flow to the overall glottal flow, neither speaker shows any significant effect of the nasal place (JZ: F(1, 58)=0.007, p>0.05; HL: F(1, 57)=0.301, p>0.05). The lack of a significant effect in nasal flow proportion in the face of a significant effect in absolute nasal flow is apparently due to the greater overall glottal flow in the context of /C_ŋ/ than that of /C_n/. But I do not have an explanation as to why there is such a difference in the overall glottal flow between these two contexts.

(15) a. Mean nasal flow $\overline{U_n}$ (ml/s) b. Mean nasal flow proportion $\frac{\overline{U_n}}{U_g}$

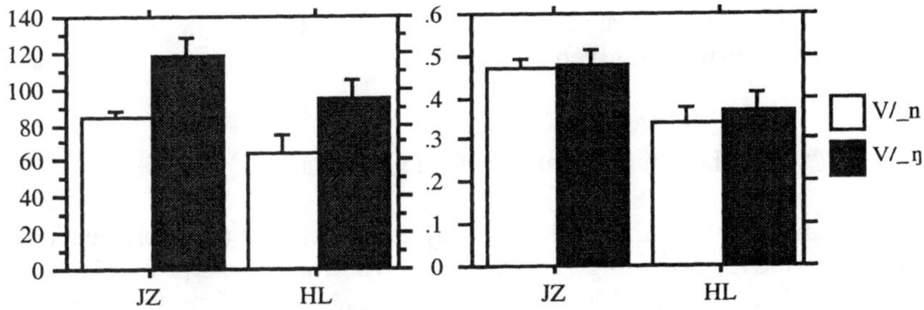

Clearly, both of the hypotheses in (9) are supported by the experimental data. The results in (14) show that the /ŋ/-coda induces a significantly longer nasal flow duration on the vowel nucleus than the /n/-coda. The results in (15) show that during the nasalized portion of the vowel, the proportion of the nasal flow to the overall flow is no less in the /C_ŋ/ context than in the /C_n/ context. Under the assumption that the oral impedance during the vowel is comparable for /CVŋ/ and /CVn/, we infer from the airflow results that the velopharyngeal opening is comparable during the nasalized portion of the vowel in /CVŋ/ and /CVn/. Then given that the nasalization is significantly longer during the vowel in /CVŋ/, we infer that the nasality induced by the /ŋ/-coda is perceptually more salient than the nasality induced by the /n/-coda.

4. An Optimality-Theoretic Account

4.1 Constraints and Universal Ranking

Intuitively, two types of constraints are crucial in the analysis of the /n/-/ŋ/ asymmetry in these Chinese dialects—faithfulness constraints and phonotactic constraints. The faithfulness constraints require the root and the suffix to be faithfully realized in the surface form, while the phonotactic constraints require the surface form to be phonotactically well-formed. The proposed faithfulness constraints that are relevant to the analyses are given in (16).

(16) a. MAX([+nas]$_{ŋ}$): preserve the nasality of /ŋ/.

b. MAX([+nas]$_{n}$): preserve the nasality of /n/.

c. REALIZEAFFIX: affixes must be realized.

The first two constraints require the nasality of /ŋ/ and /n/ to be realized in the suffixed form, respectively. The reason why we need to separate the MAX([+nas]) constraint into two will become clear in the analysis of the surveyed dialects. REALIZEAFFIX, in the cases in question, requires the diminutive suffix to be realized in the suffixed form. This can be deemed as an OT rendition of the Affix Manifestation Principle proposed by Lin (1993).

The key point to the analysis is the universal ranking between the two Max([+nas]) constraints, given in (17).

(17) MAX($[+nas]_{ŋ}$) $\underline{\gg}$ MAX($[+nas]_{n}$)
("$\underline{\gg}$": either outranks or is ranked as high as)

This universal ranking is licensed by the results of the aforementioned phonetic study, according to which, we may interpret (16a) as MAX($[+nas]_{strong}$), and (16b) as MAX($[+nas]_{weak}$). Therefore, the constraint ranking in (17) can be interpreted as a specific rendition of a general ranking schema in (18).

(18) MAX($[F]_{strong}$) $\underline{\gg}$ MAX($[F]_{weak}$)

The idea of universal rankings governed by perceptual salience scales has been entertained by many previous researchers (cf. Jun 1995, Gordon 1998a, b, Beckman 1998, Steriade 1999, among others). For example, Steriade (1999) argues that the cross-linguistic patterns of laryngeal neutralization can be understood if we employ a series of universally-ranked constraints requiring various perceptual cues for the laryngeal feature to be present and interleave them with the faithfulness constraint. Jun (1995) illustrates the necessity of universal rankings among faithfulness constraints on place features in the account of place assimilation, basing the universal rankings on the production and perception of consonants of different places. Beckman (1998) identifies cases in which a wider range of phonological contrasts is attested in prosodically strong positions, such as roots, stressed syllables, and syllable onsets, and argues that this effect can be captured by positing positional faithfulness constraints IDENT-*Position*[F] and their universal rankings with general faithfulness constraints—IDENT-*Position*[F] » IDENT[F]. The argument for such universal rankings is based on the fact that these positions are either perceptually more salient (e.g., stressed) or particularly important for lexical access (e.g., root, onset). The case under discussion here differs from the above works in that the universal ranking proposed here deals with the inherent strength of one single feature—[+nas]. The [+nas] feature tends to be more prominently preserved if it is inherently stronger, even though the difference in strength is phonetically small and phonologically non-contrastive.

The phonotactic constraints are given in (19).

(19) a. *COMPLEXCODA: no complex coda is allowed.
b. *NASALVOWEL: no nasal vowel is allowed.
c. MAXIMUMWORD: the suffixed form must be one syllable.

Intuitively, *COMPLEXCODA bans syllables with complex codas, and *NASALVOWEL bans syllables with vowels that are nasalized throughout their duration. As for MAXIMUMWORD, the motivation lies in the common Chinese preference for disyllables—since the suffixed form is usually used with another monosyllabic morpheme to form a compound word, e.g., *paŋ˦*, "side", *pjan˥ pɑ̃ɻ˦*, "radical (in Chinese writing)", it is preferred to be monosyllabic, thus guaranteeing the disyllabicity of the compound word.

Now we will give analyses for the different dialects we discussed in the survey by appealing to the constraints and their universal ranking I proposed. The dialectal variation is accounted for by different rankings of the constraints.

4.2 Case Studies

4.2.1 Beijing

The relevant data pattern in Beijing Mandarin (as well as Zhengzhou, Juxian, etc.) is recapitulated in (20).

(20) /CVn/+/ɻ/→[CVɻ]
/CVŋ/+/ɻ/→[CṼɻ]

In these dialects, upon /ɻ/-suffixation, both /n/ and /ŋ/ are lost. But only when the stem coda is /ŋ/ is the vowel nasalized after the suffix is added. These facts indicate that MAX($[+nas]_{ŋ}$) is more highly ranked than *NASALVOWEL, and *NASALVOWEL is in turn more highly ranked than MAX($[+nas]_{n}$). *COMPLEXCODA, REALIZEAFFIX and MAXIMUMWORD are never violated, and I assume that they are all undominated in the grammar. Therefore, the constraint ranking that accounts for the data pattern in Beijing Mandarin is revealed as follows:

(21) *COMPLEXCODA, REALIZEAFFIX,
MAXIMUMWORD, MAX($[+nas]_{ŋ}$)
⇓
*NASALVOWEL
⇓
MAX($[+nas]_{n}$)

The relevant tableaux for Beijing are shown in (22).

(22) a. /CVn/+/ɻ/→[CVɻ]

CVn+ɻ	*COMP CODA	REAL AFF	MAXIM WORD	MAX ([+n]$_{ŋ}$)	*NASAL VOWEL	MAX ([+n]$_{n}$)
☞CVɻ						*
CṼɻ					*!	

b. /CVŋ/+/ɻ/→[CṼɻ]

CVŋ+ɻ	*COMP CODA	REA AFF	MAXIM WORD	MAX ([+n]$_{ŋ}$)	*NASAL VOWEL	MAX ([+n]$_{n}$)
CVɻ				*!		
☞CṼɻ					*	

4.2.2Mancheng

The relevant data pattern in Mancheng is repeated in (23).

(23) /CVn/+/ɻ/→[CVɻ]
/CVŋ/+/ɻ/→[CVŋ]+[ŋəɻ]

In Mancheng, when the stem is closed by /n/, the nasal is dropped entirely upon /ɻ/-suffixation, but when the stem is closed by /ŋ/, the /ɻ/-suffix is realized in a different syllable, and the vowel remains oral, or at most partially nasalized.

To account for this data pattern, we need to make the following modification to the evaluation of the faithfulness constraints regarding the nasals: the constraints are only satisfied when the nasal itself is fully preserved in the output. They receive one violation if the nasality is only preserved on the vowel, and they receive two violations if the nasality is completely lost. This is illustrated in (24).

(24) MAX([+nas]$_{N}$): /CVN/ → [CVN] √
/CVN/ → [CṼ] *
/CVN/ → [CV] **
(N=n or ŋ)

The above modification can again be deemed as perceptually based. Under the assumption that the perception of nasality is directly related to the nasal airflow, an oral opening can significantly weaken the nasal perception, because a considerable portion of the overall airflow will be vented out through the oral cavity. Therefore, we consider the nasal segment--/n/ or /ŋ/—to render a better nasal perception than a nasalized vowel. Hence it is reasonable to posit in this case that only the complete preservation of the nasal segment satisfies the nasal faithfulness constraints, while preserving the same velum lowering gesture on the vowel incurs one violation of the constraints.

The following ranking arguments can be given to Mancheng. For the alveolar nasal case, since the oral vowel wins over the nasal vowel, *NASALVOWEL must outrank MAX([+nas]$_n$); and since the oral vowel wins over the disyllabic form, MAXIMUMWORD must outrank MAX([+nas]$_n$). For the velar nasal case, since the disyllabic form wins over both of the monosyllabic forms, MAX([+nas]$_ŋ$) must outrank MAXIMUMWORD. *COMPLEXCODA and REALIZEAFFIX are again never violated and are therefore deemed as undominated. The complete constraint ranking for Mancheng is given in (25).

(25) *COMPLEXCODA, REALIZEAFFIX, MAX([+nas]$_ŋ$)

⇓

MAXIMUMWORD , *NASALVOWEL

⇓

MAX([+nas]$_n$)

The relevant tableaux for Mancheng are shown in (26). In both (26a) and (26b), the candidate that fully preserves the nasal coda does not violate *NASALVOWEL, since we assume that the vowel preceding the nasal segment is oral, or is partially nasalized at most.[7]

(26) a. /CVn/+/ɻ/→[CVɻ]

CVn+ɻ	*COMP CODA	REAL AFF	MAX ([+nas]$_ŋ$)	MAXIM WORD	*NASAL VOWEL	MAX ([+nas]$_n$)
☞CVɻ						**
CṼɻ					*!	*
CVn +nəɻ				*!		

7 An anonymous reviewer points out that in Mancheng and Anqing (discussed in the next section), the candidate [CVŋ+ŋəɻ] for /CVŋ/+/ɻ/ (or [CVn+nəɻ] for /CVn/+/ɻ/, for that matter), violates both INTEGRITY and DEP-IO for the gemination of the nasal and the insertion of [ə] respectively. Then a candidate without [ŋ]-gemination will actually win. In response, I would like to entertain two possible explanations. In my own experience with a Hebei dialect closely related to Mancheng, the suffixed form for [CVŋ] sounds like a disyllabic word [CVŋəɻ] without [ŋ]-gemination. So the forms with [ŋ]-gemination could be due to the original fieldworker's mistranscription. Secondly, if the suffixed form does have [ŋ]-gemination, it could be due to the result of an ONSET constraint which requires syllables to have an onset and a SYLLABLE CORRESPONDENCE constraint which requires the coda of a syllable in the allomorph μ of a morpheme to remain coda of the syllable in the allomorph μ' of the same morpheme (Steriade 1995). If both of these constraints outrank INTEGRITY, then the form with [ŋ]-gemination will surface as the correct output. As for DEP-IO, we may consider that it is violated in order to satisfy an undominated constraint NUCLEUS, which requires all syllables to have a nucleus.

b. /CVŋ/+/ɻ/→[CVŋ]+[ŋəɻ]

CVŋ+ɻ	*COMP CODA	REAL AFF	MAX ([+nas]$_{\text{ŋ}}$)	MAXIM WORD	*NASAL VOWEL	MAX ([+nas]$_{\text{n}}$)
CVɻ			*!*			
CṼɻ			*!		*	
☞CVŋ +ŋəɻ				*		

4.2.3 Anqing

Anqing differs from Mancheng in only one respect: in a stem closed by /n/, upon /ɻ/-suffixation, the vowel becomes nasalized instead of staying oral, as shown in (27).

(27) /CVn/+/ɻ/→[CṼɻ]
/CVŋ/+/ɻ/→[CVŋ]+[ŋəɻ]

Therefore, the only ranking difference between Anqing and Mancheng is that in Anqing, MAX([+nas]$_{\text{n}}$) outranks *NASALVOWEL rather the opposite in Mancheng. The following constraint ranking can account for the Anqing data:

(28) *COMPLEXCODA, REALIZEAFFIX, MAX([+nas]$_{\text{ŋ}}$)
⇓
MAXIMUMWORD
⇓
MAX([+nas]$_{\text{n}}$)
⇓
*NASALVOWEL

The relevant tableaux for Anqing are shown in (29).

(29) a. /CVn/+/ɻ/→[CVɻ]

CVn+ɻ	*COMP CODA	REAL AFF	MAX ([+nas]$_{\text{ŋ}}$)	MAXIM WORD	MAX ([+nas]$_{\text{n}}$)	*NASAL VOWEL
CVɻ					*!*	
☞CṼɻ					*	*
CVn +nəɻ				*!		

b. /CVŋ/+/ɻ/→[CVŋ]+[ŋəɻ]

CVŋ+ɻ	*COMP CODA	REAL AFF	MAX ([+nas]$_ŋ$)	MAXIM WORD	MAX ([+nas]$_n$)	*NASAL VOWEL
CVɻ			*!*			
CṼɻ			*!			*
☞CVŋ +ŋəɻ				*		

As we can see from above, dialects in which there is a /n/-/ŋ/ asymmetry upon /ɻ/-suffixation can be accounted for by appealing to the universal ranking MAX([+nas]$_ŋ$) » MAX([+nas]$_n$) and inserting phonotactic constraints between these two constraints in the hierarchy.

For dialects in which /n/ and /ŋ/ behave identically upon /ɻ/-suffixation, we rank MAX([+nas]$_ŋ$) and MAX([+nas]$_n$) in the same stratum of the constraint hierarchy. Thus the constraint hierarchy will not make any distinction between the preservation of a velar nasal and that of an alveolar nasal, resulting in identical behavior of the two nasal codas. This can be seen in the Liaocheng and Jiyuan dialects below.

4.2.4 Liaocheng

In Liaocheng, both the velar and alveolar nasal codas are deleted upon /ɻ/-suffixation, and the vowels in both cases stay oral, as shown in (30).

(30) /CVn/+/ɻ/→[CVɻ]
/CVŋ/+/ɻ/→[CVɻ]

This data pattern indicates that the phonotactic wellformedness constraints *COMPLEXCODA, MAXIMUMWORD and *NASALVOWEL, as well as REALIZEAFFIX, are undominated, and they outrank the faithfulness constraints regarding the nasal codas. This constraint ranking is shown in (31).

(31) *COMPLEXCODA, *NASALVOWEL,
MAXIMUMWORD , REALIZEAFFIX
⇓
MAX([+nas]$_ŋ$), MAX([+nas]$_n$)

The relevant tableaux for Liaocheng are shown in (32). The evaluation of the faithfulness constraints regarding the nasals is back to being binary like in Beijing. Namely, it is only violated if the nasal information is completely lost in the suffixed form.

(32) a. /CVn/+/ɻ/→[CVɻ]

CVn+ɻ	*COMP CODA	REAL AFF	MAXIM WORD	*NASAL VOWEL	MAX ([+nas]$_{ŋ}$)	MAX ([+nas]$_{n}$)
☞CVɻ						*
CṼɻ				*!		

b. /CVŋ/+/ɻ/→[CVɻ]

CVŋ+ɻ	*COMP CODA	REAL AFF	MAXIM WORD	*NASAL VOWEL	MAX ([+nas]$_{ŋ}$)	MAX ([+nas]$_{n}$)
☞CVɻ					*	
CṼɻ				*!		

4.2.5 Jiyuan

The relevant data pattern in Jiyuan is shown again in (33).

(33) /CVn/+/F/→[C(Ṽ+F)]
/CVŋ/+/F/→[C(Ṽ+F)]

Recall that the diminutive suffix in Jiyuan is a feature bundle--either [+back, +round] (Duanmu 1990) or [-back, +round] (Lin 1993), not /ɻ/. Therefore REALIZEAFFIX in this case is active upon these features, not /ɻ/ as in the previous dialects.

Since for both /n/ and /ŋ/, the nasality is preserved upon suffixation by nasalization on the stem vowel, we infer that both of the nasal faithfulness constraints—MAX([+nas]$_{ŋ}$) and MAX([+nas]$_{n}$)—outrank *NASALVOWEL. *COMPLEXCODA, REALIZEAFFIX and MAXIMUMWORD are again undominated in the grammar. Therefore, the following constraint ranking accounts for the data pattern in Jiyuan.

(34) *COMPLEXCODA, REALIZEAFFIX, MAXIMUMWORD,
MAX([+nas]$_{ŋ}$), MAX([+nas]$_{n}$)
⇓
*NASALVOWEL

The relevant tableaux for Jiyuan are shown in (35).

(35) a. /CVn/+/F/→[C($\tilde{V}_F$)]

CVn+F	*COMP CODA	REAL AFF	MAXIM WORD	MAX ([+nas]$_{ŋ}$)	MAX ([+nas]$_{n}$)	*NASAL VOWEL
CV$_F$					*!	
☞C$\tilde{V}_F$						*

b. /CVŋ/+/F/→[C($\tilde{V}_F$)]

CVŋ+F	*COMP CODA	REAL AFF	MAXIM WORD	MAX ([+nas]$_ŋ$)	MAX ([+nas]$_n$)	*NASAL VOWEL
CV_F				*!		
☞$C\tilde{V}_F$						*

The analyses of Liaocheng and Jiyuan crucially depend on ranking MAX([+nas]$_ŋ$) and MAX([+nas]$_n$) on a par in the constraint hierarchy. To this end, we must acknowledge the two possible phonetic scenarios that may give rise to this ranking. One is that, as we have assumed, these dialects have the similar phonetic behavior as Beijing Mandarin. Namely, /ŋ/ induces a longer nasal flow duration and a greater nasal flow volume than /n/. But the grammar of these dialects chooses not to encode this fine phonetic difference in it. Secondly, it is possible that in these dialects, there are no significant differences between /ŋ/ and /n/ in terms of the nasal flow duration and volume. Logically, it is also conceivable that in these dialects, there is a significant effect between the two nasals in the opposite direction from Beijing, i.e., longer and stronger nasal flow for /n/ than for /ŋ/. But again, the grammar chooses not to represent this difference. We do not recognize this scenario as a possibility because if we did, then we would expect this phonetic pattern to be found in other dialects, and we would further expect that in at least some of these dialects, the phonetic differences would be picked up by the grammar, and thus create a suffix pattern like (36).

(36) /CVn/+/ɻ/→[CṼɻ]
/CVŋ/+/ɻ/→[CVɻ]

But this pattern is never attested. Regarding the first two hypotheses, without the support of empirical phonetic data, we can only lay them out at this point and hope to test them in future research.

So far, we have accounted for all the data patterns we have observed in the survey of northern Chinese dialects regarding the phonetic realization of /CV_1n/ and /CV_1ŋ/ syllables upon /ɻ/-suffixation. The analyses crucially depend on the universal ranking between the two faithfulness constraints on nasality—MAX([+nas]$_ŋ$) either outranks or is ranked as high as MAX([+nas]$_n$). The opposite data pattern in which the nasality of /n/ is more prominently preserved than /ŋ/ is not attested because the ranking MAX([+nas]$_n$) » MAX([+nas]$_ŋ$) is claimed to be universally implausible on phonetic grounds.

4.3 Further Discussion of the Analysis

If we look at the phonetic results closely, we may notice that although the differences in nasal flow duration and volume between /n/ and /ŋ/ in Beijing Mandarin are statistically significant, they are very small in absolute values. But in terms of the phonological behavior of these two nasals, they are categorically different. In the analysis I proposed, I made the assumption that these differences are the major cause, or at least one of the major causes, of the perception of nasality. Then the striking fact is, not only can very small (though statistically significant) phonetic differences be saliently perceived, but they can also incur phonological consequences. Another possibility we need to entertain is that there are other greater differences between /n/ and /ŋ/ that the phonetic study did not cover, e.g., vowel nasalization, oral flow during the nasal consonant (Wang 1997b, based on a split-mask aerodynamic study, claims that the nasal codas in Beijing Mandarin are nasal glides), etc. Therefore, the phonetic study documented here can only serve as the preliminary for a series of phonetic studies aiming to reveal the real differences between /n/ and /ŋ/ in these Chinese dialects. Moreover, a perception experiment is needed to test the hypothesis that whatever differences revealed by the aerodynamic or acoustic studies are the direct correlates of the nasal perception.

Another issue that should be raised is whether or not the analysis is best interpreted synchronically. We may imagine that historically, there were greater differences between /n/ and /ŋ/ in terms of nasality in Chinese, and they caused /n/ and /ŋ/ to behave differently phonologically. While these differences have diminished over time, their phonological consequence has not. Under this assumption, the difference between /n/ and /ŋ/ in their phonological behavior in the modern-day Chinese dialects is better explained from a historical perspective. But even so, if a perception study reveals that speakers can perceive the small phonetic differences in nasality, we cannot deny the synchronic relevance of the analysis proposed here.

5. Wang (1993, 1997a) and Duanmu (1990)

In this section, I review two previously proposed analyses of the /n/-/ŋ/ asymmetry upon /ɻ/-suffixation in Beijing Mandarin and outline the advantages of the OT account over these analyses.

5.1 Wang (1993, 1997a)—A Feature-Geometric Account

Wang (1993, 1997a) proposes a feature-geometric account for the /n/-/ŋ/ asymmetry upon /ɻ/-suffixation in Beijing Mandarin. The feature tree that Wang adopts is given in (37).

(37) The feature tree of Beijing Mandarin (Wang 1993, 1997a):

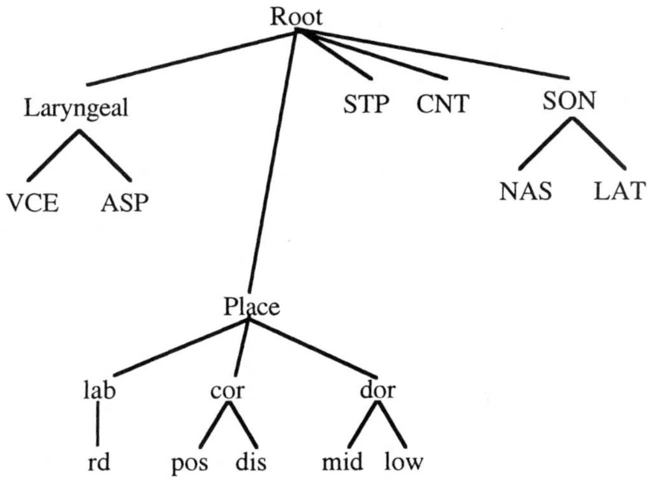

The rimes in Beijing Mandarin are grouped into two categories: coronal rimes and non-coronal rimes. Coronal rimes are rimes whose pronunciation involves the tongue tip or blade, and thus have a [cor] node under the [Place] node in the feature tree. Non-coronal rimes, on the other hand, do not involve the tongue tip or blade in their pronunciation, and therefore do not have a [cor] node in the feature tree. All the rimes that are closed by /ŋ/ are non-coronal rimes, and all the rimes that are closed by /n/ are coronal rimes.

The /ɻ/-suffix in Beijing Mandarin, as Wang proposes, is a floating feature [posterior]. Therefore, when the /ɻ/-suffix is added to the stem, if the stem has an /ŋ/ coda, and hence is a non-coronal rime, then the floating feature [pos], together with a dominating [cor] node, docks under the [Place] node of the rime, creating retroflexion. If the stem has an /n/ coda, and hence is a coronal rime, then the [cor] node of /n/ is forced to leave the tree in order to accommodate the [cor] node that comes with the [pos] feature of the /ɻ/-suffix. Data in (38a) and (38b) illustrate the suffixed forms for /CVŋ/ and /CVn/ respectively in Wang's representation. The dots indicate retroflexion.

(38) a. /p^{h}aŋ/+/ɻ/→[p^{h}ạŋ] "side" /ʈʂ^{w}əŋ/+/ɻ/→[ʈʂ^{w}ə̣ŋ] "bug"
b. /p^{h}an/+/ɻ/→[p^{h}ạɻ] "plate" /ɕin/+/ɻ/→[ɕịɻ] "heart"

If we compare Wang's phonetic representation of the Beijing data in (38) with my transcription in (1), we observe the following differences. First, in Wang's transcription, there is retroflexion on the vowels in the suffixed forms. Although there does seem to be some degree of retroflexion on the vowel, it does not seem to be the case that the whole vowel is retroflexed. This is informally tested by observing the down-trend of F2 and F3 of the vowel preceding the retroflex, indicating that not the entire vowel is affected. Therefore the retroflexion of the vowel is probably better explained by coarticulation with the following retroflex, whose exact formulation falls beyond of the scope of this paper. Second, for stems closed by /ŋ/, Wang's suffixed form is a retroflexed oral vowel followed by a retroflexed nasal. This goes against native speakers' (and well-trained phoneticians') intuition that the vowel is highly nasalized and there is no separate nasal portion to the rime in the suffixed form.

Two other problems of Wang's analysis also come to mind. One is that for stems closed by /n/, it does not explain the loss of the [+nas] feature, because the [NAS] node is independent of the [Place] node in the feature tree, and therefore should not be affected by the changes under the [Place] node. The other is that her analysis cannot be extended to account for dialects in which the stems closed by /n/ behave identically to the stems closed by /ŋ/ upon /ɻ/-suffixation, e.g., Liaocheng, Chengdu, Nanjing and Jiyuan.

None of these problems arises in the OT analysis proposed in section 4. The OT analysis clearly encodes in the representation of the suffixed forms the nasalization of the vowel in the case of /CVŋ/+/ɻ/, and the loss of the [+nas] feature in the case of /CVn/+/ɻ/. Moreover, the OT analysis easily accounts for the dialects in which /n/ and /ŋ/ behave identically upon /ɻ/-suffixation by ranking the two nasal faithfulness constraints—MAX($[+nas]_{n}$) and MAX($[+nas]_{ŋ}$)—in the same stratum in the constraint hierarchy.

5.2 Duanmu (1990)—A Syllable Structure Account

Duanmu (1990) offers a syllable structure account for /ɻ/-suffixation in Beijing and elsewhere. The basic idea for Beijing is that there is only one coda slot in the syllable structure, and it will be taken by the /ɻ/-suffix in the diminutive form. To account for the difference in vowel nasalization between the two nasals upon suffixation, he suggests that the vowel in the unsuffixed form is nasalized before a velar nasal. The derivations for a /CVn/ stem and a /CVŋ/ stem are given in (39a) and (39b) respectively.

(39) a. /gən/→[gən] /gən+ɻ/→[gəɻ]

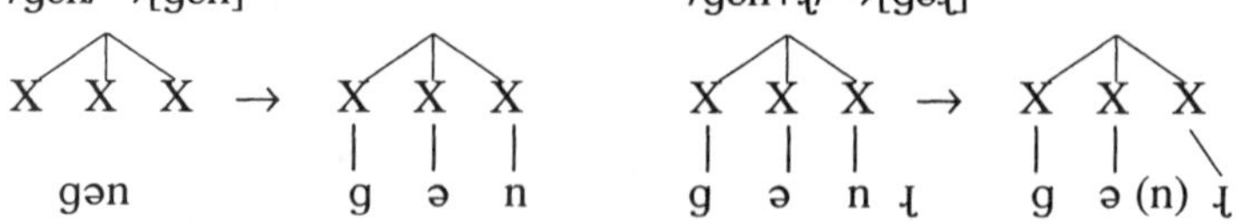

b. /gəŋ/→[gə̃ŋ] /gəŋ+ɻ/→[gə̃ɻ]

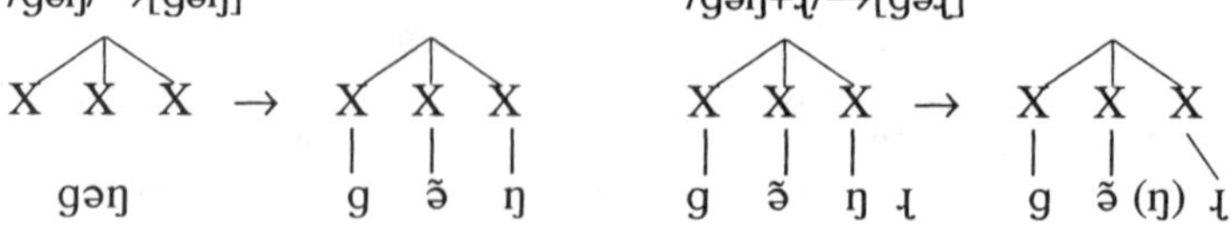

Duanmu's analysis is similar in spirit to the analysis proposed in this paper in that it acknowledges the difference in nasality between /n/ and /ŋ/. But the story seems to be more complicated than he assumes. One empirical problem with his analysis is that for the /ŋ/ case, the vowel nasalization in the suffixed form starts considerably earlier than the unsuffixed form. This is observed in an informal study of my own speech. Moreover, this analysis cannot be easily extended to Mancheng and Anqing in which the velar nasal has to be completely preserved, thus resulting in disyllables for the suffixed forms, while the alveolar nasal is simply replaced by the /ɻ/-suffix. Lastly, analysis in this line will run into serious problems with Jinan, a dialect spoken in Shandong province, which displays the following behavior as in (40) (Qian 1995).

(40) Jinan (Qian 1995)

/CV_1/+/ɻ/→[CV_1ɻ]:	/fa/+/ɻ/→[faɻ]	"method"
	/p^hɛ/+/ɻ/→[p^hɛɻ]	"tablet"
/$C\tilde{V}_1$/+/ɻ/→[CV_1ɻ]:	/p^hã/+/ɻ/→[p^hɛɻ]	"plate"
	/p^hẽ/+/ɻ/→[p^heɻ]	"(wash)basin"
/CV_1ŋ/+/ɻ/→[$C\tilde{V}_1$ɻ]:	/ʐaŋ/+/ɻ/→[ʐãɻ]	"pulp"
	/ɕiŋ/+/ɻ/→[ɕiə̃ɻ]	"star"

If we interpret Duanmu's analysis in OT terms as the effect of IDENT constraints (McCarthy and Prince 1995) regarding nasality, then we would expect a nasalized vowel in the output realization of /$C\tilde{V}_1$/+/ɻ/ and an oral vowel for the output realization of /CV_1ŋ/+/ɻ/. But from the data in (40), it seems that the vowel nasalization shows up in exactly the wrong places.

Again, the OT analysis formulated in section 4 does not have the problems mentioned above. It appeals to MAX([+nas]) constraints rather than IDENT constraints, therefore where the nasality shows up in the suffixed form is not crucial. It naturally accounts for Mancheng and Anqing by the higher ranking of the MAXIMUMWORD constraint. And for the case of Jinan, if we assume that the nasality for a nasalized vowel is weaker than the nasality of a real nasal, then a universal constraint ranking—MAX($[+nas]_{ŋ}$) » MAX($[+nas]_{\tilde{V}}$)—with the phonotactic constraint *NASALVOWEL ranked in between will generate the correct suffixed forms in (40).

6. Theoretical Implications

To this end, if we accept the assumptions of the OT analysis discussed in sections §3.2 and §4.3, namely, the differences in nasal flow duration and volume are the major correlates for the perception of nasality, then two theoretical implications can be drawn from the proposed analysis.

Regarding the nature of correspondence constraints MAX, not only can they refer to features, as suggested by McCarthy and Prince (forthcoming), Lombardi (1998) and Pulleyblank (1996), but they can also be distinguished by small and non-contrastive phonetic differences, for example, the nasality difference between /n/ and /ŋ/. Regarding phonetically governed universal constraint rankings, not only can they be posed on faithfulness constraints regarding different prosodic positions (Beckman 1998) or on different places of articulation (Jun 1995), but they can also be posed on a single feature with different degree of phonetic strength. Specifically, the cases under discussion here illustrate that it is more important to preserve the nasal feature when it is phonetically stronger and thus perceptually more salient. It is the universal ranking between MAX($[+\text{nas}]_{ŋ}$) and MAX($[+\text{nas}]_{n}$) that delivers the explanation to the /n/-/ŋ/ asymmetry upon /ɻ/-suffixation in northern Chinese dialects.

References

Abramson, A., P. Nye, J. Henderson, and C. Marshall (1981). Vowel Height and the Perception of Consonantal Nasality. *Journal of the Acoustical Society of America* 70: 329-339.

Beckman, J. (1998). *Positional Faithfulness.* Ph.D. dissertation. University of Massachusetts, Amherst.

Bell-Berti, F. and T. Baer (1983). Velar Position, Port Size, and Vowel Spectra. *Proceedings of the 11th International Congress on Acoustics* 4: 19-21. Paris, France.

Benguerel, A.-P. (1974). Nasal Airflow Patterns and Velar Coarticulation in French. In Gunnar Fant (ed.), *Speech Communication: Proceedings of the Speech Communication Seminar* 2: 105-112. Almqvist and Wiksell, Stockholm.

Chen, S.-J. (1988). Hebei Mancheng Fangyan de Tedian (Idiosyncrasies of the Mancheng Dialect of Hebei Province). *Fangyan* (Dialects) 1988: 103-112.

Cohn, A. (1990). *Phonetic and Phonological Rules of Nasalisation.* Ph.D. dissertation, UCLA. Distributed as *UCLA Working Papers in Phonetics* 76.

Cohn, A. (1993). Nasalisation in English: Phonology or Phonetics. *Phonology* 10: 43-81.

de Jong, K. and B. Zawaydeh (1999). Stress, Duration, and Intonation in Arabic Word-Level Prosody. *Journal of Phonetics* 27: 3-22.

Delattre, P. (1954). Les Attributs Acoustiques de la Nasalité Vocalique et Consonantique. *Studia Linguistica* 8: 103-108.

Delattre, P. and M. Monnot (1968). The Role of Duration in the Identification of French Nasal Vowels. *International Review of Applied Linguistics in Language Teaching* 6: 267-288.

Dow, F. D. M. (1972). *An Outline of Mandarin Phonetics.* Australian National University Press.

Dow, F. D. M. (1984). *An Introduction to the Pronunciation of Chinese*. Dept. of Chinese, University of Edinburgh.

Duanmu, S. (1990). *A Formal Study of Syllable, Tone, Stress and Domain in Chinese Languages*. Ph.D. dissertation, MIT.

Gao, B.-T. and A.-S. Zhang (1997). *Yinchuan Hua Yindang* (A Record of the Yinchuan Dialect). In J.-Y. Hou (ed.), *Xiandai Hanyu Fangyan Yinku* (Records of Modern Chinese Dialects). Shanghai Jiaoyu Zhubanshe (Shanghai Education Publishing House).

Gordon, M. (1998a). *Syllable Weight: Phonetics, Phonology and Typology*. Ph.D. dissertation, UCLA.

Gordon, M. (1998b). The Process Specific Nature of Weight: The Case of Contour Tone Restrictions. *Proceedings of WCCFL-17*.

Hao, N. (1982). Anqing Fangyan Cihui (The Vocabulary of the Anqing Dialect). *Fangyan* (Dialects) 1982: 297-313.

He, W. (1981). Jiyuan Fangyan Jilüe (A Brief Record of the Jiyuan Dialect). *Fangyan* (Dialects) 1981: 5-26.

He, W. (1982). Huojia Fangyan Yunmu de Fenlei (The Rime Categories of the Huojia Dialect). *Fangyan* (Dialects) 1982: 22-36.

Hou, J.-Y. (1989). Erwei, Erhua, Ziwei ("Er" Suffix, "Er" Coloring, "Zi" Suffix). In J.-Y. Hou, *Jinyu Yanjiu* (Studies of the Jin Dialects). Institute for the Studies of Languages and Cultures of Asia and Africa, Tokyo University of Foreign Studies.

House, A. and K. Stevens (1956). Analog Studies of the Nasalisation of Vowels. *Journal of Speech and Hearing Disorders* 21: 218-232.

House, A. (1957). Analog Studies of Nasal Consonants. *Journal of Speech and Hearing Disorders* 22: 190-204.

Huffman, M. (1990). *Implementation of Nasal: Timing and Articulatory Landmarks*. Ph.D. dissertation, UCLA. Distributed as *UCLA Working Papers in Phonetics* 75.

Jun, J (1995). *Perceptual and Articulatory Factors in Place Assimilation: An Optimality Theoretic Approach*. Ph.D. dissertation, UCLA.

Krakow, R. and M. Huffman (1993). Instruments and Techniques for Investigating Nasalization and Velopharyngeal Function in the Laboratory: An Introduction. In Marie K. Huffman and Rena A. Krakow (eds.), *Phonetics and Phonology, Vol. 5, Nasals, Nasalization, and the Velum*: 3-59. Academic Press, San Diego, CA.

Li, B. (1981). Changhai Fangyan de Erhua yu Ziwei (The "Er" and "Zi" Suffixes of the Changhai Dialect). *Fangyan* (Dialects) 1981: 93-103.

Li, Y.-M. (1996). Miyang Fangyan de Erhua ji Erhua Shanyin (The "Er" Suffix and the "Er" Tap in the Miyang Dialect). *Fangyan* (Dialects) 1996: 302-305.

Lin, T. and L.-J. Wang (1992). *Yuyinxue Jiaocheng* (A Course in Phonetics). Beijing: Beijing Daxue Chubanshe (Beijing University Press).

Lin, Y.-H. (1993). Degenerate Affixes and Templatic Constraints: Rime Change in Chinese. *Language* 69: 649-682.

Liu, D.-Q (1997). *Nanjing Hua Yindang* (A Record of the Nanjing Dialect). In J.-Y. Hou (ed.), *Xiandai Hanyu Fangyan Yinku* (Records of Modern Chinese Dialects). Shanghai Jiaoyu Zhubanshe (Shanghai Education Publishing House).

Liu, S.-H. (1993). Xiangcheng Fangyan Yinxi (The Sound System of the Xiangcheng Dialect). *Fangyan* (Dialects) 1993: 284-294.

Lombardi, L. (1998). *Evidence for MaxFeature Constraints from Japanese.* Ms., University of Maryland, College Park.

Lu, J.-W. (1992). *Zhengzhou Fangyan Zhi* (A Record of the Zhengzhou Dialect). Beijing: Yuwen Chubanshe (The Philology Publishing House).

Luo, F.-T. (1995). Muping Fangyan Cidian Yinlun (Introduction to the "Muping Dialect Dictionary"). *Fangyan* (Dialects) 1995: 1-16.

Maeda, S. (1982). Acoustic Correlates of Vowel Nasalization: A Stimulation Study. *Journal of the Acoustical Society of America* 72: S102.

Max, L. and P. Onghena (1999). Some Issues in the Statistical Analysis of Completely Randomized and Repeated Measures Designs for Speech, Language, and Hearing Research. *Journal of Speech, Language, and Hearing Research* 42: 261-270.

McCarthy, J. & A. Prince (1995). Faithfulness and Reduplicative Identity. In J. Beckman, L. W. Dickey & S. Urbanczyk (ed.), *University of Massachusetts Occasional Papers in Linguistics 18: Papers in Optimality Theory*: 249–384. Amherst: GLSA.

McCarthy, J. and A. Prince (forthcoming). Faithfulness and Identitiy in Prosodic Morphology. In René Kager, Harry van der Hulst and Wim Zonneveld (ed.), *The Prosody Morphology Interface.* Cambridge University Press, Cambridge.

Pulleyblank, D. (1996). Neutral Vowels in Optimality Theory: A Comparison of Yoruba and Wolof. *Canadian Journal of Linguistics* 41: 295-347.

Qian, Z.-Y. (1995). Jinan Fangyan Cidian Yinlun (Introduction to the "Jinan Dialect Dictionary"). *Fangyan* (Dialects) 1995: 242-256.

Shi, M.-Y. (1995). *Juxian Fangyan Zhi* (A Record of the Juxiang Dialect). Beijing: Yuwen Chubanshe (The Philology Publishing House).

Steriade, Donca (1999). Phonetics in Phonology: The Case of Laryngeal Neutralization. In Matthew K. Gordon (ed.), *UCLA Working Papers in Linguistics, Papers in Phonology* 3: 25-146.

Takeuchi, S., H. Kasuya, and K. Kido (1975). On the Acoustic Correlate of Nasality. *Journal of the Acoustical Society of Japan* 31: 298-309.

Wang, Z.-J. (1993). *The Geometry of Segmental Features in Beijing Mandarin.* Ph.D. dissertation, University of Delaware.

Wang, Z.-J. (1997a). Erhuayun de Tezheng Jiagou (The Feature Geometry of R-Rimes). *Zhongguo Yuwen* (Chinese Philology), 1997: 2-10.

Wang, Z.-J. (1997b). Ying-Han Biyunwei de Butong Xingzhi (The Quality Differences in Nasal Codas between English and Mandarin).

Whalen, D. H. and P. Beddor (1989). Connections between Nasality and Vowel Duration and Height: Elucidation of the Eastern Algonquian Intrusive Nasal. *Language* 65: 457-486.

Yin, S.-C. (1995). Harbin Fangyan Cidian Yinlun (Introduction to the "Harbin Dialect Dictionary"). *Fangyan* (Dialects) 1995: 17-25.

Yuan, J.-H. (1989). *Hanyu Fangyan Gaiyao* (An Overview of Chinese Dialects), 2nd Edition. Beijing: Wenzi Gaige Chubanshe (Writing-System Reformation Publishing House).

Zhang, H.-Q. (1995). *Liaocheng Fangyan Zhi* (A Record of the Liaocheng Dialect). Beijing: Yuwen Chubanshe (The Philology Publishing House).

Zhou, L. (1994). Wulumuqi Fangyan Cidian Yinlun (Introduction to the "Wulumuqi Dialect Dictionary"). *Fangyan* (Dialects) 1994: 241-251.

Index